The Politics
of
Dissatisfaction

Bureaucracies, Public Administration, and Public Policy

Kenneth J. Meier
Series Editor

THE STATE OF PUBLIC BUREAUCRACY
Larry B. Hill, Editor

THE POLITICS OF DISSATISFACTION
Citizens, Services, and Urban Institutions
W. E. Lyons, David Lowery, and Ruth Hoogland DeHoog

THE DYNAMICS OF CONFLICT
BETWEEN BUREAUCRATS AND LEGISLATORS
Cathy Marie Johnson

THE POLITICS OF TELECOMMUNICATIONS REGULATION
The States and the Divestiture of AT&T
Jeffrey E. Cohen

WOMEN AND MEN OF THE STATES
Public Administrators at the State Level
Mary E. Guy

Bureaucracies, Public Administration,
and Public Policy

The Politics
of
Dissatisfaction
Citizens, Services,
and Urban Institutions

W. E. LYONS
DAVID LOWERY
RUTH HOOGLAND DeHOOG

M. E. Sharpe, Inc.
Armonk, New York
London, England

Library of Congress Cataloging-in-Publication Data

Lyons, William E., 1935–   .
The politics of dissatisfaction : citizens, services, and urban institutions /
by W. E. Lyons, David Lowery, Ruth Hoogland DeHoog.
p.   cm. — (Bureaucracies, public adminstration, and public policy)
Includes bibliographical references and index.
ISBN 0-87332-898-1
1. Local government—United States—Public opinion.
2. Metropolitan government—United States—Public opinion.
3. County services—United States—Public opinion.
4. Municipal services—United States—Public opinion.
5. Public opinion—United States.
6. Social choice—United States.
I. Lowery, David.
II. DeHoog, Ruth Hoogland.
III. Title.
IV. Series.
JS323.L97   1992
321.8'0973—dc20
91-35287
CIP

Printed in the United States of America

The paper used in this publication meets the minimum requirements of
American National Standard for Information Sciences—
Permanence of Paper for Printed Library Materials,
ANSI Z39.48–1984.

MV   10   9   8   7   6   5   4   3   2   1

To Some Pretty Good Spouses

Contents

List of Tables ix

List of Figures xiii

Foreword xv

Preface xvii

Acknowledgments xix

Chapter
1. Introduction: The Lexington and Louisville Study 3

2. The Sources of Citizen Satisfaction 18

3. Responding to Dissatisfaction: The EVLN Model 46

4. Testing the EVLN Model 68

5. A Closer Look at the Tiebout Model 89

6. Institutions and Citizen Attribution Error 115

7. Fragmentation and Suburban Ghettos 144

8. Citizenship in the Metropolis 160

9. Designing Urban Institutions 185

Appendix A: Glossary of Multi-item Variables 195

Appendix B: Citizen Response to Dissatisfaction: Questionnaire 198

References 210

Index 219

List of Tables

1.1 Characteristics of Matched Cities/Neighborhoods 12

1.2 Summary of Survey Site Households, Telephones Surveyed, and Response Rates 13

1.3 Difference in Means/Proportions for Paired Research Sites for Selected Demographic Variables 14

2.1 Services in Lexington/Fayette and Jefferson County Sites 29

2.2 Difference-of-Means Tests for Quality and Bias in Quality for Consolidated/Nonconsolidated Research Sites 31

2.3 OLS Regression Results of Tests of Five Models of Citizen Satisfaction with Local Public Services 36

2.4 Comparison of OLS Regression Site Dummy Estimates for Consolidated/Nonconsolidated Research Sites 39

2.5 Comparison of OLS Regression Site Dummy Estimates for Black and White Research Sites in Lexington–Fayette County 40

2.6 OLS Analyses of Jurisdiction-level Determinants of the Pattern of Stage One Site Coefficients 41

3.1 Hypothesized Relationships between Propensity to Invoke Responses to Dissatisfaction and the Determinants of Responses 58

3.2 Hypothesized Relationships between Determinants of Responses to Dissatisfaction and Level of Correspondence 61

4.1 Estimates for Original EVLN Dissatisfaction Model 73

4.2 Estimates for Respecified EVLN Dissatisfaction Model 81

4.3 Estimates for Respecified VOICE Model by Paired Research Sites 82

4.4 Estimates for Respecified LOYALTY Model by Paired Research Sites 83

4.5 Estimates for Respecified NEGLECT Model by Paired Research Sites 84

5.1 Primary Governmental Jurisdiction Orientation of Fragmented Arrangement (Louisville) Case Respondents 107

5.2 Perceptions of Alternatives by Institutional Arrangement—
Matched Lexington and Louisville Sites   107

5.3 Service Level Perceptions: Difference-of-Means Tests across Institutional Arrangements—Matched Lexington and Louisville
Sites   108

5.4 Differences in Number of Services Perceived to be Provided
from Actual Number of Total and Most Local Services   109

5.5 CURRENT DISSATISFACTION Difference-of-Means Tests
across Alternative Institutional Arrangements—Matched
Lexington and Louisville Sites   109

5.6 CURRENT DISSATISFACTION Difference-of-Means Tests
across Neighborhoods/Cities within Alternative Institutional
Arrangements   110

5.7 INVESTMENT Difference-of-Means Tests for Alternative
Institutional Arrangements—Matched Lexington and Louis-
ville Sites   111

5.8 Likelihood of Moving for Regime/Government Reason by
Institutional Arrangement—Matched Lexington and
Louisville Sites   111

5.9 VOICE Difference-of-Means Tests for Alternative
Institutional Arrangements—Matched Lexington and
Louisville Sites   112

5.10 Considered Privatized Services (EXIT-PRIV) by Institutional
Arrangement—Matched Lexington and Louisville Sites   113

5.11 NEGLECT Difference-of-Means Tests for Alternative
Institutional Arrangements—Matched Lexington and
Louisville Sites   114

5.12 LOYALTY Difference-of-Means Tests for Alternative
Institutional Arrangements—Matched Lexington and
Louisville Sites   114

6.1 Decomposition of Attribution Errors in Service Evaluations   123

6.2 Frequency Distribution of Numbers of Errors in Evaluations
Made by Fragmented- and Consolidated-Government
Respondents   128

6.3 Difference of Means on Numbers of Errors by Matched
Consolidated/Fragmented Institutional Arrangements   130

6.4 Difference of Means on Biases in Evaluations by Matched
Consolidated/Fragmented Institutional Arrangements   132

6.5 Difference (Bias) in Observed Mean Evaluation and True
Mean Evaluation   135

6.6 OLS Regression of Satisfaction with Government on
Real Service Evaluation, Evaluation Biases, and Controls—
Consolidated Cases   137

6.7   OLS Regression of Satisfaction with Government on Real
Service Evaluation, Evaluation Biases, and Controls—
Fragmented Cases   138
6.8   Predicted Satisfaction with Government with No Biases and
with Mean Level of Biases   139
7.1   Dissatisfaction, Disaffection, and Political Participation
Difference-of-Means Tests across Alternative Institutional
Arrangements—Green Acres and Newburg   152
7.2   Dissatisfaction, Disaffection, Participation Difference of
Means Tests across Neighborhoods/Cities within Alternative
Institutional Arrangements   153
7.3   Dissatisfaction, Disaffection, Participation Difference
between Consolidated and Fragmented Black Communities'
Differences from Corresponding White Communities   155
8.1   Summary of Conceptual, Behavioral, and Structural
Implications of Liberal and Communitarian Notions of
Citizenship as Applied to Metropolitan Governance   162
8.2   Probit and OLS Estimates of the Extended EVLN Models   176
8.3   PSYCHOLOGICAL ATTACHMENT Difference-of-Means
Tests for Alternative Institutional Arrangements—Matched
Lexington and Louisville Sites   180

List of Figures

3.1 EVLN Dimensions of Responses to Dissatisfaction, Response Types, and Illustrative Behaviors   54

3.2 Illustrative Scenarios of High and Low Correspondence between the Boundaries of Social and Political Worlds   60

4.1 A Sequential Choice Model of Responses to Dissatisfaction   85

6.1 Average Bias in Satisfaction by Average Number of Attribution Errors — Five Consolidated and Five Fragmented Communities   141

8.1 Mean Levels of EXIT by Levels of PSYCHOLOGICAL ATTACHMENT   177

8.2 Mean Levels of NEGLECT by Levels of PSYCHOLOGICAL ATTACHMENT   178

8.3 Mean Levels of VOICE by Levels of PSYCHOLOGICAL ATTACHMENT   178

8.4 Mean Levels of LOYALTY by Levels of PSYCHOLOGICAL ATTACHMENT   179

Foreword

The M. E. Sharpe, Inc. series on bureaucracies, public policy, and public administration is designed as a forum for the best work on bureaucracy and its role in public policy and governance. Although the series is open with regard to approach, methods, and perspectives, especially sought are three types of research. First, the series hopes to attract theoretically informed, empirical studies of bureaucracy. Public administration has long been viewed as a theoretical and methodological backwater of political science. This view persists despite a recent accumulation of first-rate research. The series seeks to place public administration at the forefront of empirical analysis within political science. Second, the series is interested in conceptual work that attempts to clarify theoretical issues, set an agenda for research, or provide a focus for professional debates. Third, the series seeks work that challenges the conventional wisdom about how bureaucracies influence public policy or the role of public administration in governance.

The Politics of Dissatisfaction: Citizens, Services, and Urban Institutions is destined to be a classic in public administration and public policy; it makes major theoretical and empirical contributions to the literature in both fields. *The Politics of Dissatisfaction* is a rigorous empirical attempt to assess the public choice view of citizenship and local government. Traditional public administration has long advocated the consolidation of urban governments to provide for equitable treatment of all citizens and to gain the benefits of economies of scale in government services. Public choice theory has challenged this prescription, arguing that fragmentation has its benefits. Multiple small jurisdictions, the argument goes, allow individuals to choose the service/taxation combination that they desire. Providing such choices, public choice contends, will foster the development of an informed democratic citizenry.

The Politics of Dissatisfaction represents the systematic destruction of this public choice perspective on urban government. An elaborate theoretical assessment of public choice conclusions reveals a variety of limitations and inconsistencies. Using an extensive citizen survey of ten urban communities, the authors find that the hypotheses of public choice theory simply are not true. Contrary to the predictions of public choice, citizens in small, fragmented urban areas are not better informed about issues involving local government, they are not more likely to participate in politics, they are not more likely to feel they can influence government, and they are not more satisfied with local government services than are citizens living in consolidated urban governments. Professors Lyons, Lowery, and DeHoog have exposed public choice approaches to urban governance as exercises in wishful thinking.

Given, then, that fragmented urban communities do not provide for better development of democratic citizenship, the normative contrast between consolidation and fragmentation weighs heavily in favor of consolidation. Consolidation provides a larger tax base, a greater opportunity to address significant urban policy problems, and the ability to address questions of economic and political equity. Advocates of municipal reform now have the evidence needed to refute the public choice challenge.

The work presented here does not address other applications of public choice theory to politics. Given the theory's inadequacies in an area where a series of axiomatic internally consistent arguments was presented, scholars would be wise to examine public choice approaches in other areas. Professors Lyons, Lowery, and DeHoog have demonstrated that rigorous empirical evaluation of such theories is possible and have provided a blueprint for others to do so.

Kenneth J. Meier

Preface

The research upon which this book is based was founded on conversations between two of its authors, W. E. Lyons and David Lowery, during the early 1980s. We were frustrated with the state of scholarly debate over the content of urban political behavior and institutions. While the urban political behavior literature offered a rich mix of assertions, hypotheses, and even grand theoretical analyses, it was, simply put, a mess. With some important exceptions that we consider in some detail, little or no attention was given to how the various political behaviors observed in real urban settings and studied through a variety of methods relate to each other, or to how citizens select among them when they are dissatisfied with local government. Just as frustrating was the urban institutions literature, which had by then hardened into a fixed competition between proponents of governmental fragmentation and supporters of the traditional reform theory of jurisdictional consolidation. Their competing and dramatic claims struck us as ignoring the complexity of behaviors found in actual urban settings. And the research designs linking institutions to behaviors were simply not up to the task of unraveling their complex linkages, even assuming that we had some broader theoretical guidance about just what linkages to look for. But while frustrated, we realized that such intellectual untidiness should be better viewed as intellectual opportunity.

The key turning point was our exposure to Caryl Rusbult's Exit, Voice, Loyalty, and Neglect (EVLN) model of responses to dissatisfaction, which significantly extended Albert Hirschman's work by dimensionalizing the categories of response and, more importantly, pointing to a set of theoretical antecedents governing how individuals select among the responses. Though developed to account for behaviors within interpersonal relationships, we recognized that the model was sufficiently powerful to organize much of the political behavior literature. Moreover, the determinants of selection, especially the concept of alternatives, allowed us to consider the role of institutional boundaries, the central variable in the dispute between traditional reformers and public choice scholars. With the support of the National Science Foundation under Grant No. SES85–20155, we then developed and implemented a research design to test the model.

This project provided the data that constitute the Lexington and Louisville study.

Having completed our test of the EVLN model, we were fully prepared to retire our data. Fortunately, Ruth Hoogland DeHoog then joined the project. Ruth extended the study by compelling us to consider more fully the implications of our findings for public choice prescriptions about how best to organize local government. She also asked why it was that citizens become dissatisfied in the first place, long before they invoke some political response to dissatisfaction. And she asked perhaps the most important question of all: how these research findings bear on the content and conduct of citizenship. With Ruth now on the team, we discovered a new depth in the Lexington and Louisville study that took us beyond its initial goals.

The Lexington and Louisville study points to two general conclusions. The first is that the complexity of the local political world—why citizens become dissatisfied and how they then respond politically—can be parsimoniously understood by focusing on a few variables that define the actual situation in which citizens find themselves. We expect that this conclusion will be well-received in the discipline given that we are not alone in our frustration with the fragmented state of knowledge about urban political behavior. But we do not expect such a positive reception for our second conclusion: that in the design of urban institutions, the hypotheses of the traditional reformers, as opposed to those of public choice scholars, are more often supported than not. With this finding, we necessarily take one side in the longest-standing controversy in the study of urban politics.

Though our findings rather clearly compel us to side with the traditional reformers, we fully recognize that the Lexington and Louisville study cannot be the last word in such a long-standing controversy. Rather, just as the important work of public choice scholars during the last two decades raised the quality of the debate between those supporting institutional fragmentation and proponents of governmental centralization, we hope that our findings stimulate new theoretical and empirical analyses of urban politics. And we especially hope that the EVLN model, which shares much with public choice analyses of urban institutions, will provide a new theoretical tool that can be usefully employed by those supportive of a broad range of institutional forms.

We are deeply indebted to an important and unknown group of scholars who made the research reported here far better than it might otherwise have been. Many of the analyses reported here appeared previously in different form as a series of journal articles. It is the reviewers of these research reports whom we must thank. Their selfless and entirely anonymous efforts to make us reach deeper, think harder, and write more clearly offered us immediate pain for the long-term benefit of better scholarship. We also thank Ken Meier for his prompt and enthusiastic support of this book. Each of us—Lyons, Lowery, and DeHoog—believes that any remaining faults in the analysis are the full responsibility of our coauthors.

Acknowledgments

We acknowledge with gratitude the support provided for this project by the National Science Foundation under Grant No. SES85–20155. While this support was essential to our completing the project, all opinions, findings, and conclusions are our own, and do not necessarily reflect the views of the National Science Foundation.

Part of chapter 2 is adapted from Ruth Hoogland DeHoog, David Lowery, and William E. Lyons, "Citizen Satisfaction with Local Governance: A Test of Individual, Jurisdictional, and City Specific Explanations," *Journal of Politics 52* (August 1990): 807–37, by permission of the *Journal of Politics* and the University of Texas Press.

Chapter 3 is adapted from William E. Lyons and David Lowery, "Citizen Responses to Dissatisfaction in Urban Communities: A Partial Test of a General Model," *Journal of Politics 51* (November 1989): 842–68, by permission of the *Journal of Politics* and the University of Texas Press.

Chapter 4 is adapted from William E. Lyons and David Lowery, "The Organization of Political Space and Citizen Responses to Dissatisfaction in Urban Communities: An Integrated Model," *Journal of Politics 48* (May 1986): 321–46, by permission of the *Journal of Politics* and the University of Texas Press.

Elements of chapter 5 are adapted from David Lowery and William E. Lyons, "The Impact of Jurisdictional Boundaries: An Individual-Level Test of the Tiebout Model," *Journal of Politics 51* (February 1989): 73–97, by permission of the *Journal of Politics* and the University of Texas Press.

Other parts of chapter five are adapted from William E. Lyons and David Lowery, "Governmental Fragmentation Vrs. Consolidation: Five Public Choice Myths about Creating Informed, Involved, and Happy Citizens," *Public Administration Review 49* (November/December 1989): 533–43. Reprinted with permission from *Public Administration Review,* © 1989 by the American Society for Public Administration (ASPA), 1120 G Street NW, Suite 500, Washington, DC, 20005. All rights reserved.

Chapter 6 is adapted from David Lowery, William E. Lyons, and Ruth Hoogland DeHoog, "Institutionally Induced Attribution Errors: Their Composition and Impact on Citizen Satisfaction with Local Governmental Services," *American Politics Quarterly 18* (April 1990): 169–96, by permission of Sage Publications, Inc.

And elements of chapter 7 are adapted from Ruth Hoogland DeHoog, David Lowery, and William E. Lyons, "Metropolitan Fragmentation and Suburban Ghettos: Some Empirical Observations on Institutional Racism," *Journal of Urban Affairs 13* (Number 4, 1991): 479–93, by permission of the *Journal of Urban Affairs* and JAI Press, Inc.

The Politics
of
Dissatisfaction

1

Introduction:
The Lexington and
Louisville Study

More than two decades ago, Robert Lineberry asserted that urban governments in the United States are responsible for providing the majority of the nation's population those services that are "most vital to the preservation of life, liberty, property, and public enlightenment."[1] Although he posed this argument during the heyday of federal spending on various urban-oriented programs, little has happened during the ensuing years to invalidate its veracity. In fact, President Reagan's "New Federalism," coupled with reductions in levels of funding for most domestic programs throughout the Reagan-Bush era, have added to the importance and significance of urban governments and the services they provide.[2] Cities, as well as states, are no longer simply the delivery agencies for programs and policies designed and funded by the national level of government; they now serve—in policy areas ranging from homelessness through racial strife to the tragedy of AIDS—on the front lines of many of the social and economic crises confronting our nation.

This important and growing role alone, though, cannot itself justify special attention to urban citizens and their services. If the relationships between citizens and their municipal governments were no different from similar ties at the state and/or national levels, we could simply generalize from the voluminous research on state and federal political participation back to the local level. But with varying degrees of effort and success, the thousands of local governments serving our urban areas attempt to deliver vital services under rather unique and often frustrating circumstances. On the one hand, local governments operate under significant legal and fiscal limitations imposed by their respective states, not to mention the federal government. In addition, they must deal with major economic constraints created by national and international forces over which they have little, if any, control.[3] And at the same time, they are called upon to deliver many of these services in an environment in which large segments of their populations have the opportunity directly to observe and experience their performance on a daily basis. Potholes in the streets and the activities of local police and sanitation workers are much more visible to citizens of urban areas on a day-to-day basis than most state or federal programs.[4] The immediacy and visibility of municipal services and the sometimes exogenous origins of the problems they are designed to address make urban services and urban politics special.

Given the special nature of urban services and the rather unusual circumstances under which they are provided, it is not surprising that urban researchers have been interested in understanding the public opinion dynamics that underlie them. *Why are some citizens more satisfied with urban governance and city services than others? And how do they respond politically when satisfaction turns into dissatisfaction?* Indeed, we will see that a rather sizable body of literature has developed around each of these questions. Some of the answers that have been developed to our questions are quite normative and prescriptive in character. And much of the literature is heavily descriptive, relying on a single city case method that provides only a limited basis for sound inference about theoretically derived hypotheses. But even if we ignore these parts of the literature, there remains a large body of work that develops and empirically tests many important theoretical propositions concerning citizen evaluations of urban services and the political behaviors predicated on those evaluations. It is this body of research—its theoretically based hypotheses and its empirical analyses—that is the focus of our inquiry and to which we hope to contribute.

Research on Satisfaction and Dissatisfaction

To begin with, several contending explanations of how and why citizens become satisfied or dissatisfied with local services have been examined in the literature. One of these is firmly grounded in the traditional political participation literature, and emphasizes the role of such *individual-level* demographic factors as race and income,[5] as well as such attitudinal considerations as political efficacy and community disaffection, in structuring citizen evaluations of services.[6] Other explanations focus on a variety of *city- and/or neighborhood-specific* factors, including patterns of civic leadership and management, special neighborhood needs and characteristics, and unique historical or cultural circumstances.[7]

A third approach that will receive special attention in our analysis stresses the importance of various institutional or *jurisdiction-level* factors, including the much-debated effects of having local services provided and therefore evaluated within a highly fragmented versus a more integrated or consolidated system of local government for urban areas. For more than thirty years, debate over how to organize and analyze urban governments in the United States has been structured around these two perspectives. The classic civic reform tradition that developed during the early 1900s has, from its inception, emphasized the socioeconomic interdependencies found in America's urban areas while lamenting the fragmentation of the governmental systems that have attempted to service them. The solution, according to this reform tradition, was simple and straightforward: reduce the number of units of government in each urban area, preferably to a single, unified unit of government for each urban area. According to the civic reformers, this type of institutional arrangement would not only produce economies and efficiencies in the delivery of local services, it would also focus political responsibility and assure a more integrated governmental response to areawide problems.

The public choice or Tiebout model, on the other hand, emphasizes the unique nature of the tax–service needs and expectations of each individual and each household. And, since individuals and households with similar needs and desires tend to cluster in particular neighborhoods and sections of our urban areas, the public choice approach stresses the need to establish and maintain numerous units of local government in each urban area in order to maximize opportunities for these spatially defined groups to choose a tax-service package that best suits their needs. The resulting government system has been termed polycentric, with many different types and sizes of overlapping jurisdictions providing a wide array of services for local and regional needs. Proponents of this fragmented system believe not only that it provides citizen choice and local control, but that it also improves the efficiency and effectiveness of service delivery.[8]

An equally impressive body of theoretical and empirical work has developed around the related question of how citizens politically respond to dissatisfaction with local services. Citizen evaluations of local services and municipal governance have been linked to a broad array of political attitudes and behaviors, ranging from withdrawal and nonparticipation in local politics to protesting and rioting.[9] In addition, citizen satisfaction, or the lack thereof, has been linked to such conventional types of activities as supporting or opposing tax increases or service cutbacks, exiting or leaving a local jurisdiction in search of a better tax and service package, and various types of citizen-initiated contacting behaviors.[10] Thus, citizens' evaluations of local services are politically meaningful.

This body of literature offers any number of accounts of how, when, and why citizens invoke these varied behavioral responses to dissatisfaction, contending explanations that highlight an array of *individual-level, city- and/or neighborhood-specific,* and *systemic or jurisdiction-level* variables. In addition to the individual-level traits of race, income, and education, various types of citizen responses to dissatisfaction with local services have been linked to such attitudinal predispositions as political efficacy, perceived need for certain services, and individual interest in and knowledge about local governments and the tax and service packages they offer. Other explanations focus on the effects of differing neighborhood conditions, including the socioeconomic composition and objective service needs of various spatially defined communities. Others attempt to include such city-specific structural variables as whether or not there is a centralized complaint agency or bureau in the municipal government under the expectation that such institutional features can facilitate or inhibit citizens' efforts to redress grievances.[11]

Some of the most important and enduring theoretical propositions concerning citizen responses to dissatisfaction with their local tax and service packages can again be found in the long-standing debate between advocates of the public choice approach and the traditional civic reform model for organizing local government. These propositions concern not only the effects of metropolitan governmental fragmentation or consolidation on the availability and use of the classic Tiebout notion of exit, or "voting with one's feet," they also address the potential impacts of these institutional features on a wide range of citizen responses to dissatisfaction, including the use of various types of contacting or "voice" behaviors.[12]

Given these broad and deep literatures on the sources of satisfaction with urban governance and the nature of political responses to dissatisfaction, one might think that social science has a firm and well-developed understanding of these phenomena. Unfortunately, this is not the case. Despite the centrality of citizen evaluations of local services in urban politics research, our understanding of the sources and consequences of these evaluations under varying structural and institutional arrangements remains quite fragmentary and incomplete for two reasons.

First, while the literature contains a number of theoretical propositions specifying why citizens will be satisfied with urban governance, and how, in turn, they respond when dissatisfied, many, including the much-discussed public choice notion that citizens will "vote with their feet," have never been directly or adequately tested. Simply put, the research designs employed by urban scholars have not provided an analytic base of sufficient strength to enable us simultaneously to examine many of the competing propositions. As a result, the empirical literature is comprised of and compromised by too many partial answers that cannot be compared with sufficient confidence to justify strong inferences about many of the literature's contending hypotheses.

Admittedly, the study of these phenomena—like the study of urban politics generally—continues to be a "painfully eclectic field" utilizing differing measures, methodologies, and levels of analyses.[13] Some of the blame for this can be attributed to the persistent problem of finding sufficient resources to enable urban researchers interested in these types of questions to do much more than rely on single city case studies or on secondary analyses of data collected for other purposes. As we will see, developing and implementing the kinds of research designs needed to conduct comprehensive tests of many of the theoretical propositions is costly in both time and resources. Much of the responsibility, however, must be shared by those of us who have conducted research on these questions over the years. Like many urbanists, researchers interested in these particular kinds of questions have often failed, in the words of Bryan Jones, "to link theory and data very carefully."[14]

Second, and perhaps more important, the field remains disjointed because we lack an integrated theoretical account of these phenomena. All too often, theoretical propositions are developed concerning one political response to dissatisfaction without considering how that response relates to others, or specifying how citizens select among them. Several hypotheses about exiting behaviors, for example, fail to consider how exit relates to citizen complaining behaviors, ritualistic support for local government in the face of dissatisfaction, and/or withdrawal from local politics. At least in part, this problem too is a function of our inadequate research designs; one is hardly driven to develop a comprehensive theory of satisfaction or responses to dissatisfaction if the available testing procedures can address only a limited set of propositions at any one time. Yet, many of these propositions clearly are related at some fundamental level. And until these linkages are theoretically specified and tested, a comprehensive understanding of the politics of dissatisfaction will remain elusive.

Purpose, Data, and Methods

In this volume, we attempt to strengthen the links between theory and data concerning the origins, nature, and consequences of citizen satisfaction or dissatisfaction with urban services. The core of the analysis is comprised of a number of recently published and several as yet unpublished findings from a study sponsored by the National Science Foundation. But the analysis is more than the sum of partial answers to partial questions about urban governance. The individual studies on which this volume is based collectively overcome, we believe, the twin problems of inadequate and limited research designs and the lack of comprehensive theoretical integration of the many propositions on satisfaction and responses to dissatisfaction. While no study will provide a complete understanding of any phenomenon, our goal is to present and empirically test a comprehensive, integrated theory of satisfaction and responses to dissatisfaction with urban services.

Several steps were taken from the inception of this study to help insure the success of the endeavor. In addition to following such basic research protocols as trying to clarify and give consistent meaning to key theoretical concepts and assumptions,[15] the entire research program was designed to provide a broader and more integrated theoretical and empirical foundation for understanding the causes and effects of citizen satisfaction/dissatisfaction with urban services. For example, we integrate and test a variety of existing theoretical propositions concerning the *relative effects* of various individual, systemic, and city-specific factors on the formation of citizen evaluations of urban services. We also develop and empirically test an expanded version of Albert Hirschman's more generalized "exit," "voice," "loyalty" model for understanding and explaining citizen responses to dissatisfaction with urban services.[16] In addition to incorporating the notion of "neglect" as yet another kind of response that citizens can choose, our Exit, Voice, Loyalty, and Neglect (EVLN) model also examines several theoretically relevant variables that govern how citizens choose from among these four possible types of responses to dissatisfaction with urban services.

As is often the case, our examination of these broader theoretical issues raises a number of more specific questions about citizens' evaluations of public services that cannot easily be addressed within the more comprehensive models mentioned above. Among the important questions requiring somewhat separate examination is whether and to what extent fragmented versus consolidated systems lead citizens to make various types of "errors" in evaluating local services. Other questions include the extent to which various institutional arrangements enhance or inhibit the creation of informed, involved, and satisfied citizens, and whether such arrangements work differently for black majority communities in metropolitan areas than for white majority neighborhoods. We also use these findings to examine the broader question of the meaning of citizenship in urban settings.

Perhaps the most important step taken to strengthen the linkages between theory and data regarding the sources and consequences of urban service dissatisfaction inheres in the rather unique data set generated for this project. To meet our objectives, especially the goal of theoretically integrating and simultaneously testing the key propositions of the various approaches that have been taken to explaining these phenomena, we needed an unusually robust research design. First, we needed to generate survey data from independent samples of individuals living in a wide variety of neighborhoods in a number of different urban settings. And second, we needed data about respondents living under both fragmented and consolidated systems of local government in order to tap the effects of several systemic or jurisdiction-level variables highlighted in the literature.

Obviously, it would be prohibitively expensive to survey independent samples of every conceivable type of neighborhood defined in terms of age, income, racial, or life-style characteristics, or to replicate such a study in a large number of urban areas operating under widely differing levels of governmental fragmentation. Indeed, in our original proposal to the National Science Foundation, we planned to conduct telephone interviews with approximately 300 respondents drawn from each of only five different types of neighborhoods in only six different metropolitan areas in the United States. Even the most basic and conservative version of a budget for that project amounted to well over $400,000, most of which would have been spent on simply sampling and conducting long-distance telephone interviews with approximately 9,000 respondents.

At the request of the National Science Foundation, we scaled down the number of urban areas to two, thereby reducing the number of planned telephone interviews by 60 percent. To further reduce the cost of this project, we sampled respondents from five matched pairs of distinct socioeconomic communities or neighborhoods located in two quite different urban areas in close proximity to the University of Kentucky where the telephone surveys were to be conducted.

Fortunately, we were able to find two urban areas that met all of our basic requirements, including the fragmentation-consolidation contrast, within seventy-five miles of the campus. The two urban areas selected were Lexington–Fayette County, Kentucky, and Louisville–Jefferson County, Kentucky.

The Lexington and Louisville Surveys

Lexington–Fayette County, with a population (1980) of 204,000, is a growing, relatively affluent, urban community situated in the heart of the famous bluegrass region of Kentucky. Its diversified economy is centered on a large IBM facility and related light industries, the University of Kentucky, and various hospitals and medical facilities that make Lexington a regional medical center. It has increasingly become the central or regional home for many corporate offices, while maintaining its historical role of servicing the surrounding agricultural economy.

In 1972, the voters of Lexington–Fayette County approved a plan to consolidate the governments of the City of Lexington and the County of Fayette. That plan or charter was put into effect in January of 1974,[17] thereby providing us with an opportunity to examine the sources and consequences of citizen dissatisfaction with urban services in an environment in which a single local government serves a wide variety of spatially defined socioeconomic communities. While relatively few urban areas have been able to consolidate their local governments along the lines of the Lexington model, many of the basic systemic conditions found in the Lexington setting can also be found in a large number of the burgeoning urban areas in the Sun Belt where, through either annexation or consolidation, governmental fragmentation is much less extensive.

Louisville–Jefferson County, with a population (1980) of 685,000, on the other hand, is a more industrialized urban area located on the Ohio River. Although its economy has become more service-oriented in recent decades, it continues to rely heavily on basic manufacturing and assembly plants. Population growth shifted almost exclusively to the suburbs and more recently to surrounding counties as the City of Louisville began to experience absolute declines in population starting in the early 1960s.

Although several efforts have been mounted over the years to consolidate the governments of Louisville and Jefferson County, the most recent of which were defeated in 1982 and again in 1983, residents of this urban area continue to be served by almost 100 units of general-purpose local governments, not to mention numerous special districts and authorities. Many of the ninety-plus incorporated municipalities located on the fringes of the City of Louisville are very small and serve quite homogeneous socioeconomic communities, making the Louisville–Jefferson County setting quite typical of the governmentally fragmented urban environment found in most of the older industrial centers in the nation. Because of its relatively high level of governmental fragmentation, coupled with the general tendency for urban residents to cluster in space in terms of various socioeconomic and life-style characteristics, the Louisville setting offers us numerous opportunities to study respondents from a wide variety of neighborhoods served by local governments whose boundaries also coincide with the contours of these spatially defined "social worlds."

Aside from its practicality, these two research settings offered several other advantages. First, both share the same "individualistic–traditionalistic" cultural milieu based on Elazar's well-known scheme for classifying political cultures among the various states.[18] Second, the school systems in both Louisville–Jefferson County and Lexington–Fayette County are consolidated. This allows us to focus squarely on the impacts of fragmented versus consolidated institutional arrangements on citizen evaluations of tax–services packages other than education, which often involves issues and concerns such as court-ordered desegregation plans that may not be relevant to evaluating other types of local services. Third, both research sites are in the same state, thereby holding constant such factors as state/local fiscal centralization, differing patterns of tax reliance, and legal requirements pertaining to the provision of local tax–service packages. And fourth, the use of matched pairs of independent surveys of individuals residing in neighborhoods from the greater Louisville and Lexington settings allows us to employ two levels of control for extraneous influences in our examination of the sources and consequences of citizen dissatisfaction with urban services. In addition to the control arising from matching our research sites, we are able to introduce individual-level controls for the impact of the standard socioeconomic and attitudinal determinants found in the traditional political participation literature. In sum, the inferences that we draw about individuals and communities from contrasts on key theoretical variables should have a high degree of internal validity.

But what of external validity or our ability to generalize from the Lexington and Louisville study findings to other urban settings? In part, our goal of developing and testing a comprehensive model of satisfaction and responses to dissatisfaction with urban governance necessarily places a premium on the internal validity of our research design, an emphasis that can lead to sacrifices in the external validity of any project. The influence of individual-level, systemic, and neighborhood- and city-specific determinants of satisfaction and responses to dissatisfaction cannot be simultaneously examined with any degree of internal validity using the kind of inexpensive, national survey that ensures easy generalizability. Unless resources on the order of at least those requested in our initial National Science Foundation proposal are available, trade-offs must be made.

Our decision to maximize internal over external validity is not uncommon in research on urban politics, as evidenced by the often cited public choice analyses of St. Louis and Indianapolis.[19] But as a border state in the upper south, Kentucky and its municipalities share a mix of many social, economic, and political characteristics with both northern and southern states and cities. As noted above, for example, Lexington–Fayette County shares many institutional features with the fast-growing cities of the Sun Belt, while Louisville–Jefferson County is more sim-ilar in structure to the older cities of the industrial north, though both operate within the same geographic, legal, and cultural setting. Thus, while no study of this type can be said to ensure external validity, our two research settings have much in common with many other metropolitan areas across the nation.

After examining the census data for all of the incorporated municipalities in Jefferson County, Kentucky, other than the City of Louisville, plus all of the tract and block data for various sections of Lexington–Fayette County, we were able to identify five matched pairs of spatially defined socioeconomic communi-ties in these two urban areas. The five types of communities that were ultimately chosen, as seen in Table 1.1, varied in terms of such factors as socioeconomic status (SES), race, age, and levels of familistic versus nonfamilistic life-styles.

Although socioeconomic status is a very relative term, the definitions used in our selection process were based on conventions related to household income and education. Familism and nonfamilism were determined on the basis of cen-sus data indicating the presence or absence of children in a majority of house-holds.[20] While it is possible to identify neighborhoods or subcommunities composed of younger, nonfamilistic households, we decided, in this instance, to focus on nonfamilistic areas that also happen to be composed of relatively large numbers of persons over sixty-five years of age. This strategy allowed us not only to include nonfamilistic life-styles as a defining characteristic among the limited number of research sites that we could sample in this study, but it also enabled us to introduce more variations on the age dimension. Two factors were held relatively constant in selecting the five communities in both research set-tings—type of dwelling and occupancy status. All of the research sites in both the Louisville–Jefferson County and the Lexington–Fayette County settings were predominantly composed of single-family units that were heavily owner-occu-pied. These, of course, are the kinds of communities most directly addressed by the Tiebout locational choice hypothesis.

The only major difference between the two sets of research sites is that the "boundaries" for each of the five neighborhoods in the Louisville setting also happened to correspond to the official boundaries of an incorporated municipal-ity, whereas their demographic "mirror images" in the Lexington setting were served by a single governmental entity that embraced all of these communities. The defining characteristics of the five matched pairs of neighborhoods selected for this study are noted in Table 1.1.

Households located within each of these ten research sites were identified from the most current Municipal Directory published by R. L. Polk for each of the urban areas in question.[21] Approximately 300 households were selected in each of the ten communities to provide a total of approximately 3,000 potential respondents for this study. In four instances—two in the Lexington area and two in the Louisville area—the number of households with listed telephone numbers

Table 1.1

Characteristics of Matched Cities/Neighborhoods

Lexington–Fayette neighborhood (consolidated)	Louisville–Jefferson independent city (fragmented)	Characterization
Blueberry	Minor Lane Heights	Moderate to low SES; younger; more familistic; predominantly white
Chinoe	Beechwood Village	Moderate to low SES; more elderly; less familistic; predominantly white
Stonewall	Barbourmeade	Moderate to high SES; middle age; more familistic; predominantly white
Crestwood/Shadeland	Windy Hills	Moderate to high SES; more elderly; less familistic; predominantly white
Green Acres	Newburg	Moderate to low SES; younger; more familistic; predominantly black

was less than or equal to our desired goal of 300. In these cases, the University of Kentucky Research Center (UKSRC), which conducted the telephone interviews, was instructed to survey the universe of households. In the other six cases, the UKSRC was instructed to use random sampling techniques to identify the 300 households with listed telephone numbers to be surveyed. In all cases, random selection techniques were used to select the adult in the household to be interviewed. A total of 2,867 households were contacted during the fall of 1986. After deleting persons who refused to be interviewed or who reported that the telephone number assigned to them was no longer attached to a household located in the particular local governmental jurisdiction in question, the UKSRC was able to complete a total of 2016 interviews for a response rate of 70.3 percent. Table 1.2 summarizes the number of households contacted and the response rates for each of the ten research sites.

To assess whether the five matched pairs of socioeconomic communities selected on the basis of 1980 census data were in fact comparable pairs of research sites, tests of differences in means or proportions were performed using data from the telephone surveys concerning such demographic traits as age, income, education, race, homeownership status, and the number of children under eighteen years of age living at home. For the most part, the differences

Table 1.2

Summary of Survey Site Households, Telephones Surveyed, and Response Rates

Consolidated/fragmented government matched sites	N of households with listed phone no.	N valid phone no. surveyed	N of completed interviews*
LEX: Blueberry	310ᵁ	259	211 (81.5%)
LOU: Minor Lane Heights	307ᵁ	240	157 (65.4%)
LEX: Chinoe	753ˢ	329	225 (68.4%)
LOU: Beechwood Village	497ˢ	303	188 (62.0%)
LEX: Stonewall	661ˢ	319	254 (79.6%)
LOU: Barbourmeade	290ᵁ	254	173 (68.1%)
LEX: Crestwood/Shadeland	858ˢ	316	253 (80.1%)
LOU: Windy Hills	657ˢ	301	181 (60.1%)
LEX: Green Acres	302ᵁ	268	208 (77.6%)
LOU: Newburg	891ˢ	278	166 (59.7%)

*Percentages indicate the proportion of valid telephone numbers called that resulted in completed interview.

ᵁIndicates that all households with telephone numbers listed in the municipal directory were defined as a universe to be surveyed.

ˢIndicates that a random sample of approximately 300 households was drawn from the list of all households with telephone numbers listed in the municipal directory.

were small and statistically insignificant.

As seen in Table 1.3, however, a few statistically significant differences were observed. Most seemed to have little substantive import. For example, significant differences in racial composition were found in three of the matched pairs of research sites even though we had selected our survey sites to be predominantly white or predominantly black. In all three cases, however, the racial composition of the paired sites was as predicted from the 1980 census data: they were predominantly and overwhelmingly white or black despite statistically significant differences in proportions computed from information provided by respondents. Simply put, in each case, one of the matched pair of sites had somewhat more black (or white) respondents than the other, although both, as expected, had very, very few blacks (or whites). Similar arguments can be made for the statistically significant differences observed for most of our other nominal and ordinal measures of demographic variables. The only interval level measures tested were age and number of children under eighteen, neither of which evidenced discernible differences in means across research sites.

While the observed differences across the matched sites are small and of probably limited significance, many of the analyses to be presented incorporate individual-level values of these variables to supplement the control provided through the matching process itself. As we have noted, this is one of the internal

Table 1.3

Difference in Means/Proportions for Paired Research Sites for Selected Demographic Variables

Demographic variables[†]

Research site		AGE	EDUC.	IN-COME	RACE	OCCU.	RENT/OWN	NKIDS
LEX:	Blueberry	41.2	4.59	2.88	0.92	4.14	0.90	1.89
LOU:	Minor Lane	43.6	3.15*	2.30*	0.99*	3.20*	0.92	1.99
LEX:	Stonewall	51.2	5.47	4.92	0.96	4.75	0.98	1.72
LOU:	Barbourmeade	49.9	5.42	4.88	0.96	4.94	0.99	1.76
LEX:	Crestwood	54.9	5.50	3.57	1.00	5.14	0.94	1.41
LOU:	Windy Hills	56.4	5.35	4.14*	0.95*	4.56*	0.98*	1.48
LEX:	Chinoe	52.8	5.59	3.39	1.00	4.79	0.75	1.53
LOU:	Beechwood	53.4	5.05*	3.21	1.00	4.98	0.91*	1.52
LEX:	Green Acres	44.9	3.46	2.33	0.12	3.28	0.82	1.91
LOU:	Newburg	43.8	3.52	2.16	0.07	3.17	0.86	1.93

* = difference significant at $p < 0.05$
† Variables: AGE: number of years since birth; EDUCATION: 1 = 8 years of school or less, 2 = 9–11 years, 3 = completed high school, 4 = high school plus business or technical training, 5 = some college, 6 = completed college, 7 = graduate or professional school beyond college; TOTAL HOUSEHOLD INCOME: 0 = < $10,000, 1 = $10K–$20K, 2 = $20K–$30K, 3 = $30K–$40K, 4 = $40K–$50K, 5 = $50K–$60K, 6 = $60K–$70K, 7 = $70K–$80K, 8 = > 80K; RACE: 1 = white, 0 = black; OCCUPATION: 1 = laborer, machine operator, 2 = clerical or retail sales, 3 = skilled technician, 4 = manager or supervisor, 5 = owner or chief executive officer, 6 = professional; RENT/OWN: 0 = rent, 1 = own; NKIDS: number of children under eighteen living at home.

validity advantages of our research design. But while we incorporate individual-level controls in a number of the analyses, comparisons of the resulting OLS regression results with comparable difference of means/proportions tests of the matched sites generally yielded similar findings, suggesting that our matching procedures were generally effective. At several points, therefore, we rely on the simpler difference of means/proportions tests for ease of presentation.

All of the individual-level socioeconomic variables used in this study are measured as listed in the notes accompanying Table 1.3. All other variables will be defined and discussed as needed in the presentation of our analyses and findings. A summary of these variables and their operationalizations is also presented in appendix A. A complete copy of the questionnaire used by the University of Kentucky Research Center for interviewing respondents for this study is provided in appendix B.

Overview of the Book

We will begin with a presentation of our basic findings concerning the sources and consequences of citizen dissatisfaction with local services and the governments that provide them. Chapter 2, therefore, presents our findings on the relative merits of individual-level, systemic or jurisdiction-level, and city- or neighborhood-specific explanations of the sources of satisfaction with local services. To the best of our knowledge, these findings represent the first direct attempt to confront this issue in a comprehensive manner using a research design that clearly allows for such comparisons to be made in a systematic and valid manner. Chapter 3 presents our expanded version of Hirschman's model of responses to dissatisfaction. The EVLN model both conceptually organizes "exit," "voice," "loyalty," and "neglect" behaviors as responses to dissatisfaction and specifies how citizens select among them. Chapter 4 presents the results of a partial empirical test of this model using data from the Lexington and Louisville study, followed by a presentation and test of a respecified version of the model. While very similar to the EVLN model presented in chapter 3, this respecified model is predicated on positing attitudes and behaviors associated with the notion of "loyalty" as the default or ritualistic reaction of those who are basically satisfied with their local tax–service packages rather than as a response to dissatisfaction. Taken together, chapters 2, 3, and 4 provide a comprehensive and integrated account of satisfaction and responses to dissatisfaction with urban services.

As we will see, the findings presented through chapter 4 contrast sharply with some of the empirical findings of proponents of the public choice model of local government organization. We believe that the roots of this disagreement lie in some of the underlying assumptions of the public choice approach, especially as represented by the influential Tiebout exiting hypothesis and applied to assessing the relative merits of fragmented and consolidated local governmental arrangements. Therefore, we explore a number of underlying assumptions and propositions drawn from the rather large body of literature on the public choice model much more thoroughly in chapter 5. Our findings raise serious questions about the theoretical underpinnings of the public choice preference for government fragmentation.

Simply raising questions about the public choice model does not, however, provide an intellectual justification for the alternative institutional recommendations of traditional civic reformers. That is, pointing out the limitations of fragmentation cannot, in and of itself, demonstrate the advantages of consolidation.

We therefore attempt to develop and test three independent, political justifications for consolidation in chapters 6, 7, and 8. In chapter 6, we develop and test a model of institutionally induced attribution errors in citizens' evaluations of and satisfaction with public services. Chapter 7 presents an even more finely detailed examination than that provided by chapter 5 of the implications of fragmentation versus consolidation for blacks living in socioeconomically similar communities in our two types of urban settings, an issue that has generated its own rather voluminous literature. And in chapter 8, we examine several models of citizenship in urban communities, linking the behavioral responses of the EVLN model to governmental institutions and individual-level attachment to the community. Taken together, the results presented in these chapters suggest that citizens in consolidated metropolitan settings are better able to evaluate accurately the services provided by their local governments, are provided a more equitable distribution of services, and are more likely to respond in a constructive manner when they become dissatisfied.

Our concluding chapter, chapter 9, focuses on the implications of all of these findings for designing urban political institutions. In a very real sense our findings force us to think again about many of the basic assumptions and propositions about the alleged virtues of having our urban areas served by a highly fragmented government system versus a larger, more inclusive, and more structurally unified system. At minimum, they offer some theoretically and empirically grounded arguments that will help to improve the quality of the debate about metropolitan structure that has been waged for almost half a century between advocates of the public choice model and the traditional civic reformers.

In this debate, our findings lead us to fall squarely on the side of the traditional reformers. In an age where most Americans are no longer novices at living in or thinking about large-scale metropolitan settings, our findings raise provocative questions about the extent to which the mere size of local political entities can be used to define the nature and content of citizenship. It may even be time, we believe, to reassess the utility of such notions as a "community of limited liability" that served to characterize the loosening of traditional ties and attachments to local jurisdictions among urban dwellers during the 1950s and early 1960s.[22] With new institutions, we may be able to establish new ties and attachments that might provide the foundation for a more civil urban life.

Notes

1. Lineberry (1977, p. 10).
2. See Conlan and Walker (1986) for a discussion of President Reagan's "New Federalism."
3. Peterson (1981); Kantor (1988); and Wong (1988).
4. See Yates (1977, pp. 18–20); Sharp (1986, pp. 1–5); and Lineberry (1977, pp. 1–12).
5. For a quick sampling of this literature, see Aberbach and Walker (1970); and Hero and Durand (1980).
6. A reading of Stipak (1977), along with, say, Brown and Coulter (1983), will provide a basic understanding of the thrust and scope of this literature.
7. Yates (1977), along with Talbot (1969), and Ferman (1985), provide insights into the issue of civic leadership and management. Lineberry (1977) and Sharp (1986), among others, address the effects of neighborhood needs and characteristics. A discussion of the possible effects of unique historical and cultural factors on how urban citizens evaluate local services and governments can be found in Elazar (1970).
8. See Ostrom, Tiebout, and Warren (1961), Phares (1989), Wood (1961a), and

Zimmerman (1972) for summaries of these two classic approaches to understanding a wide range of issues and questions pertaining to urban government and politics, including the important question of how best to structure urban political systems so that most, if not all, citizens will be basically satisfied with their local services and the government or governments that provide them.

9. The classic works concerning these types of responses can be found in Bachrach and Baratz (1970), and Sears and McConahay (1973).

10. See, for example, Fowler (1974); Beck, Rainey, Nicholls, and Traut (1987); Tiebout (1956); Ostrom, Tiebout, and Warren (1961); Sharp (1986); and Coulter (1988), for a solid introduction to each of these themes.

11. See Sharp (1986) and especially Sharp (1984c) for excellent summaries of the literature on these subjects.

12. A discussion of the Tiebout response and its theoretical underpinnings can be found in Tiebout (1956), and Ostrom, Tiebout, and Warren (1961).

13. Goodman (1977, p. 245).

14. Jones (1989, p. 38).

15. Concepts such as "local political efficacy," to mention just one example, are used in several studies to explain why citizens develop particular feelings about the quality and quantity of urban services, as well as why they do what they do in response to those feelings. Unfortunately, similar substantive meanings can be found in the literature concerning the effects of such related concepts as "community disaffection." See Beck et al. (1987), and Stipak (1977). Then there is the confusion created by confounding such things as "citizen interest," "awareness," "information," and "knowledge" with feelings of being able to influence government decisions concerning local services. See Beck et al. (1987); Vedlitz and Veblen (1980); and Hero (1986).

Sometimes these types of conceptual problems raised serious measurement problems as well. Perhaps the most glaring measurement problem confronted in this study concerned the notion of "exit," or "voting with one's feet," as a response to dissatisfaction with local services. As will be noted in detail later in this book, all of the measures used to test hypotheses concerning exit behaviors prior to this study were based on reported moves or intentions to move regardless of motive or reasons. As such, they fail to distinguish between those who are "exiters" because of job transfers or personal reasons and those who are moving or intend to move to another local jurisdiction that offers a more satisfactory tax–service package. Only the latter type of exiter meets the underlying assumptions of the Tiebout model.

16. Hirschman (1970).

17. Lyons (1977).

18. The Elazar classification scheme of "Traditionalistic," "Individualistic," and "Moralistic" political cultures has been discussed in numerous places. For a concise description of these terms see Elazar (1972).

19. See Ostrom, Tiebout, and Warren (1961), for a summary of the research findings from these studies.

20. See Lyons (1971, pp. 398–408) for a discussion of survey versus aggregate measures of familistic versus nonfamilistic life-styles.

21. A simple random digit dialing technique was not a viable option since telephone numbers, including the first three prefix numbers, are rarely assigned to conform to the kinds of spatial considerations that were imperative for this project.

22. For discussion of this term and its relevance to the events that were taking place as the "outward explosion" of America's urban areas was beginning to take shape in late 1950s and early 1960s, see Janowitz (1967).

2

The Sources of
Citizen Satisfaction

As former Chicago Mayor Michael Bilandic discovered when he was swept from office, getting the snow removed from city streets in a timely manner is not a trivial issue. Nor is it one that has gone unstudied by social scientists. Citizen satisfaction with public services has long been linked to a broad array of political behaviors, a linkage that is one of two central themes of this book. But why do citizens become satisfied or dissatisfied with their local governments in the first place? Answering this question is an appropriate starting point for our assessment of citizens' political behaviors in response to local government services.

Despite substantial scholarly attention, our knowledge about the origins and determinants of citizen satisfaction remains fragmentary. As noted in chapter 1, the literature offers three basic kinds of explanations of citizen satisfaction with urban services: (1) those focusing on various kinds of individual-level factors; (2) those stressing varying types of systemic or jurisdictional-level factors; and (3) those emphasizing city- or neighborhood-specific determinants of satisfaction.[1] While potentially additive and complementary, these approaches have seldom been compared or tested in combination. Moreover, their fragmentary and sometimes contradictory findings often raise as many questions as they answer.

Our fragmentary understanding of the determinants of satisfaction is not due, we believe, to a lack of theoretical imagination, but rather to limits in our tools of investigation. The inferential limits of the city-specific case study have been recognized for many years. But even the more systematic research designs employed by political scientists have been less than ideally suited for disentangling the three accounts of citizens' satisfaction with urban governance. In this chapter we provide a more detailed examination of these three types of explanations, along with an assessment of the research designs and techniques that have been used to investigate them. And we will argue that the Lexington–Louisville data provide us with a unique opportunity to assess the three explanations of satisfaction simultaneously, an assessment that points to a very straightforward account of how citizens evaluate the services provided by their local governments.

Three Explanations of Citizen Satisfaction

Individual-level Explanations

Given that much of the political behavior literature concentrates on individual attitudes and actions, it is not surprising that the dominant approach to understanding satisfaction focuses on individual-level factors. In particular, two individual-level approaches characterize the literature, although it should also be noted that the best analyses link both in more complex causal models of citizen satisfaction.[2] The first and older body of research in this tradition focuses on *demographic* variables. For example, several studies have suggested that, on average, blacks rate service quality far lower than do whites,[3] even though systematic social-class or racial biases generally have not been found to matter as much as they used to in determining the actual distribution of services within individual cities.[4] Other studies have suggested that age, income, gender, occupation, homeownership, marital status, and size of household may affect some service evaluations, but again, there is little consensus about the importance of these variables.[5]

While there is a long tradition of examining the demographic correlates of satisfaction with public services, these analyses usually do not clarify just why any observed empirical relationship should exist. All too often, the finding that a particular demographic variable is related to satisfaction remains simply an unexplained empirical observation. In other analyses, however, the demographic variables are interpreted as proxies for more immediate attitudes and beliefs presumed to be directly influencing citizens' satisfaction with services. And these underlying attitudes and beliefs constitute the second set of individual-level factors discussed in the literature.

Prominent in this set of factors is the concept of *political efficacy*. Although many researchers have accepted Balch's argument that political efficacy is a government-specific phenomenon, few have totally abandoned the use of the standard measure of general political efficacy found in the general political participation literature.[6] Accordingly, many urban scholars now attempt to distinguish between general political efficacy as measured by the traditional Survey Research Center (SRC) index, and the notion of *local political efficacy* as it relates to particular local governments.

Efforts along this line have been subsumed under a variety of labels and indicators. Beck et al. and Stipak deal with the general notion of *local political efficacy* under the heading of community disaffection and found it to be strongly associated with service satisfaction.[7] Similarly, in a study of citizen evaluations of police protection, another measure closely resembling Balch's notion of local political efficacy was found to be positively and significantly related to satisfaction.[8] But, while the role of disaffection and/or local political efficacy in shaping service evaluations has been studied, some considerable ambiguity remains, especially in regard to its measurement. This is an issue we consider more fully below.

Social investment, or what Sharp calls "stakeholding,"[9] on the part of citizens might also be expected to influence service evaluations. By social investment, we mean the degree to which citizens are socially and psychologically attached to the community. Those who are highly invested in and attached to their community are hypothesized to be more satisfied with their local governments and more loyal to them. Although the findings on this hypothesis have been mixed, some of the more complex analyses have found community attachment or investment to be related to service evaluations, albeit indirectly.[10]

On the basis of such analyses, we can formalize the individual-level model of citizen satisfaction with urban services in the following manner:

$$\text{SATISFACTION}_i = a + b_1 \text{ GENDER}_i + b_2 \text{ RACE}_i + b_3 \text{ INCOME}_i + b_4 \text{ AGE}_i$$
$$+ b_5 \text{ HOMEOWNERSHIP}_i + b_6 \text{ LOCAL EFFICACY}_i$$
$$+ b_7 \text{ GEN'L EFFICACY}_i + b_8 \text{ INVESTMENT}_i,$$

where the first five variables are self-explanatory individual-level demographic factors; LOCAL EFFICACY is local political efficacy; GEN'L EFFICACY is general political efficacy; and INVESTMENT is the level of social and psychological attachment to the community.

Jurisdiction-level Explanations

Our second approach to understanding the sources of satisfaction focuses on systemic jurisdiction-level phenomena. We should point out, however, that in some cases the boundary between this approach and the individual-level models can be quite fuzzy. For example, a number of aggregate-level analyses and multiple-city surveys have suggested that several of the individual-level demographic factors discussed above may have jurisdiction-level analogs that influence satisfaction over and above their individual-level impacts. Although none of the studies reporting significant variations in satisfaction across cities on the basis of aggregate differences in the size of the nonwhite population or differences in mean per-capita income has been able to ascertain whether they were due to individual- or jurisdiction-level causes,[11] the possibility that the jurisdiction-level dimension of such variables may have an added impact remains theoretically plausible. The percentage of blacks in a city's population may affect service perceptions of individual blacks and/or whites if evaluations are based on how responsive residents believe the municipality has been to the needs of various racial communities. Similarly, whether the population of a city is wealthy or poor on average may be more important in determining satisfaction than the personal wealth of a given citizen. In any event, factors such as RACE and INCOME must be examined at both levels of analysis.

Another and somewhat broader interpretation of this same general orientation emphasizes the larger *societal and economic context* in which local citizens conduct their daily lives, rather than specific jurisdiction-level demographic characteristics such as race and income. Williams, for example, asserts that individuals and household units search for access to a broad range of "life-style maintaining" conditions by locating in specific neighborhoods within a given urban area, thereby segregating themselves into discreet social worlds.[12]

This type of clustering of households into relatively homogeneous neighborhoods has been discussed extensively in the literature, a body of work that we discuss more thoroughly in chapter 3. It is also thought to be associated with differing service expectations and, therefore, differing evaluations of local tax–service packages. Indeed, several studies have reported significant differences in the service expectations of various types of neighborhoods, with upper-class areas displaying strong interests in "amenities," while working-class communities stress "housekeeping services," and lower-status areas push for "social services."[13] If variations in service expectations across communities are independent of or have an intensifying effect on individual-level socioeconomic and life-style considerations, they should be considered in trying to understand differences in satisfaction with local services and the governments that supply them.

A third class of jurisdiction-level factors focuses on various features of local *governmental structures*. While a number of variables are noted in the literature (e.g., strong mayor versus manager systems or district versus at-large representation), one of the most important and most widely discussed is the distinction between having an urban area served by a highly fragmented versus a more integrated or even a fully consolidated system of local government. As noted previously, the debate over this structural issue has been waged for decades between advocates of public choice theory as represented by the Tiebout exiting hypothesis and supporters of the more traditional civic reform approach to governing urban areas. The core idea underlying the public choice approach is that citizens living in highly fragmented systems of local government can shop for the kind of tax–service package they want from among numerous local jurisdictions competing for consumers of (and taxpayers for) their services. Citizens living under such a competitive, quasi-market arrangement, the argument continues, will experience higher levels of service performance and accessibility, as compared to those who are forced to receive their services from a more unified or consolidated government monopoly.[14] The traditional civic reform view, in contrast, argues that larger and more comprehensive units of local government, including consolidated ones, can be more cost-effective due to economies of scale, provide clearer lines of political accountability, and offer greater opportunities for applying professional expertise to the complexities of urban life.[15] In the end, both views assert that their preferred institutional arrangement better promotes citizen satisfaction.

Not surprisingly, these competing hypotheses have attracted the attention of urban researchers. Although efforts have been made to examine a broader range of urban services, much of the attention given to these questions has been directed at satisfaction with local police services.[16] Most of these studies use some form of comparison group design. As we shall see, however, the designs that have been used often do not enable researchers meaningfully to examine the effects on satisfaction of the alternative structural arrangements referred to above. Still, assuming for the moment that they actually do tap into the impacts of fragmentation or consolidation, rather than simply the size of local jurisdictions, these studies tend to provide strong support for the public choice view, with Rogers and Lipsey's bivariate comparison of general satisfaction in two Nashville metropolitan jurisdictions being perhaps the most directly relevant example.[17]

Another type of systemic or jurisdiction-level consideration that might be related to the formation of citizen evaluations of urban services concerns actual differences in the level and quality of the services provided. It might be argued that, all other things being equal, local jurisdictions offering more and higher-quality services may be perceived more favorably by their citizens than those with fewer and poorer services. While this might seem obvious, it is by no means clear that satisfaction is directly related to service levels and quality. Previous research indicates that subjective evaluations of services do not always reflect objective service quality, nor, as we will see in chapters 5 and 6, are these evaluations laden with accurate information about actual governmental activities and performance.[18] Citizens who have had prior contacts with local officials appear to be somewhat more accurate judges of service quality, but these kinds of citizens are in the minority. Putting off for the moment the question of accuracy, these previous findings do not rule out the possibility that jurisdiction-level variations in service levels and quality might influence citizen satisfaction.

Taken together, this analysis of various systemic or jurisdiction-level determinants of satisfaction suggests the following model:

$$\text{SATISFACTION}_i = a + b_1 \text{ RACE-J}_i + b_2 \text{ INCOME-J}_i +$$
$$b_3 \text{ SOCIAL CONTEXT}_i + b_4 \text{ ALTERNATIVES}_i +$$
$$b_5 \text{ NO. OF SERVICES}_i + b_6 \text{ SERVICE QUALITY}_i,$$

where RACE-J indicates the dominant racial composition of a jurisdiction; INCOME-J indicates the average income level; SOCIAL CONTEXT indicates the "socioeconomic matrix" of a community; ALTERNATIVES indicates whether a jurisdiction operates under a consolidated urban–county government or a fragmented system offering many alternative municipalities within a metropolitan area; NO. OF SERVICES is the actual number of services provided in the jurisdiction; and SERVICE QUALITY is the actual quality of services provided.

City and Neighborhood-specific Explanations

After we have accounted for individual- and jurisdiction-level systemic influences on citizen satisfaction with urban services, what remains? Two possibilities exist. On the one hand, the remaining variance could be due to simple random error. This assumption is frequently built into analyses relying on single surveys of individuals living in multiple jurisdictions. On the other hand, unique, but not strictly random, city- or neighborhood-specific factors could be accounting for much of this unexplained variance. While not directly concerned with studying citizen satisfaction with services per se, a rich case literature in urban politics suggests that a wide variety of such factors, including unique historical events, the quality of local political leadership, and/or local management practices, can have a considerable impact on the quality of services and on how citizens evaluate them.[19]

Enumerating a complete list of such city- and neighborhood-specific influences would be a difficult and perhaps unending task, not to mention the problems that would be created if such an exhaustive list of unique factors had to be incorporated into a meaningful but parsimonious model of citizen satisfaction with urban services. To be inclusive, such a list would need to identify everything from the specific history of a given city to its mayor's leadership style, management practices, and unique policies. Some of these factors, moreover, can become easily confounded with several of the systemic or jurisdictional-level explanations that we have outlined. Changes in civic leadership or an influx of new residents with different service needs and expectations, for example, can lead to significant changes in the kind and quality of local services offered. They can also help to alter or reinforce existing views about various structural questions, including whether it is better to fight or to welcome such integrative efforts as annexation or consolidation.

These difficulties do not mean, however, that it is pointless to include such unique city- or neighborhood-specific considerations into the study of how and why citizens develop positive or negative evaluations of urban services and the local governments that supply them. Indeed, the case literature suggests that they are very important. The difficulty, of course, is developing a research design that allows us validly to separate the influence of such variables from the more general random variation in services and their evaluations that might be expected to pervade phenomena that many regard as having low salience. While the problems confronting such a design will be discussed more fully below, it is possible to specify a rather simple, if not very informative, formal model for explaining the effects of city- and/or neighborhood-specific determinants of citizen satisfaction. This basic model would read as follows:

$$\text{SATISFACTION}_i = a + b_1 \text{COMM1}_i + b_2 \text{COMM2}_i + \ldots b_n \text{COMM}n_i,$$

where the coefficients represent the mean levels of each neighborhood or community within an urban area relative to the score of a reference neighborhood or community as captured by the constant term. Such a model implies rather simplistically that the residents of each neighborhood/city will have a unique mean level of satisfaction with governance as a function of a unique array of circumstances.

The Limits of Research Design

How do the three types of explanations of citizen evaluations relate to the research strategies commonly used in the literature? More important, are these designs adequate to the task of decomposing the determinants of citizens' satisfaction with local government services? Two types of research designs are commonly employed, each of which offers strengths and weaknesses relative to the three modes of explanation.

The most common type of analysis, a survey of individuals living in a single city,[20] has the advantage of allowing scholars to assess the individual-level determinants of satisfaction directly. Unfortunately, such analyses, by their very nature, tell us little about either the jurisdiction-level systemic or the city-specific determinants of satisfaction. The influence of these variables on service evaluations is lost in the intercept term in empirical analyses of data where the values they must take are constant. A variant on this approach is found in the use of separate surveys of a limited number of cities, usually two or three cities in a single state or two or three neighborhoods in a single city. While providing the foundation for some very sophisticated analyses, most of these studies include too few cities to account for jurisdiction-level systemic and neighborhood- or city-specific influences. There is simply not enough variation in these two sources of influence in two or three sites to sort out their relative importance in determining satisfaction levels.[21]

The second research strategy employs single surveys of citizens from multiple jurisdictions.[22] While such designs are better able to sort out both individual- and jurisdiction-level systemic determinants of satisfaction, so few individuals are typically surveyed in any one city that it is difficult to measure the impact of neighborhood- or city-specific influences. It is unlikely that the relatively few respondents from any one city are sufficiently representative of that municipality to justify inferences about city-specific influences on satisfaction, let alone anything about neighborhood-specific influences. The variance created by such factors becomes lost in the residual term of these analyses.

Noting the limitations of studies using these two research strategies in no way invalidates many of their specific research findings. If one is interested in making inferences about the individual-level determinants of satisfaction, as Beck

and his colleagues were, then use of a city-specific survey is probably appropriate. But if one is interested in simultaneously accounting for all three types of
determinants of satisfaction, such an approach is clearly inadequate because of
insufficient variance in jurisdiction-level influences. Instead, we need a research
design that will allow us to disentangle the two systemic influences on citizen
evaluation of city services—individual- and jurisdiction-level influences—while
controlling for community-specific determinants.

The research that, to this point, has best approximated these requirements is
the comparative jurisdiction work of several public choice analysts on general
satisfaction with services, and satisfaction with police services in particular.[23]
These studies generally employ multiple surveys of citizens living in a variety of
institutional arrangements *within* a metropolitan setting. Unfortunately, the survey sites that were purposely selected in these analyses were not designed to
provide clear contrasts on some of the key jurisdiction-level variables in which
their authors were purportedly interested. By contrasting large and small jurisdictions *within* a single metropolitan area, rather than similar communities across
fundamentally different metropolitan area institutional arrangements (i.e., a pure
consolidated government versus a pure fragmented system), these analyses can
tell us more about the impact of city size within a common metropolitan institutional setting than about the intrinsic impact of institutional arrangements per se.
When, as is typical, they are coupled with an exclusive reliance on bivariate
analyses, these studies clearly are of limited utility in fully accounting for the
sources of citizen satisfaction.

Testing the Satisfaction Explanations

To test the relative merits of the three explanations of citizen satisfaction with
urban services, as well as the relative importance of the factors subsumed under
each of these explanations, it is imperative that we turn to the kind of research
design described in chapter 1. By using survey data from our five matched pairs
of spatially defined socioeconomic communities located in the highly fragmented greater-Louisville versus the more consolidated Lexington setting, we
can move a long way toward accomplishing both of these goals. We will have
sufficient variation in both individual- and jurisdiction-level variables to meaningfully assess their roles in determining citizen satisfaction. Given this basic
research strategy, the remaining challenge is to design theoretically relevant
measures and estimation procedures that allow us to maximize the full potential
of the research design.

Variables and Their Measurement

The dependent variable, SATISFACTION, is based on responses to two questions: (i) "Would you say that you are currently VERY SATISFIED, SATIS-

FIED, DISSATISFIED, or VERY DISSATISFIED with the way [name of local government] is doing its job?" and (ii) "In general, how good a job do you feel [name of local government] is currently doing in providing services—would you say that it is doing EXCELLENT, GOOD, or a POOR job?" Since the two items were moderately to strongly correlated ($r = 0.67$), the responses were combined to form a seven-point index, ranging from zero to six. Importantly, this is a very general or bottom-line measure of satisfaction that presumably addresses both the service and tax-cost components of the citizen's evaluation of his or her local government.

Although it might be argued that these two questions are tapping separate dimensions of satisfaction, separate SAS LOGIST analyses of the two components of this combined SATISFACTION index on the separate models outlined above produced nearly identical results. This similarity was maintained for the combined models as well. The signs of the coefficients were the same, and those that were statistically significant using the combined measure were also significant using the two separate or component measures of satisfaction.[24] Therefore, we present results only for the full SATISFACTION index.

Turning to the independent variables identified under the individual-level explanation, we see that RACE and GENDER are dichotomous measures with a value of one, indicating that the respondent is white and male, respectively. Similarly, a value of one for the dummy variable HOMEOWNERSHIP indicates that the respondent owns his or her own home. The remaining individual-level, demographic variables—INCOME, AGE, and EDUCATION—were coded as indicated in notes accompanying Table 1.3 presented in the previous chapter.

Several social-psychological variables were also included in the individual-level model of SATISFACTION. The four standard items developed by Campbell, Gurin, and Miller were considered for inclusion in an indicator of GENERAL EFFICACY (alpha = 0.54).[25] Although there is some controversy over the meaning of the traditional four-item measure,[26] an abbreviated GENERAL EFFICACY scale made up of the first two items shown in the GENERAL EFFICACY measure defined in appendix A (alpha = 0.68), generated nearly identical empirical results as the full, four-item scale. Therefore, the four-item scale is employed in this analysis.

As has been noted, urban scholars have found it important to distinguish between general and local political efficacy, although no standard measurement convention has yet emerged. Unfortunately, many of the measures that have been used to tap this concept confound citizen information and knowledge about local government with feelings about being able to influence government decisions.[27] Indeed, Hero employs the Seligson–Sharp indicator as a measure of awareness, rather than as a measure of efficacy.[28] Our measure instead follows the lead suggested by Balch in 1974, who simply directed the focus of the items included in the traditional efficacy scale onto a particular level or unit of government.[29] Thus, our measure of LOCAL EFFICACY, as noted in appendix A, consists of four items: belief that *local officials* don't care about you; not caring what happens in *local government* and politics; thinking it is not worth paying attention to *local issues*; and believing that it is useless to complain to *local officials* (alpha = 0.69).

Five items were combined to tap the concept of individual-level social and psychological INVESTMENT in the community. As noted in appendix A, these items focused on the degree of emotional attachment respondents had to the community, how sorry the respondent would be to leave his or her immediate neighborhood or community, the number of friends and relatives who live in the area, and length of residence (alpha = 0.53). Somewhat surprisingly, the rent/own item used here as a demographic variable did not scale well with the five items included in INVESTMENT, suggesting that the levels of psychological attachment to and social involvement in a neighborhood are distinct from the most common form of capital or economic investment.

Contrasts on three of the six types of systemic or jurisdiction-level determinants of satisfaction identified in the literature—fragmented versus consolidated government, social context, and racial composition—were built into our comparison group design. Since five of our research sites are located in the highly fragmented greater-Louisville setting, while the other five in Lexington operated within a consolidated system, we were able to create a dummy indicator labeled ALTERNATIVES to capture this important variable. Respondents from the greater-Louisville setting were assigned an ALTERNATIVES value of one, indicating that they live in a fragmented government environment in which citizens have many *alternative* municipalities in which to reside within their metropolitan area. ALTERNATIVES for their counterparts from the Lexington setting was coded as zero, indicating that they have few choices in selecting among municipalities in which to reside within their consolidated metropolitan area. These five matched pairs of research sites were also used to create four dummy variables to capture the effects of differing social and economic environments, with MATCH1 through MATCH4 representing the first four matched pairs of research sites listed in Table 1.1, while the poorer and predominantly black neighborhoods of Newburg and Green Acres serve as our reference category for this variable.

The racial composition of the research site was a third jurisdiction-level variable of concern. As noted in the previous chapter, two of our research sites were composed of large black majority populations. Thus, we might use a dummy variable indicator that is the mirror image of the social worlds MATCH variables, scored one for the residents of the two predominantly black communities, to tap this jurisdiction-level variable. The problem, of course, is that this indicator, in combination with the MATCH and ALTERNATIVES indicators, would introduce perfect collinearity into any multivariate analysis. A better way to interpret the systemic effects of the jurisdiction-level racial composition variable is to focus on expectations about our social context dummy variables. Support for the social context view, for example, suggests that the four MATCH coefficients for the four predominantly white pairs of communities should differ not only from the black community referents, but among themselves as well. Support for the racial implications of the systemic or jurisdictional approach, on the other hand, should result in our finding few, if any, significant differences in satisfaction between respondents from our four predominantly white MATCH pairs of communities, but very sharp differences between these white communities and our predominantly black community referents. By interpreting the MATCH coefficients with these expectations in mind, then, we need not add a separate racial composition dummy to the analysis.

While this will comprise our major approach to assessing this particular dimension of the racial factor, we will at times also employ RACE-J, which is a measure of the proportion of the population of each research site that is white, as an alternative indicator that is less than perfectly collinear with the MATCH indicators when combined with the ALTERNATIVES measure. We will also use INCOME-J, which is a measure of the mean income for each of the ten research sites, as an alternative way to assess the jurisdictional-level impact of wealth above and beyond its individual-level equivalent discussed earlier.

The fifth jurisdiction-level variable is NO. OF SERVICES—the actual number of services provided in each Lexington neighborhood or its matched incorporated municipality in the Louisville–Jefferson County setting. This indicator is an index made up of dummy variables referring to the services listed in Table 2.1 that are actually provided by the incorporated municipalities in the greater-Louisville setting and the neighborhoods in Lexington. Inclusion of just the number of services supplied by the small cities in the former setting, however, risks confounding the fragmentation/consolidation status of the local governmental jurisdiction with the number of services. For, as noted in Table 2.1, the Jefferson County respondents receive some services from the county government and/or from special service districts in addition to those supplied by their particular incorporated municipality. To avoid this potential problem, we included another variable, labeled NO. OTHER SERVICES, which is the number of services that each of our five Jefferson County sites receives from among the eleven services listed in Table 2.1 from the county and/or the metropolitan sewer district. For the Lexington–Fayette respondents, NO. OTHER SERVICES is coded zero. Both of these service variables are employed in our analysis to assess the independent impact of the number of municipal service on citizen satisfaction.

The last jurisdiction-level variable is SERVICE QUALITY. Although we lack an objective measure of service quality, we were able to construct a proxy measure based on respondent evaluations of the services listed in Table 2.1. After providing them with a list of services, respondents were asked: "Would you say that the [service in question] is EXCELLENT, GOOD, FAIR, POOR, or IS NOT PROVIDED by the [Name of Local Government]?" Those responding with one of the first four categories were coded as having evaluated

Table 2.1

Services in Lexington/Fayette and Jefferson County Sites

Services	Lexington–Fayette Neighborhoods[a]					Jefferson County Cities[b]				
	1	2	3	4	5	1	2	3	4	5
Police protection	UCG	UCG	UCG	UCG	UCG	City	City	City	City	County
Trash collection	—	UCG	—	—	UCG	City	City	City	City	—
Street lighting	UCG	UCG	—	UCG	UCG	City	City	City	City	City
Parks & recreation	UCG	UCG	UCG	UCG	UCG	—	City	—	—	County
Road maintenance	UCG	UCG	UCG	UCG	UCG	City	City	City	City	City
Public transportation	UCG	UCG	UCG	UCG	UCG	—	—	—	—	County
Public health	UCG	UCG	UCG	UCG	UCG	County	County	County	County	County
Sanitary sewers	UCG	UCG	1/2 UCG	UCG	UCG	MSD	MSD	—	—	MSD
Planning & zoning	UCG	UCG	UCG	UCG	UCG	County	County	County	County	County
Storm sewers	UCG	UCG	UCG	UCG	UCG	MSD	—	—	—	County
Social services	UCG	UCG	UCG	UCG	UCG	County	County	County	County	County
Total serv.	10	11	8.5	10	11	9	9	7	7	10
City serv.	10	11	8.5	10	11	4	5	4	4	2

[a]UCG is the Urban–County Government. County is Jefferson County, and MSD is the Metropolitan Sewer District.
[b]The respective research sites are numbered in the order they appear in Table 1.1.

the service as one that was provided by their most immediate unit of local government (e.g., a Jefferson County municipality or the Lexington–Fayette Urban–County Government). Actual evaluations of service quality ranged between one (POOR) and four (EXCELLENT). Respondent scores for all services that were evaluated were combined to develop an individual's mean evaluation of service quality. Since we have conceptualized SERVICE QUALITY as a jurisdiction-level variable, the individual mean rankings of service quality were combined to form a mean evaluation score for each of our ten research sites.

Obviously, this proxy indicator suffers from a number of potential problems, the most important of which concerns the errors that individuals might make in evaluating service quality.[30] Two very different types of errors are possible. First, citizens might incorrectly evaluate the quality of a local service. This would be an *assessment error*. While we cannot correct our measure for this type of error, it is unlikely to have a systematic impact given our conception of SERVICE QUALITY as a jurisdiction-level variable. Individual-level random error of this type will wash out when we use community mean evaluations of quality.

Furthermore, the mean community rankings correspond well to our impressions of the actual quality of services provided in the ten jurisdictions, as purged of an important source of bias, as seen in Table 2.2. For instance, the lowest mean ranking of service quality shown in this table is for the fragmented site in MATCH5, which is the predominantly black City of Newburg. Newburg's services can be accurately described as almost nonexistent due to serious financial difficulties that will be discussed further in chapter 6. Also, the mean rankings of service quality across the five consolidated sites are very similar, which should be the case since all of them are served by the consolidated Lexington–Fayette government. In contrast, there is greater variation in SERVICE QUALITY across the five sites located in the fragmented Louisville setting, which would be expected given the different service providers. In short, we believe that the SERVICE QUALITY proxy used here is a valid indicator of actual service quality; it generates markedly similar and markedly different scores where they are expected.

A second, and more troubling source of error in citizen evaluations of services occurs when such evaluations are based on a misunderstanding of what services are actually the government's responsibility. Such *errors in attribution* can occur when a citizen: (1) fails to recognize that a particular unit of local government is providing the service in question; (2) holds a unit of local government responsible for providing a service that is not being provided by any of several local governments; or (3) holds a local government responsible for a service actually provided by another local government. Such errors, as we will see in chapter 6, can bias both individual-level *and* community-level mean evaluation scores. Although a detailed discussion of this problem and our method for decomposing such evaluations into their biased and unbiased components is presented later in this book, it should be noted that the mean SERVICE QUALITY scores reported in the top half of Table 2.2 are unbiased with respect to attribution error and have been computed using the methodology described in chapter 6.[31]

Since, as we will see in Chapter 6, bias due to attribution error is greater in fragmented than in consolidated settings, we used the biased component that was

Table 2.2

Difference-of-Means Tests for Quality and Bias in Quality for Consolidated/Nonconsolidated Research Sites

Matched sites[a]	Consolidated-site	Fragmented-site	Difference	t-value
Variable = SERVICE QUALITY				
MATCH 1	2.498	2.737	−0.239***	3.040
[106/81]	(0.105)[b]	(0.605)		
MATCH 2	2.746	2.769	−0.023	0.682
[88/109]	(0.343)	(0.467)		
MATCH 3	2.498	2.235	0.263***	3.450
[82/116]	(0.437)	(0.637)		
MATCH 4	2.612	2.658	−0.046	0.530
[72/75]	(0.510)	(0.537)		
MATCH 5	2.546	1.897	0.649***	6.470
[121/70]	(0.524)	(0.738)		
Variable = BIAS IN SERVICE QUALITY				
MATCH 1	−0.064	0.184	−0.248***	8.300
[133/86]	(0.105)	(0.265)		
MATCH 2	0.001	−0.306	0.307***	10.670
[223/115]	(0.007)	(0.308)		
MATCH 3	−0.013	−0.043	0.030	1.330
[140/126]	(0.066)	(0.245)		
MATCH 4	−0.018	−0.181	0.163***	4.420
[135/100]	(0.060)	(0.363)		
MATCH 5	0.001	−0.386	0.387***	6.950
[206/88]	(0.018)	(0.522)		

$* = p < 0.10$; $** = p < 0.05$; $*** = p < 0.01$.

[a]The matched pairs of sites are in the order presented in Table 1.1. The number of cases is given in the left column with the first number listed referring to the consolidated-government case and the second to the fragmented-government case.

[b]Figures in parentheses are standard deviations.

purged from the SERVICE QUALITY measure to form an additional jurisdiction-level variable known as BIAS IN QUALITY. This variable, the community
means of which are noted in the bottom half of Table 2.2, should allow us to
ascertain the effects of this particular consequence of fragmented versus consolidated government for determining citizen satisfaction with local governmental
services, and, therefore, should allow us to make a more informed interpretation
of the overall impact of the concept underlying our more general ALTERNA-
TIVES variable. Negative scores for this variable indicate that bias due to attribution errors inflates the observed mean evaluations of local services.

One other problem with the quality indicators mentioned above concerns their
relation to our dependent variable, SATISFACTION. If the specific service evaluations used to construct SERVICE QUALITY reflect a common, underlying, or
global assessment of government, rather than thoughtful judgments about the
quality of local services, and if SATISFACTION is also a product of this kind of
global assessment, then there will be a built-in tautological relationship between
these indicators.

We do not believe that this potential tautology applies to this case, however.
The correlation between the individual-level SERVICE QUALITY index (from
which the community-level proxy is constructed) and SATISFACTION is strong
($r = 0.65$), but less than perfect, as might be expected if both were reflecting the
same underlying general orientation toward government. Furthermore, if the
evaluations of specific services reflected a common, global assessment, service
rankings would not vary *across* services by individual respondents. Yet, substantial variation is evident. Indeed, the technique of decomposing mean rankings
into their biased and unbiased components in terms of attribution error mentioned above, and explored more fully in chapter 6, would not work without
variances in evaluations across services within individuals. Finally, by purging
the individual rankings of attribution error bias and then combining them to form
community mean SERVICE QUALITY, a jurisdiction-level variable, the indicator is at least two steps away from any global individual-level assessment that
may have been tapped by our dependent variable. The simple correlation between the bias purged jurisdiction-level version of SERVICE QUALITY and
SATISFACTION is only 0.46. While sizable, this is indicative of something less
than a tautology.[32]

Our final set of indicators is associated with the city- and/or neighborhood-
specific explanations of satisfaction. They consist of nine dummy variables, one
for each of the first nine spatially defined socioeconomic communities listed in
Table 1.1. A score of one indicates that a respondent resided in that dummy's
research site, with the reference site being the predominantly black City of
Newburg in Jefferson County. The use of Newburg as our reference, we will see,
facilitates some of the comparisons that will be made about the jurisdiction-level
impact of race. While the account of service satisfaction provided by this class of
explanations does not specify the many kinds of possible city- and/or neighbor-

hood-specific factors that may influence citizen evaluations, the use of the city/neighborhood-specific dummies will allow us to capture a wide range of such potential influences, albeit in somewhat of a naive manner.

Testing and Estimation Procedures

Having examined the variables to be used in this analysis, it is obvious that we cannot test simultaneously all three of the models specified above. Perfect collinearity would be guaranteed due to just the jurisdiction-level MATCH variables and the city- and neighborhood-specific dummy variables. Even when the MATCH variables were dropped from the analysis, severe collinearity problems (tolerance levels greater than 0.01) were encountered. This was especially true with regard to the site dummies and the several jurisdictional-level explanation variables. This is not surprising since these measures are site-specific.

Because of this problem, our analysis is conducted in two stages. In the first stage, the model is estimated with only the individual-level variables and the city- and neighborhood-specific explanation site dummies, thereby allowing the site dummies to account for all of the variance associated with site-specific phenomena, including those associated with the systemic jurisdictional-level determinants. A second stage of analysis is then undertaken that features an examination of the impacts of the site dummy coefficients in relation to the jurisdictional-level variables of INCOME-J, RACE-J, SERVICE QUALITY, BIAS IN SERVICE QUALITY, social context (MATCH), and ALTERNATIVES. This two-stage process, we will see, allows us to disentangle the two sources of non-individual-level variation, namely those created by jurisdiction-level and city- and/or neighborhood-specific variables.

Finally, given the limited range (zero to six) and the finite number of values of SATISFACTION, OLS regression may be less than an ideal estimation procedure. Thus, tests of the models were conducted using both OLS regression and SAS LOGIST. The LOGIST estimates generated nearly identical results as those produced from OLS estimation. The signs of the coefficients were identical, and the coefficient probability values pointed to the same substantive conclusions.[33] Given the more general familiarity with OLS among researchers in this field, we present the OLS results.

Findings

The OLS regression results for the three basic models and their variants are presented in the first four columns of Table 2.3. In the first column of the table, the results from estimating a model with just the individual-level variables are presented. Overall, these results are similar to those reported in the literature based on single-city surveys. Two of the attitudinal variables—INVESTMENT and LOCAL EFFICACY—and the RACE and INCOME demographic measures are significant at the 0.05 level or better. The coefficients indicate that white, lower-income, highly socially and/or psychologically attached, and more locally efficacious citizens tend to have higher levels of satisfaction.

Two of the findings from this initial analysis are somewhat surprising, however. First, general efficacy appears to be only weakly related to satisfaction with services. Given the tolerance value of 0.75, the low t-value for GEN'L EFFICACY (1.34) cannot be attributed to collinearity. Thus, satisfaction with local government services is more a function of local phenomena than global efficacy levels. Second, three of the demographic variables failed to generate significant coefficients: GENDER, HOMEOWNERSHIP, and AGE. However, in more sophisticated causal analyses of citizen satisfaction, these variables usually are viewed as only indirectly influencing satisfaction levels through more proximate attitudes about government.[34] Once measures of these more proximate attitudes are included, as they are in this case, their independent, direct influence on satisfaction levels might be expected to diminish.

The second column of Table 2.3 presents the results for a truncated version of the jurisdiction-level model. The five MATCH dummy variables used to tap the social context explanation were excluded because they, not surprisingly, generated severe collinearity problems (no change in R^2 and no significant coefficients). Even so, this truncated version of the model generates quite strong results. All of the coefficients are significant at the 0.01 level or better, and all have the expected sign. SATISFACTION, it would appear, is significantly higher among respondents living in predominantly white, higher-income neighborhoods served by consolidated governments that offer more and higher-quality services. It is also likely to be higher in sites with high attribution error bias, suggesting that many local governments are being given false credit for services they don't really supply, a point we consider more fully in chapter 6.

Column three presents the results for our model of site uniqueness and includes only the nine site dummy variables. While these results are not especially interesting in and of themselves, being products of a naive model, it is worth noting the sizable differences across the dummy variable coefficients, indicating that SATISFACTION levels do vary by city and/or neighborhood.

It appears, then, that each of the three models "works" to some degree when considered on its own terms. This becomes especially evident when we discover that the R^2 values generated by each of these models are nearly identical. Interestingly, however, the R^2 for the city- and neighborhood-specific model is the highest (0.267), which suggests that the substantive explanations embedded in the individual-level and jurisdictional-level models do not take us much further in understanding the roots of citizen satisfaction than a simple naive model that alerts us that each site is unique. While this finding may give some comfort to those wedded to the unique-event hypothesis found in much of the descriptive case literature, a final judgment about the substantive merits of this model must be reserved until we can complete our two-stage analysis of all three models.

The results of the terminal regression for the first stage of our comparative analysis of these models are presented in the fourth column of Table 2.3. This combined model contains the site-specific dummies to pick up the impacts of both the jurisdiction-level and the city- and neighborhood-specific explanations, as well as the variables associated with the individual-level explanations of satisfaction. Overall, the model performs as expected. The R^2 value of 0.42, in contrast to the R^2 values for the three separate models, suggests that both individual- and site-specific factors contribute to citizen satisfaction with urban services. More importantly, eight of the site dummies generated discernible coefficients, indicating that at least these eight sites have mean satisfaction levels different from that of the Newburg reference site. Also, two of the individual-level attitudinal variables (LOCAL EFFICACY and INVESTMENT) that generated significant coefficients in the first model did so in the combined model as well. The only important difference to be noted when comparing the results of columns one and four concerns the coefficients for RACE and INCOME, which were significant in the individual-level model, but are not in the combined analysis. This suggests that the earlier individual-level RACE and INCOME results might be artifacts of mean differences across research sites, or that they are a function of jurisdictional- rather than individual-level race or income characteristics. We will examine these hypotheses in greater detail below.

At this point, we are limited in what we can say about the site-specific dummies. While the results presented in column four of Table 2.3 indicate that most of the cities or neighborhoods differ from Newburg, the reference site, we cannot say whether this is a function of systematic variation in jurisdiction-level variables or truly city- and neighborhood-specific effects. To distinguish these separate site-level influences, we must turn to the second stage of our analysis. Here we examine the pattern of dummy variable site coefficients to see if they coincide with patterns that would be expected if jurisdiction-level racial and income composition, actual levels and quality of services, and fragmented versus consolidated governmental arrangements actually have the hypothesized impacts on SATISFACTION. If not, we will be left with the conclusion that the dummies reflect unique factors associated with each research site and not any of the defined jurisdiction-level characteristics included in the analysis.

Table 2.4 reports a set of more specialized t-tests contrasting pairs of the dummy variable generated in the first-stage analysis, or, more specifically, comparing the differences in the first-stage dummy coefficients across the matched Lexington–Fayette and Louisville–Jefferson County sites. Such comparisons are valid given the two levels of control for extraneous influences built into the design; the sites were deliberately matched to control for the influence of demographic variables, and many of those same demographic variables were also included as controls in the model generating these coefficients.

As expected by both traditional civic reformers and public choice proponents, sizable differences in the matched site dummy coefficients are evident in

Table 2.3

OLS Regression Results of Tests of Five Models of Citizen Satisfaction with Local Public Services

Independent variable	Model 1 Individual- level model	Model 2 Partial- jurisdiction model	Model 3 City/neigh- borhood- specific model	Model 4 Partial combined model	Model 5 Final model
GENDER	0.163* (0.092)[a]	—	—	0.046 (0.083)	0.076 (0.083)
RACE	0.503*** (0.127)	—	—	0.313 (0.231)	−0.196 (0.138)
INCOME	−0.058** (0.025)	—	—	−0.018 (0.024)	−0.008 (0.023)
AGE	−0.001 (0.003)	—	—	0.000 (0.003)	0.000 (0.003)
HOMEOWNERSHIP	−0.084 (0.159)	—	—	−0.095 (0.145)	−0.062 (0.147)
INVESTMENT	0.170*** (0.024)	—	—	0.146*** (0.022)	0.143*** (0.022)
GENERAL EFFICACY	0.026 (0.042)	—	—	0.030 (0.038)	0.029 (0.039)
LOCAL EFFICACY	0.330*** (0.028)	—	—	0.281*** (0.026)	0.291*** (0.026)
ALTERNATIVES	—	2.450*** (0.778)	—	—	—
INCOME-JURIS.	—	0.429*** (0.078)	—	—	—
RACE-JURIS.	—	−0.013*** (0.003)	—	—	—
NO. OF CITY SERVICES	—	0.307*** (0.073)	—	—	0.065* (0.039)
NO. OTHER SERVICES	—	−0.311** (0.134)	—	—	0.019 (0.057)

(continued)

Table 2.3 *(continued)*

Independent variable	Model 1 Individual-level model	Model 2 Partial-jurisdiction model	Model 3 City/neighbor-hood-specific model	Model 4 Partial combined model	Model 5 Final model
SERVICE QUALITY	—	1.384* (0.721)	—	—	2.241*** (0.268)
QUALITY BIAS	—	−2.951*** (0.414)	—	—	−1.217*** (0.231)
BLUEBERRY	—	—	1.290*** (0.208)	0.898*** (0.269)	—
STONEWALL	—	—	1.312*** (0.221)	0.748** (0.300)	—
CRESTWOOD/ SHADELAND	—	—	1.592*** (0.229)	0.951*** (0.303)	—
CHINOE	—	—	1.825*** (0.223)	1.074*** (0.299)	—
GREEN ACRES	—	—	1.320*** (0.212)	1.169*** (0.190)	—
BARBOURMEADE	—	—	0.009 (0.216)	−0.363 (0.295)	—
WINDY HILLS	—	—	1.938*** (0.228)	1.433*** (0.304)	—
MINOR LANE HEIGHTS	—	—	0.817*** (0.226)	0.666** (0.295)	—
BEECHWOOD VILLAGE	—	—	2.331*** (0.208)	1.609*** (0.291)	—
INTERCEPT	−2.632	−5.718	2.308	2.529	2.231
R^2	0.262	0.262	0.267	0.422	0.401

* $= p < 0.10$; ** $= p < 0.05$; *** $= p < 0.01$.
[a]Figures in parentheses are standard errors.

Table 2.4. Contrary to both sets of expectations, however, the direction of these differences does not follow a pattern. For two of the matched pairs (MATCH 3 and MATCH 5), the consolidated Lexington–Fayette County site coefficient was greater than its fragmented counterpart in Louisville–Jefferson County. But the reverse was true in two other cases—MATCH 2 and MATCH 4. Thus, it would seem that fragmentation versus consolidation has little direct influence on SATISFACTION. This finding highlights the importance of surveying multiple jurisdictions. It also suggests that Rogers and Lipsey's finding that satisfaction was higher in a small, independent city that had been exempted from the Nashville–Davidson County consolidation than it was in a matched neighborhood served by that government was likely an idiosyncratic result based on a single comparison.[35]

The results in Table 2.4 can also be used to assess the jurisdiction-level social context explanation, which predicts differences in the site coefficients across the five types of socioeconomic communities *within* Fayette County and *within* Jefferson County. Differences in social context, we have argued, might alter expectations about what the government should do, which in turn can influence citizen evaluations. Moreover, this explanation would lead us to expect no discernible differences in the site coefficients *across* the matched sites. Since both sites in each pair have nearly identical social characteristics, they should exhibit similar satisfaction levels. As noted in Table 2.4, however, significant differences in coefficients are evident for four of the five matched pairs of sites, with MATCH 1 (Blueberry and Minor Lane Heights) providing the lone exception. Indeed, the Lexington neighborhood of Green Acres (MATCH 5) has the highest site coefficient for the consolidated sites, while its matched site of Newburg has the second lowest site score (zero, since the site dummies are measuring the other nine sites relative to Newburg) among the fragmented sites. Thus, the pattern of dummy variable coefficients provides little support for the hypothesis that satisfaction is largely conditioned by the socioeconomic context resulting from spatial segregation.

But what of jurisdiction-level racial differences? Earlier we observed that the individual-level race variable, which was significant in the model including only the individual-level explanation measures, was no longer statistically discernible when the site dummies were included in the model. Was the individual-level race finding an artifact of jurisdiction-level racial influences on satisfaction? In other words, does black dissatisfaction arise from their minority/majority status in a community rather than from race per se? Our findings offer a mixed answer to this question. Some evidence for a jurisdiction-level race effect is evident for the Louisville–Jefferson County case. As seen in the fourth column of Table 2.3, the coefficients of three of the predominantly white sites are higher than for Newburg, the predominantly black reference category. However, the Lexington–Fayette case provides little support for the racial composition hypothesis. As seen in the *t*-tests presented in Table 2.5, all of the differences between the

Table 2.4

Comparison of OLS Regression Site Dummy Estimates for Consolidated/Nonconsolidated Research Sites (N = 735)

Matched sites[a]	Consolidated-site	Fragmented-site	Difference	t-value
MATCH 1	0.898 (0.269)[b]	0.666 (0.295)	0.232	0.900
MATCH 2	1.074 (0.299)	1.609 (0.291)	−0.535**	2.240
MATCH 3	0.748 (0.300)	−0.363 (0.295)	1.111***	5.575
MATCH 4	0.951 (0.303)	1.433 (0.304)	−0.482***	5.660
MATCH 5	1.169 (0.190)	0.000 —	1.169***	6.138

* = $p < 0.10$; ** = $p < 0.05$; *** = $p < 0.01$.
[a]The matched pairs of sites are in the order presented in Table 1.1.
[b]Figures in parentheses are standard errors.

coefficient of the Green Acres site and those of the four predominantly white sites carry the wrong sign and none is significant. The residents of Green Acres were, on average, more satisfied with their municipal government than the residents of the four predominantly white research sites in that city.

Can these mixed results be taken as evidence of jurisdiction-level racial differences? Not necessarily. Any answer that might be drawn from these empirical results is complicated by the fact that Newburg, in contrast to all of the other cities, was a relatively new entity, having incorporated only several years prior to our study. Given the desire to include a predominantly black, independent city in the analysis, however, we had little choice but to study Newburg. No other predominantly black, independent city exists among the more than ninety incorporated municipalities in Jefferson County. Still, the financial and administrative strains associated with launching a new city government can be severe and may account for our finding on the jurisdiction-level racial composition hypothesis. Indeed, the strains in this case proved fatal. As we will see in chapter 7, Newburg disincorporated within two years after our survey largely because of serious fiscal problems. For this reason, and also in light of the sharply divergent Lexington–Fayette County results, we are hesitant to conclude that jurisdiction-level racial composition influences citizen service satisfaction.

The fourth jurisdiction-level influence is assessed by INCOME-J, the average

Table 2.5

Comparison of OLS Regression Site Dummy Estimates for Black and White Research Sites in Lexington–Fayette County ($N = 735$)

| Predominantly white sites | | Predominantly black Green Acres | | |
Site	Coefficient	Coefficient	Difference	t-value
Blueberry	0.898 (0.269)[a]	1.169 (0.190)	−0.271	0.656
Chinoe	1.074 (0.299)	1.169 (0.190)	−0.095	1.112
Stonewall	0.748 (0.300)	1.169 (0.190)	−0.421	0.603
Crestwood/ Shadeland	0.951 (0.303)	1.169 (0.190)	−0.218	0.254

* $= p < 0.10$; **$= p < 0.05$; *** $= p < 0.01$.
[a]Figures in parentheses are standard errors.

income of the ten research sites. As in the case of race, both individual- and jurisdiction-level income effects were hypothesized, and the statistically discernible impact of the individual-level income variable in the individual-level model results reported in Table 2.3 sharply declined when the site dummies were added. Since the mean income of a jurisdiction is an interval measure instead of a simple dichotomy like ALTERNATIVE and RACE-J, it is no longer appropriate to use simple contrasts of the matched site coefficients of the type used in Tables 2.4 and 2.5 to evaluate the impact of INCOME-J on SATISFACTION. But if the average level of income in a jurisdiction influences satisfaction, we should find that the pattern of site coefficients (Newburg = 0) reported in the fourth column of Table 2.4 is associated with average jurisdiction income. This hypothesis is tested in the first column of Table 2.6, which reports the results of regressing the ten site coefficients on INCOME-J. As indicated by the R^2 value of 0.003 and the insignificant t-value, the hypothesis receives no support.

The second and third columns of Table 2.6 report some additional regression results on the jurisdiction-level race and consolidated/fragmented government hypotheses tested earlier. The coefficients in the second column were generated by regressing the site dummy coefficients on the ALTERNATIVES dummy variable. Again, little support is found for the contention that either fragmented or consolidated systems help to promote citizen satisfaction. Column 3 of Table 2.6 reports the results from regressing the site coefficients on RACE-J (the proportion of white respondents), and again little support is found for the juris-

Table 2.6

OLS Analyses of Jurisdiction-level Determinants of the Pattern of Stage One Site Coefficients (N = 10)

Independent variable	Dependent: Site Dummy Coefficients–Table 2.3 Model 4			
	Model 6	Model 7	Model 8	Model 9
INCOME-JURISDICTION	0.032 (0.227)[a]	—	—	—
ALTERNATIVES	—	–0.311 (0.399)	—	—
RACE-JURISDICTION	—	—	0.004 (0.006)	—
NO. CITY SERVICES	—	—	—	0.107* (0.044)
NO. OTHER SERVICES	—	—	—	0.078 (0.064)
SERVICE QUALITY	—	—	—	1.728*** (0.312)
QUALITY BIAS	—	—	—	–2.236*** (0.518)
INTERCEPT	0.880	0.787	1.995	–4.549
R^2	0.003	0.024	0.071	0.942

* = $p < 0.10$; ** = $p < 0.05$; *** = $p < 0.01$.
[a]Figures in parentheses are standard errors.

diction-level race explanation given the small R^2 value and the nonsignificant slope coefficient.

Our last jurisdiction-level explanation addresses the level and quality of services. Because NO. OF SERVICES, NO. OF OTHER SERVICES, SERVICE QUALITY, and QUALITY BIAS are interval measures, we test this explanation in the same manner as the jurisdiction-level income hypothesis. And as seen in the fourth column of Table 2.6, strong support is found for the service-based explanation. All of the service coefficients are significant except for NO. OF OTHER SERVICES, which was included simply as a control for county and special district services in the fragmented Jefferson County sites. The results indicate that citizens are more satisfied when they receive more services, when those services are of higher quality, and when attribution error bias is low.

Importantly, the four service-related variables account for almost all of the variance in the site dummy coefficients ($R^2 = 0.94$) generated in the model presented in the fourth column of Table 2.3. In other words, the level and quality of services account for almost all of the unique city and neighborhood and jurisdiction-level and, thus, site-related variance in individual satisfaction scores. And if anyone is skeptical about regression results based on only ten cases and four independent variables, we should also note that very similar findings were obtained in an alternative model including only the number of services variable.

Based on this second-stage analysis of the site dummy coefficients, a new combined model was estimated. As indicated in the last column of Table 2.3, this version of the model includes only the individual-level variables and the four service level and quality variables. Again, when we examine the individual-level variables, only the LOCAL EFFICACY and INVESTMENT coefficients are significant. And again, the three services variables found to be significant in Table 2.6 are significant when reintroduced into the respecified combined model.

Reestimation with just these significant variables yields the following simplified model ($R^2 = 0.40$) of citizen satisfaction with local services:

$$SATISFACTION_i = -2.057 + 0.276 \text{ LOCAL EFFICACY}_i +$$
$$(0.024)$$

$$0.149 \text{ INVESTMENT}_i + 0.059 \text{ NO. OF SERVICES}_i +$$
$$(0.021) \qquad\qquad (0.016)$$

$$2.011 \text{ SERVICE QUALITY}_i - 1.234 \text{ QUALITY BIAS}_i,$$
$$(0.187) \qquad\qquad (0.219)$$

where all of the coefficients are significant at the 0.001 level.

Discussion

By using a research design that allows us directly to contrast individual-level, jurisdiction-level, and city- and neighborhood-specific explanations, we have been able to develop a parsimonious account of citizen satisfaction with urban services. This account emphasizes individual citizen efficacy relative to local government, social and psychological attachment to or investment in local communities, and actual numbers and quality of services provided by local governments. Those who are invested in a community and who have higher local efficacy will tend to be more satisfied. Further, citizens living in jurisdictions with more services and higher-quality services will tend to be more satisfied.

This does not mean that we have fully explained satisfaction with local services. We were not able to consider the specific impact of tax costs of services on citizens' satisfaction levels, although our very general, bottomline measure of SATISFACTION probably taps some consideration of taxes as well as services.

Also, we examined only one of several possible structural variables. Although many of these were controlled for through our selection of research sites, they could still be very important to a more general understanding of satisfaction. In addition, we have relied on proxies for some key variables. Aside from the obvious case of SERVICE QUALITY, our indicator of service levels—NO. OF SERVICES—did not account for variations in levels of specific services (e.g., a full range of police services versus a part-time patrol officer). While we believe they are valid, these measures contain random error, and more objective and/or comprehensive measures should be examined. And we have not attempted to develop a more complex causal model to account for the sources of local efficacy, service levels, or service quality. Still, because we were able to begin to sort out the competing explanations of satisfaction, we believe that our findings represent a contribution to our understanding of local government.

Finally, we must note that our model offers a very encouraging view of the relationship between citizens and their local governments. Far from resting on indirect demographic determinants or reference to local history, our results offer a very understandable account of levels of citizen satisfaction with local government. On the individual's side of the relationship, we find an important role for local government efficacy and attachment to or investment in a community. And on the government's side of the relationship, our model points to what local officials actually do for citizens—namely, provide some level and quality of services. On each side, then, we have factors that seem consistent with what democratic theory (or at least a liberal understanding of democratic theory, as we will see in chapter 8) would suggest should matter in defining how citizens judge their governments.

There is, however, one important caveat to our findings, especially our findings in regard to the impact of fragmented or consolidated government institutions. Despite our failure to find that such structures directly influence satisfaction levels, ALTERNATIVES may still have some indirect impact. We know from Table 2.1, for example, that there are very large differences in the number of services provided by the consolidated government in the Lexington setting and the independent cities in Louisville–Jefferson County, and that more services lead to more positive service evaluations. Thus, consolidated or fragmented governmental institutions do influence evaluations of service provision, but their influence is expressed through differences in the average number of services provided by the two types of systems. In short, consolidated local government is associated with somewhat higher citizen satisfaction. Further, as will be shown in chapter 6, attribution error seems to falsely inflate service perceptions in fragmented systems to a greater extent than in consolidated governmental systems. With this caveat in mind, and having offered an account of satisfaction with local government, we can now turn to considering how citizens respond politically when they become dissatisfied.

Notes

1. A fourth approach to citizen evaluations suggested in this literature provides some evidence that citizens who have had contacts with public officials about services tend to have a more accurate, and generally positive, assessment of services (see Fitzgerald and Durand, 1980; Cole, 1975; Parks, 1984; Hero and Durand, 1980). Thus, it would appear that contact with public officials itself shapes citizens' views, but this relationship is not entirely a clear one (see Brown and Coulter, 1983).

It must also be noted, however, that some scholars have suggested a rather different relationship between citizen evaluations and citizen contacting—i.e., that low service evaluations imply citizens' need to contact, and that those with low satisfaction may well have a greater motive to engage in contacting behavior than those who are satisfied with services (see Jones, 1980; Sharp, 1982; Thomas, 1982). Thus, we have a reverse causation question: is contacting an independent variable, or a dependent variable? Preliminary analysis of this model using the Kentucky data provided no basis for the assertion that contacting/complaining produces more positive general service evaluations. Rather, those who contacted officials were more likely to give negative public service assessments, suggesting that contacting is a response to unsatisfactory services (see chapter 4 of this volume). Therefore, contacting behavior should not be included as an independent variable in the present model.

2. Beck, Rainey and Traut (1986).

3. See Aberbach and Walker (1970); Durand (1976); Schuman and Gruenberg (1972); and Brown and Coulter (1983).

4. Lineberry (1976); Jones (1980); and Mladenka (1981).

5. Brown and Coulter (1983); Hero and Durand (1980); Fitzgerald and Durand (1980); and Brudney and England (1982a).

6. Balch (1974); and Sharp (1986).

7. Beck et al. (1986) and Stipak (1977, 1979).

8. Brown and Coulter (1983).

9. Sharp (1986, pp. 70–73).

10. Beck et al. (1986).

11. Fowler (1974); and Schuman and Gruenberg (1972).

12. Williams (1971).

13. For a good summary of the literature on this score, see Sharp (1986, pp. 69–71).

14. Ostrom, Bish, and Ostrom (1988); Ostrom, Tiebout, and Warren (1961); and Bish (1971).

15. Knott and Miller (1987).

16. E. Ostrom (1986); and E. Ostrom and Smith (1976).

17. Rogers and Lipsey (1974).

18. See Stipak (1977, 1979); and Parks (1984).

19. See Lyons (1977); Yates (1977); Rakove (1975); Talbot (1969); Ferman (1985); Swanstrom (1985); Kotter and Lawrence (1974); and Elazar (1970).

20. Orbell and Uno (1972); Brudney and England (1982b); Coulter (1988); Hero and Durand (1980); and Aberbach and Walker (1970).

21. For example, Beck et al. (1986); Beck, Rainey, Nichols, and Traut (1987); and Sharp (1986) analyze survey data from three cities.

22. Fitzgerald and Durand (1980); and Sharp (1984b).

23. Rogers and Lipsey (1974); E. Ostrom (1976); and Ostrom and Smith (1976).

24. For example, when Model 5 in Table 2.3 was estimated using SAS LOGIST rather than OLS, all of the coefficients were again significant and all carried the same sign.

25. Campbell, Gurin, and Miller (1954).

26. Abramson (1983).

27. Vedlitz and Veblen (1980); Seligson (1980); and Sharp (1982, 1986).

28. Hero (1986).

29. Balch (1974).

30. Brudney and England (1982b); and Percy (1986).

31. In chapter 6 we specify the direction and size of the bias introduced by three sources of attribution error: (a) SUBSET error, which occurs when citizens fail to evaluate a service because they do not realize that it is provided by their most immediate unit of local government; (b) MISSET error, which happens when citizens evaluate a service that they think is provided by their most immediate unit of local government, but that is really provided by another level or unit of local government operating in the urban area; and (c) NONSET error, which occurs when citizens evaluate a service that they think is provided by some local government but that is in fact not provided by any local government. The direction of the bias is indicated by the difference between the mean of the invalid service evaluations and the mean of the valid service evaluations. And the total impact of the bias would be the product of this difference and the proportion of services incorrectly included in the service set upon which the citizen forms his or her overall evaluation and the size of the observed service set upon which that assessment is based. We then combine these three sources of attribution errors with the citizen's initial or observed evaluation of governmental performance to determine his or her true evaluation.

32. The correlation between QUALITY BIAS and SATISFACTION was only –0.04.

33. Comparison of the SAS LOGIST discussed in note 24 with the OLS results presented in the fifth column of Table 2.3 illustrates the similarity of the results generated by the two procedures.

34. Beck et al. (1986).

35. Rogers and Lipsey (1974).

3

Responding to Dissatisfaction: The EVLN Model

Unlike the residents of certain south seas islands, the citizens of metropolitan America can rarely be described as "happy campers." The problems of crime, drug use, deteriorating services, escalating taxes, and official corruption are fruitful sources of dissatisfaction with urban life, dissatisfaction that is often directed toward local government and governmental leaders. As we have seen in the last chapter, the roots of this government-focused dissatisfaction are, at least in part, understandable. Three major and quite different theoretical accounts of satisfaction were simultaneously tested in an appropriate research design, leading to a parsimonious explanation largely based on the number and quality of services provided to citizens. Having examined the sources of satisfaction and dissatisfaction, we now turn to considerably more difficult questions: what do citizens do when they become dissatisfied and why do they do it?

While social scientists have developed a number of concepts useful in developing thoughtful, theory-based reflections on these questions, comprehensive answers remain elusive. For more than three decades, for example, the "spatial dimensions of urbanism"[1] have provided an important theoretical tool for studying a broad range of questions pertaining to urban government and politics, including the question of citizen responses to dissatisfaction with local governmental services. Starting with the work of Shevsky and Bell, the concept of differing "social worlds" or neighborhoods based on socioeconomic and lifestyle considerations has been a major theoretical theme in the literature.[2] The early work of Tiebout, Ostrom, and more recently Bish continues to prompt research based on their market model for explaining the behavior of both individuals and local governmental units operating within spatially segmented urban areas.[3] Similarly, considerable attention has been given to the broader version of the Tiebout model embracing spatially defined socioeconomic as well as political worlds found in the work of Williams in political science and Cox and others in geography.[4]

Unfortunately, the now rather voluminous literature concerning various aspects of the spatial dimensions of urbanism—like the study of urban politics generally—remains a "painfully eclectic field," utilizing differing measures, methodologies, and levels of analyses.[5] This has been especially true in the refining and testing of various theoretical propositions about the linkages between differing interpretations of the "spatial dimensions of urbanism" and citizen responses to dissatisfaction with local services. Moreover, little attention has been given to integrating the many theories on citizen responses to dissatisfaction, especially as they relate to the structural arrangements or institutions of local government.

Although many of the empirical and measurement problems found in the literature remain quite serious, the basic purpose of this chapter is to specify a more integrated theoretical model of responses to dissatisfaction.[6] We start by examining the linkages between the "spatial dimensions of urbanism" and forms of local political participation as responses to dissatisfaction. An integrated model of responses to dissatisfaction is then presented—the EXIT, VOICE, LOYALTY, and NEGLECT [EVLN] model—and applied to urban communities. In short, we try to develop a comprehensive and parsimonious answer to the questions of how and why citizens respond to dissatisfaction that mirrors the analysis of the sources of dissatisfaction offered in the last chapter. Finally, we use the model to generate a number of hypotheses about the impacts of varying levels of correspondence between the boundaries of social and political worlds on modes and levels of participation as a response to dissatisfaction.

Existing Models and Their Limitations

Most, if not all, of the literature concerning the impacts of the "spatial dimensions of urbanism" on individual political attitudes and behavior at the local level traces its theoretical roots to several sets of propositions advanced by the Tiebout and Williams models. Although they differ in a number of ways, these two models share at least one basic theoretical assumption that is directly relevant to this discussion. Both assert the now well-documented proposition that "families [and households] with similar resources, beliefs, and habits" tend to cluster in urban space.[7] We accept this proposition as a given, and posit it as a fundamental theoretical premise for the model to follow.

The Tiebout and Williams models, however, differ rather sharply in terms of such things as the basic motives behind the locational choices made by individuals and household units. The Tiebout market-oriented model argues that individuals and household units shop for an optimal package of public goods at the lowest cost available in a competitive "market" of differing tax–service packages offered by various local governmental jurisdictions operating within a given urban area. The broader Williams model, on the other hand, asserts that individuals and household units search for access to a broad range of "life-style maintaining" conditions in the community of choice. Tax–service packages may be an important aspect of the calculus of making and maintaining a locational choice under the Williams model, but they are not the only consideration. Many life-style-maintaining conditions, it is argued, are also supplied by the private sector, or can be consumed by commuting to other local governmental jurisdictions within a given urban area. Given the empirical evidence concerning the motives for individual locational choices, we accept this broader interpretation regarding the bases for individual and household locational choices.[8]

Of perhaps greater concern is the question of what people do after they have made a locational choice. The Tiebout model is rather specific about the behavior of individuals and households following their initial locational decision within a particular urban area. Given a competitive market situation, people will vote with their feet or move to another local jurisdiction if: (i) their original, spatially delimited local governmental jurisdiction fails to deliver the promised tax–service package; or (ii) changes occur in the individual's tax–service preferences due to changing needs, resources, or circumstances. Although the original Williams model is not as straightforward on this score, the concept of "exit," to use Hirschman's term, is clearly implicit in it. Unfortunately, few efforts have been made in the literature flowing out of the Tiebout-Williams model to expand upon the range of possible behavioral responses to dissatisfaction with local tax–service packages other than "exit." Despite the growing evidence from separate streams of research indicating that individuals engage in a variety of activities to rectify or improve local governmental policies and performance,[9] only limited efforts have been made toward linking these two bodies of literature.[10]

At least two other problems remain. First, while considerable emphasis continues to be placed on active forms of individual responses to dissatisfaction with local services and governance, only limited attention has been given to more passive types of responses such as "loyalty." "Exit" and "voice" type behaviors, to use Hirschman's terms, both require some form of active response—moving out of the local jurisdiction or engaging in some form of active participation in local affairs to rectify problems causing dissatisfaction. Even Sharp's innovative exploration of "loyalty" conceptualizes this response to dissatisfaction as a residual category holding a variety of very different attitudes and behaviors ranging from such positive or regime-supportive activities as defending local government against criticisms to such negative or regime-destructive alternatives as withdrawal from participation.[11]

To be effective, an integrated model must capture both the "active–passive" as well as the "constructive–destructive" dimensions of attitudes and behaviors associated with local political participation as a response to dissatisfaction. This broader range of attitudinal and behavioral alternatives also needs to be tied to theoretically relevant antecedents that will enable researchers to test meaningful hypotheses concerning types and levels of citizen responses to dissatisfaction, antecedents about which the literature says virtually nothing at all.

A second but related problem found in the literature flowing out of the Tiebout and Williams models concerns the question of correspondence—or lack thereof—between the spatial contours of neighborhoods and the boundaries of local political jurisdictions operating within a given urban area. On the surface, the Tiebout and Williams models seem to solve the problem by assuming that the boundaries of urban political units, especially those found in the suburbs, embrace relatively homogeneous populations that share common needs, values, interests, and socioeconomic characteristics. To accommodate situations where socioeconomic and political boundaries do not coincide, the underlying thesis has been that the urbanization process tends to produce relatively homogeneous tax–service preferences in local government jurisdictions in terms of subjective demand, even if not always in terms of "objective" socioeconomic need.[12]

Unfortunately, much of the relevant empirical literature has failed to confront directly the veracity of these assumptions. Guest and Lee,[13] for example, have reported some interesting findings about the values, attitudes, and behaviors of individuals living in neighborhoods that display traits associated with such notions as "urban villagers,"[14] versus a "community of limited liability" as described by Greer and especially Janowitz.[15] But their definition of "community" is based on a "list of widely recognized unincorporated neighborhoods" and "local areas" in the city of Seattle and in King County, Washington, that accords little attention to the implications of the widely differing political boundaries that embraced them.[16]

Guest and Lee are not the only researchers who have been forced to rely on surveys of adults living in neighborhoods that may have little to do with the underlying spatial structure of a local political system. Orbell and Uno, for instance, examined exit and voice as problem-solving techniques using a survey of households in the *entire metropolitan* area of Columbus, Ohio. Responses were analyzed in terms of various census criteria that lumped respondents into socioeconomic and racial categories that had little or no connection with the spatial notion of "neighborhood" which they posed as their purported unit of analysis. Moreover, they were unable to examine variations in their findings on responses to dissatisfaction across the several political jurisdictions that operate in the highly fragmented world of local governments in the greater Columbus area.[17]

More than a decade later, Sharp used a 1978 nationwide Harris poll of urban dwellers to explore the utility of Hirschman's notions of exit, voice, and loyalty within the context of local urban government organizations.[18] While interesting and quite suggestive in many respects, Sharp's findings provide only limited and inferentially tenuous answers to questions about the linkages between various aspects of the "spatial dimensions of urbanism" and the attitudes and behaviors of individuals living in particular local government jurisdictions. As we saw in the last chapter, such questions simply cannot be addressed using data from a single nationwide poll.

For the most part, of course, these limitations are due to resource constraints that compel researchers to limit their theoretical scope of inquiry in order to utilize data collected for other purposes or to make sampling decisions that served more limited purposes. Regardless, the result has been to evade the implications of such spatial concepts as *neighborhoods* and *local political jurisdictions* that underlie many of the basic propositions concerning citizens' political responses to dissatisfaction.

Furthermore, recent trends in the urbanization process, particularly the shift of population to the Sun Belt and to smaller urban areas, has compounded the problem. The scenario that grew alongside the development of the Tiebout and Williams models during the 1950s and 1960s was based on the then-realistic assumption that the "outward explosion of urban populations," to use Willbern's expression,[19] would take place within a world of numerous, relatively small, political jurisdictions on the periphery of core cities. For a while, these models were able to accommodate the growing heterogeneity of suburbia taken as a whole. The spatial clustering by income, occupation, and life-style occurred within the context of numerous, highly specialized suburban political jurisdictions, each serving relatively homogeneous populations. The only troublesome question was what to do with the myriad, spatially defined social and economic worlds found within the jurisdictional boundaries of our core cities. Even this question did not seem to pose too many problems, as evidence accumulated suggesting that core cities were becoming more and more homogeneous in terms of race and income, until the neighborhood government movement began to call attention to the continuing socioeconomic differences among various clusters of core city dwellers during the early 1970s.[20]

What cannot be easily accommodated by the original versions of the Tiebout and Williams models, however, are the realities of contemporary urbanization in the Sun Belt. This phenomenon developed following a quite different scenario of the urbanization process from that based on the experience of our older, industrial cities in the Northeast and upper Midwest. Since most of the growing areas of the Sun Belt follow the southern model of local government (i.e., with strong county governments, few incorporated municipalities, stringent municipal incorporation requirements, and/or more lenient annexation laws), the trend has been for urban growth to spill over large areas served by a single local municipality.[21] Spatial clustering based on various social, economic, and life-style considerations continues to happen in these areas. However, the opportunity for making a locational choice that results in choosing a local government jurisdiction composed exclusively of similar types of people, or of people with very similar tax–benefit expectations, is highly restricted in such settings.

The Basis for an Alternative Model

What is needed, then, is a broader, integrative model that accounts for the full range of political behaviors in which citizens might engage in response to dissatisfaction, specifies how they select from among those responses, and that does both in a manner that fully accounts for the important impacts of the "spatial dimensions of urbanism." Recent work based on the investment model of Thibaut and Kelly[22] concerning individual responses to dissatisfaction in individual relationships and public and private job situations,[23] provides the basis for the broader model developed below. Not only does this expanded model incorporate a broader range of attitudinal and behavioral options than those suggested by Tiebout, Williams, and even Hirschman, but it also sets forth a more theoretically robust set of antecedent factors to explain variations in responses to dissatisfaction with local governmental services and policies under various forms of correspondence and noncorrespondence between the "boundaries" of spatially defined socioeconomic worlds and the legal boundaries of local political jurisdictions.

In his discussion of responses to decline in firms, organizations, and states, Hirschman proffered a typology of responses to dissatisfaction, and outlined three general categories of reaction to deteriorating satisfaction: (a) *exit*—leaving the organization; (b) *voice*—actively and constructively attempting to improve conditions; and (c) *loyalty*—passively but optimistically waiting for conditions to improve. In several more recent studies,[24] substantial support has been found for the Hirschman model in the study of responses to dissatisfaction in interpersonal and job situations in both the public and private sectors. More important, however, these studies have also identified a fourth category of response: *neglect*—passively allowing conditions to worsen.

These four categories of response to dissatisfaction differ from one another along two dimensions—constructiveness versus destructiveness and activity versus passivity. Voice and loyalty are considered constructive behaviors that should serve to maintain or revive satisfactory working conditions or interpersonal relations, while exit and neglect are more destructive to the employment or interpersonal relationship. Stated in terms of the active/passive dimension, exit and voice are both active responses (i.e., they both require doing something), while loyalty and neglect are more passive in nature.

Rusbult and Farrell[25] have also suggested that three basic conditions affect the likelihood of an employee engaging in behaviors associated with these four responses to dissatisfaction. First, to the extent that an employee was satisfied with his or her job prior to the emergence of problems, constructive behaviors should be more likely. Thus, greater *prior satisfaction* should promote voice or loyalty over exit or neglect. Second, greater *investments* in a job or relationship should encourage constructive responses to dissatisfaction. Individuals with greater investments are more likely to choose voice or loyalty, while those with minimal or no investments are likely to exercise the destructive exit or neglect options. Third, persons with superior alternatives, such as another job offer, are more likely to enact active responses. Good *alternatives* provide the motivation to do something, and serve as a source of power for effecting change. The mode of change can be destructive to the current relationship (i.e., exit) or constructive (i.e., voice). But in the absence of a good alternative, the only options available to the dissatisfied individual are to wait passively for conditions to improve (i.e., remain loyal) or passively allow conditions to worsen (i.e., neglect behavior).

Applying the Model in Urban Settings

Application of the model to urban settings involves several steps. First, the relationship between this expanded model and the larger literature on political participation must be specified. Second, the four possible responses to dissatisfaction—exit, voice, loyalty, and neglect—must be stated in terms of attitudes and behaviors that are relevant to the political process, as opposed to job or interpersonal relationships. And third, the determinants of responses to current dissatisfaction (i.e., prior satisfaction, investments, and alternatives) must be clearly delineated in terms that are relevant to the local political and governmental aspects of citizens' lives.

Political Participation as Response to Dissatisfaction

It should be noted that the model developed here deals with a limited subset of the topics that generally appear under the heading of political participation. Clearly, most treatments of local political participation tend to conceptualize it in ways that speak more to individual predispositions than to individual responses to the circumstances in which they find themselves.[26] Here, attention is addressed instead to participation arising in response to problems—whether specific or diffuse—that affect the relationship between the citizen and his or her local government.

Although some researchers have complained that the more general "political participation literature characteristically fails to treat participation as a problem solving act,"[27] somewhat more attention is given to this theme in the literature on *local* political participation. It is certainly evident in the Tiebout model, where voting with one's feet is viewed as the preeminent response to dissatisfaction arising from unfavorable comparison of one's current tax–service package with that offered by another governmental jurisdiction located within the same urban area. It also shows up in the discussions of "need" and "perceived problems" with local government services as critical factors in explaining various forms of "particularized citizen contacting" of local officials.[28] Similarly, the "nonparticipation" of the poor and underprivileged in the model of local decision making developed by Bachrach and Baratz points to the redress of grievances as the object of political participation.[29] And even in discussions of the traditional modes of political participation, we find frequent reference to the role of dissatisfaction in engendering individual activity in the political world.[30]

The focus, then, is on one part of the subject of the larger literature on political participation: participation arising in response to dissatisfaction with local government services and policies. It should be clear, though, that we cannot ignore individual predispositions toward differing levels and forms of participation in theoretically accounting for "total" participation or in empirical tests of the specific hypotheses to be developed below. For now, however, we assume that these other factors are constant.[31]

This interpretation of political participation as a response to dissatisfaction is still incomplete unless we can specify in fairly precise terms what citizens might be dissatisfied about. After all, citizens may leave one neighborhood or local governmental jurisdiction—to use the "exit" response as an example—for any number of reasons, only some of which can be characterized as arising from dissatisfaction with local government. *To narrow our subject matter, then, we will define as relevant sources of dissatisfaction, those that arise from policies over which the local polity may be expected to have some control or responsibility.*

Although this is still very general, the Williams and Tiebout models suggest both a broad and narrow specification of this conceptualization. Clearly, the focus of the Tiebout model is more narrowly focused on the tax–service package provided by the local government. Citizens, according to this model, are expected to compare alternative packages against their interpretation of an optimal package and to migrate to the governmental unit whose package is closest to their ideal. If through this comparative evaluation the citizen finds that the difference between the package of their present jurisdiction and their optimal package is greater than the difference between that of another jurisdiction and their optimal package, he or she can be said to be dissatisfied with his or her present tax–service package.

As indicated above, the Williams model speaks to a larger set of concerns falling under the general description of "life-style-maintaining conditions." While a jurisdiction's control over and responsibility for such a broader set of issues may in many cases be quite ambiguous, we can develop a broader set of measures of such issues by following Williams's lead. In any case, the definition of dissatisfaction would be the same as that for the more restrictive specification arising from the Tiebout model. Citizens would be expected to compare their ideal sets of "life-style-maintaining conditions" to that provided by their current and neighboring jurisdictions. Similarly, dissatisfaction would be defined as an unfavorable comparison of their present local government to an alternative within the metropolitan area.

Four Responses to Dissatisfaction

Even given our restrictive focus on local political participation as a form of response to dissatisfaction, we are confronted with a large array of attitudes and behaviors to be taken into account in an integrated manner. As indicated above and as represented in Figure 3.1, four types of political participation are consid-

Figure 3.1. EVLN Dimensions of Response to Dissatisfaction, Response Types, and Illustrative Behaviors

active

EXIT

e.g.,
• leaving or contemplating leaving the jurisdiction for regime-based reason
• opting for privatized rather than city services

VOICE

e.g.,
• attending meeting to discuss problems
• belonging to organization to address problems
• contacting officials
• organizing petition drive
• talking to neighbors about community problems
• signing a petition

destructive ———————————————————— *constructive*

NEGLECT

e.g.,
• not following public issues
• believing it is useless to complain to officials
• believing that the government doesn't care about you
• not caring what happens in the community

LOYALTY

e.g.,
• trusting officials to do the right thing
• defending the community
• being patient in criticizing the government
• believing that community problems will work themselves out

passive

ered: exit, voice, loyalty, and neglect. These categories of participation are expected to vary along two dimensions: an active–passive dimension, with voice and exit anchoring one end of the continuum and loyalty and neglect the other; and a constructive–destructive dimension, with voice and loyalty constituting the former and neglect and exit the latter value.

Before examining each of these categories of response in detail, it must be noted that each captures any number of specific attitudes and behaviors. Of course, it is not always intuitively obvious that a specific behavior falls into any particular or even only one of the four categories. This is because the two dimensions underlying the typology inherently involve the intent of the citizen. Does a citizen, for example, intend to end the relationship between himself or herself and the local government (exit), or merely to send a message that he or she is dissatisfied (voice) by exercising a certain form of behavior? Or does failing to act in the face of a specific situation indicate neglect or loyalty? Is an urban riot a form of exit, voice, or neglect? For many—probably most—behaviors, such ambiguity is not a problem. But for others, especially those that are both extreme and rare forms of political behavior (riots, for example), different analysts may disagree about how specific behaviors should be categorized. These problems of operationalization can be addressed through more detailed research on specific behaviors such as that found in Sears and McConahay's analysis of the Watts riot.[32] For now, though, we limit ourselves to examples of behaviors representative of each of the four categories that are more common forms of participation in response to dissatisfaction.

Specifying the "exit" form of response to dissatisfaction is relatively straightforward, given the Tiebout and Williams models. Exit involves ending the relationship between the citizen and the local government. This may take its most general form in the citizen's leaving or intending to leave one jurisdiction and moving to another—the classic Tiebout response. Additionally, some forms of service privatization might be viewed as a more specific or targeted form of exit. In this case, the citizen severs the service relationship with his or her local government only for a specific activity, such as garbage collection or education. Whether specific or general, though, exit involves ending the relationship that is the source of dissatisfaction.

"Voice" is probably the broadest and most familiar response category. If we conceptualize voice as active and constructive efforts to improve conditions giving rise to dissatisfaction, then much of what traditionally falls under the topic of political participation can be identified as "voice," including most unconventional (e.g., some forms of demonstrations and protest activities) and conventional (e.g., contacting officials on an issue, issue-motivated party or campaign work, campaign contributions, and engaging in political discussions) modes of participation.[33]

"Loyalty" entails passively but optimistically waiting for conditions to improve. In the organizational behavior literature, this has been measured by ritualistic behavior and support of the firm, combined with generally positive attitudes about and trust in its decisions concerning the problem that gives rise to dissatisfaction. This very closely resembles the interpretation of the voting act and regime-supportive attitudes found in the political participation literature.[34] Loyalty is passive support of the system with little direct action to redress the problem giving rise to dissatisfaction.

"Neglect" is perhaps the most difficult of the responses to define. And while such concepts as disaffection, alienation, cynicism, and distrust have a long history in the general political participation literature,[35] they, and the "neglect" behaviors that might be extrapolated from them (e.g., apathy, nonvoting, tax avoidance), are rarely viewed as responses to specific sources of dissatisfaction. Rather, they are usually grouped under discussions of personal factors influencing participation that increase or decrease an individual's propensity to participate at all. While necessarily building on this literature, we are compelled to view neglect as something more, given our focus on participation as responses to dissatisfaction.

The Determinants of Responses to Dissatisfaction

While these four categories of response seem to capture and, more importantly, to organize within a single conceptual scheme most of the modes of participation behavior in response to dissatisfaction found in the existing literature, we are ultimately interested in the conditions under which each of the four responses is invoked by dissatisfied citizens. In the initial presentation of the model, three factors were discussed: prior satisfaction, investments, and alternatives.

"Prior satisfaction" with the "tax–service package" or "package of life-style-maintaining characteristics" is fairly straightforward. Those who have been satisfied in the past should have a greater motivation to adopt constructive behaviors—voice and loyalty. They know that the jurisdiction has met their needs in the past. Such knowledge, in turn, should encourage them to give the jurisdiction time to correct the source of dissatisfaction. In contrast, those with low levels of prior satisfaction would feel less confident that the jurisdiction can or will rectify the source of dissatisfaction. Accordingly, they would be more likely to adopt destructive behaviors—exit or neglect.

"Investment level" should have a similar effect. Citizens who are highly invested in a particular jurisdiction are more likely to adopt constructive behaviors since they have more to lose than poorly invested individuals who would be expected to respond by either allowing the situation to decay further (neglect), or, alternatively, moving from the jurisdiction or privatizing the service that is the source of dissatisfaction (exit). These investments can include such tangible investments as homeownership, employment, or children in the schools of the jurisdiction. They can also embrace social and psychological investments arising from long-term residence in and attachment to the jurisdiction. In either case, jurisdiction-specific commitment arising from such investments should increase the propensity of individuals to exercise voice or loyalty in the face of dissatisfaction.

The availability of good alternatives should increase the likelihood of individuals adopting active responses in the face of dissatisfaction. For our purposes, good alternatives are indicated by the availability of another jurisdiction that offers a "tax–service" or "life-style-maintaining" package that is closer to the dissatisfied individuals' interpretation of the optimal level and mix of public services or opportunities for privatization of the service that is dissatisfying. In contrast, those with poor alternatives—such as minorities restricted to the inner city by discriminatory practices or those residing in urban areas that have reduced the number of local government jurisdictions through unified government or annexation—should be more likely to adopt passive responses to dissatisfaction.

While existing models of responses to dissatisfaction specify only these three determinants of the exit, voice, loyalty, and neglect options, we believe that one additional factor must be included, one that determines not so much the type of response, but the level of response. We would expect "level of current dissatisfaction" to influence propensities to invoke each of the four response categories where "level of current dissatisfaction" is defined in terms consistent with the Tiebout and Williams models' interpretation of dissatisfaction. That is, level of current dissatisfaction is defined as the difference between the individual's level of satisfaction with his or her existing tax–service or life-style-maintaining conditions package and the level of satisfaction he or she would expect to have with the available alternative closest to his or her ideal. Those who are only mildly dissatisfied should be more likely to "exit" than those who are satisfied, but not to the degree of those who are extremely dissatisfied. Still, previous models—the Tiebout model for one—have generally assumed that response invocation is costless and that, accordingly, even minor comparative disadvantages will lead citizens to undertake the exit response.

This still leaves the problem of how to include the level of current dissatisfaction term in the model. Our expectation that "current dissatisfaction" affects level of dissatisfaction suggests that it be included in interaction with the other three determinants of responses to dissatisfaction. Against a baseline propensity to exit, voice, loyalty, and/or neglect (as determined by the variables associated with the more standard political participation literature), any individual's levels of prior satisfaction, alternatives, and investments should lead to changing patterns of exit, voice, loyalty, and/or neglect only to the degree to which he or she was dissatisfied. If the individual is not dissatisfied, the other three determinants would have no influence on the individual's propensity to adopt exit, voice, loyalty, and/or neglect behaviors beyond his baseline propensity to do so.

This is by no means the only possible way to view the impact of level of current dissatisfaction. It might seem reasonable to expect that at very extreme levels of dissatisfaction, we would not see even greater loyalty, to use the example of one response, but we might see a "phase change" whereby citizens would begin to exit, voice, or neglect. While we considered this and other possible specifications of the impact of level of dissatisfaction on the three determinants of response, we opted for the simple linear intensification interpretation. Given the types of tax–service packages involved (local government taxes and services), we would not expect to see extreme levels of dissatisfaction very often. While certainly possible (e.g., the 1978 tax revolt in California), we would expect such conditions to be fairly rare.

To this point, we have presented the main elements of the model, elements that can be summarized as:

$$\text{RESPONSE}_i = a + b_1 (\text{CURRENT} * \text{PRIOR})_i + b_2 (\text{CURRENT} * \text{ALTERNATIVES})_i + b_3 (\text{CURRENT} * \text{INVESTMENT})_i + b_5 \text{IND1}_i + \ldots b_n \text{IND}N_i \, ;$$

where RESPONSE represents the ith individual's propensity to adopt one of the

Table 3.1

Hypothesized Relationships between Propensity to Invoke Responses to Dissatisfaction and the Determinants of Responses

| | Responses to dissatisfaction | | | |
Determinants of response	EXIT	VOICE	NEGLECT	LOYALTY
PRIOR SATISFACTION	–	+	–	+
INVESTMENTS	–	+	–	+
ALTERNATIVES	+	+	–	–

responses to dissatisfaction (EXIT, VOICE, LOYALTY, or NEGLECT); PRIOR, ALTERNATIVES, and INVESTMENT represent the individual's value on the three determinant variables of the model; CURRENT is level of current dissatisfaction; and IND1 to INDN represent control variables for the individual and social determinants of individual participation found in the more general political participation literature. The specific hypotheses on the signs of the relationships between the determinants of responses, ignoring for the moment the role of current dissatisfaction, since it is presumed to have a positive interactive effect on all of the relationships, are presented in Table 3.1. Levels of prior satisfaction and investments should be positively related to the propensity to invoke the constructive voice and loyalty responses and negatively related to the propensity to invoke the relationship-destructive exit and neglect responses. And the availability of alternatives should be positively related to the propensity to invoke the active exit and voice responses and negatively related to the propensity to invoke the passive loyalty and neglect responses.

We can make this presentation more concrete by illustrating how the model might be applied in four prototypical cases of response to dissatisfaction where we assume that the "level of dissatisfaction" is fixed, since it influences the propensity to invoke each response type in the same manner. The first case falls into cell A of Figure 3.1, the exit response. The typical exiter is the Tiebout citizen who votes with his or her feet in the face of an increase in the comparative dissatisfaction with the tax–service package of his or her present community. These individuals would have minimal investments in the jurisdiction (i.e., complete mobility from the perspective of the Tiebout model), and there would be a large number of competing jurisdictions (i.e., good alternatives). However, the Tiebout model assumes that even minor comparative disadvantages are sufficient to generate exit. While similar to the Tiebout model, our interpretation of exit takes into account the degree of dissatisfaction and the base from which it is calculated.

Alternatively, the prototypical citizen who invokes the voice response (cell B) is one who has a high level of prior satisfaction, a high level of investment in his or her current jurisdiction, and good alternatives. Unlike the exiters, voicing citizens have some reasonable expectations that the jurisdiction can satisfy their demands (they were satisfied in the past) and are invested in the community. Still, they have good alternatives and could leave, albeit at some cost. This would lead them to seek actively to alter the conditions giving rise to dissatisfaction: voice. These individuals would contact city officials, write letters to the editor, campaign for political candidates addressing the issue they are concerned with, and adopt other, similar "voice" activities to redress their grievances. Given their large investments in the community and the availability of alternatives, local officials would have some incentive to meet their demands, making voice a viable response to dissatisfaction.

In cell D, we find loyalists. These individuals, like those in the previous response set, have a high level of investment in the community and a high level of prior satisfaction. Unlike those exercising voice, however, their alternatives are poor. There may be no neighboring community to which they might move, or if there are other communities, their service packages are clearly inferior to those provided by their present community. In such a situation, voice would not be an effective option since the availability of exit is the threat necessary to make voice credible.[36] Loyalty or passive support of the community would be the likely response.

Finally, the neglect response in cell C can be illustrated by the political behavior of disadvantaged citizens of the urban core. Given few viable alternatives (perhaps associated with poverty and racial discrimination), exit is not possible and voice is unlikely to be effective. Indeed, the attempted voice of such citizens is likely to be dismissed in the form of "nonissues" as suggested by Bachrach and Baratz.[37] The low levels of prior satisfaction found among such citizens are unlikely to encourage loyalty, passively waiting for conditions to improve. Accordingly, political behavior will be expressed in the form of neglect.

The Impact of Organizing Political Space

Although the model outlined above is considerably more elaborate than those employed by Orbell and Uno, Sharp, and others, it does not yet explicitly address how various levels of correspondence between spatially defined social and political worlds influence citizen responses to dissatisfaction with local governance.

While many urban dwellers in the United States may not live in one of the purely polar situations suggested below, positing and intellectually exploring the extremes of a theoretically important, but continuous, variable is often useful in assessing its full implications. "Polar Scenario I" in Figure 3.2 represents the situation where the "boundaries" of several, quite different, spatially defined "social worlds" or neighborhoods square perfectly with the legal boundaries of

Figure 3.2. **Illustrative Scenarios of High and Low Correspondence between Boundaries of Social and Political Worlds**

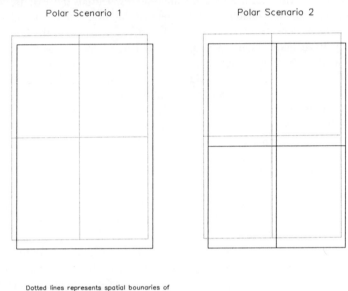

Polar Scenario 1   Polar Scenario 2

Dotted lines represents spatial bounaries of
social worlds A, B, C, and D
Solid line represents government boundaries.

local government jurisdictions (e.g., municipalities, townships, counties, and/or local school districts). These differing neighborhoods may be defined by racial or ethnic, social class, or life-style considerations. But each has its own local government, which, therefore, serves a relatively homogeneous population.

In "Polar Scenario II" these same neighborhoods are located in an environment in which there is no correspondence between their boundaries and the legal boundaries of local governmental jurisdictions. In this situation, a single local government jurisdiction contains a wide variety of differing social worlds embracing populations with widely varying values, interests, and policy preferences.

Although considerable variation actually exists, urban areas—especially suburban areas—located in the Northwest and upper Midwest that were the focus of the urban literature in the 1960s and 1970s come closest to approximating the conditions described in "Polar Scenario I." In contrast, the closest approximation of "Polar Scenario II" are those situations discussed earlier under the urbanization scenario developing primarily in the Sun Belt where massive annexation or city–county consolidation has occurred.

With these polar cases in mind, we can now assess how the organization of political space can be analyzed using the EVLN model. We expect level of correspondence to influence how the responses of dissatisfaction are exercised

Table 3.2

Hypothesized Relationships between the Determinants of Responses to Dissatisfaction and Level of Correspondence

| | Determinants of responses to dissatisfaction | | | |
	PRIOR SATISFAC-TION	INVEST-MENTS	ALTERNA-TIVES	CURRENT DISSATISFAC-TION
LEVEL OF CORRE-SPONDENCE	+	+	+	+

through its impact on the three determinants discussed above—prior satisfaction, investments, and alternatives—as well as the current dissatisfaction interaction term.

First, and as shown in Table 3.2, we expect level of correspondence to be positively related to levels of prior satisfaction. Despite our finding in chapter 2 on the impact—or rather, the lack of impact—of ALTERNATIVES (fragmented or consolidated governmental structure) on citizen satisfaction with local governance, this expectation is firmly embedded in the work of Ostrom and Tiebout, and starts with the assumption that metropolitan areas will be characterized by some level of heterogeneity in tastes for packages of "taxes and services" or "life-style-maintaining" conditions."[38] Low-correspondence political jurisdictions like those found in Polar Scenario II—encompassing a full range of heterogeneous styles of urban living—will be less likely, it is argued, to provide a level and mix of public services that will be satisfying to a greater proportion of citizens than those serving more homogeneous populations: the high correspondence of Polar Scenario I jurisdictions. And contrary to our finding in chapter 2, a number of empirical analyses suggest that citizen satisfaction tends to increase as the size of the jurisdiction decreases.[39] We should expect, then, that prior satisfaction will be higher in metropolitan areas with boundaries drawn in such a way that high levels of correspondence exist between social worlds and political jurisdictions.

Since the model suggests that low levels of prior satisfaction will lead to invocation of the destructive responses to dissatisfaction, we would expect to find a greater tendency toward exit and neglect in situations approximating those found in Polar Scenario II, all other things being equal. Conversely, we expect to find greater tendencies toward the constructive responses (i.e., voice and loyalty) among those living in situations approximating Polar Scenario I. This latter expectation may be surprising in that the Tiebout model generally assumes that exit is the primary device through which citizens express themselves. Yet, in the absence of any direct test of the Tiebout model,[40] we cannot rule out the possibility that the very achievement of the Tiebout-type correspondence situation might tend to decrease use of the very mechanism that is deemed to drive that model in the first place. We will, however, explore this issue more fully in chapter 5.

Second, we expect level of correspondence to be positively related to levels of investment. To the extent that a high level of correspondence implies smaller, more homogeneous political jurisdictions, we might expect greater social and psychological investment in the political community in the higher-correspondence cases—those approximating Polar Scenario I. Ostrom, for example, suggests that citizens are more likely to be attached to smaller political communities.[41] While the empirical veracity of this assumption has yet to be tested and will be considered more fully in chapters 5 and 8, the assumption is one given wide currency in both the public choice and communitarian literatures. But even if this assumption were validated, we would not expect this effect to be determinant in most cases. Many of the investments of the type addressed by the model—proximity to a job, family, homeownership, etc.—are determined by the individual and are little influenced by boundaries. To the extent it has some effect, though, high levels of correspondence should decrease tendencies toward constructive responses; lower levels of psychological attachment, for example, will decrease the likelihood of voice and loyalty and increase the likelihood of exit and neglect.

Third, we expect the level of correspondence to be positively related to the availability of alternatives. If we assume that opportunities for privatization are constant, then, quite simply, more alternatives will be available in high-correspondence situations like those found in Polar Scenario I than in a case of low correspondence represented by Polar Scenario II.[42] The impact of alternatives should be clear. Many alternatives increase the likelihood of active responses while few increase the probability of passive responses. Thus, the high-correspondence case environment not only encourages higher *levels* of exit, but also higher *levels* of voice. Although the former response is seemingly self-evident and consistent with the propositions of the Tiebout model, the latter is also indicated as a viable possibility given the model developed here.

Fourth, because the basic model outlined earlier posits current dissatisfaction to have a positive interactive effect on the other three determinants of response to dissatisfaction, and because we also expect levels of correspondence to influence levels of current dissatisfaction, we expect levels of current dissatisfaction to affect the degree or magnitude of the other effects posited in the model. This argument rests on the comparative sense in which the term "level of current dissatisfaction" was originally defined in the model: as a function of direct comparisons of the citizen's level of satisfaction derived from his or her current tax–service package and/or life-style-maintaining conditions and the expected satisfaction from relocating to an alternative jurisdiction.

The fact that high levels of correspondence such as that found in Polar Scenario I are consistent with the existence of many alternatives makes it more likely that one will be closer to the citizen's optimal package than his or her present package. In contrast, in situations similar to that found in Polar Scenario II, the low-correspondence condition, there are likely to be few, if any, other tax–service packages to compare to the one the citizen now consumes. Relative to the alternatives, such an individual may have a low level of dissatisfaction even though his or her existing package of services and taxes may be far from optimal. To put it simply, one is unlikely to ask whether the grass is greener on the other side of the fence if there are no fences around. Thus, the level of current dissatisfaction should be higher in cases like those illustrated by Polar Scenario I than in those illustrated by Polar Scenario II.

And because the level of current dissatisfaction term is included in the model interactively with the three determinants of response (alternatives, investments, and prior satisfaction), the effects of these determinants on the responses should be enhanced in the high-correspondence case and depressed in the low-correspondence case. Other things being equal, the level of responses—exit, voice, loyalty, and/or neglect—one finds in the high-correspondence case will be greater than one finds in the low-correspondence case.

What then is the ultimate or net impact of varying levels of correspondence between the "boundaries" of social and political worlds on the propensity of invoking the response types? This is an extremely difficult question to answer given the complexity inherent in the model. With three determinants of responses to dissatisfaction, and their interaction with levels of correspondence, simple effects are unlikely.

One approach is simply to look for consistencies in effects hypothesized by the model across the alternative polar scenarios presented in Figure 3.2. When this is done, we find that voice is the only response category for which level of correspondence has a consistent effect on all four terms of the model: prior satisfaction, investments, alternatives, and the interactive effects associated with current dissatisfaction. In the presentation of the model, we have seen that high prior satisfaction, high levels of investment, good alternatives, and high levels of current dissatisfaction serve to increase the propensity to exercise "voice" behaviors. And in the discussion of the impact of level of correspondence, we have seen that each of these conditions is associated with the high-correspondence situation. Given these consistent patterns, we can expect that mean levels of voice behaviors for members of any given social world or neighborhood will be higher in situations approximating Polar Scenario I situations than for members of the corresponding neighborhood in settings more similar to Polar Scenario II.

Unfortunately, the net impact of varying levels of correspondence is not so clear regarding the other categories of response. With exit, for example, the model suggests that a high propensity to exercise exit behaviors is associated with low prior satisfaction, weak investments, good alternatives, and high current dissatisfaction. Yet, based on the arguments presented above, the level of correspondence is expected to influence the mean levels of these variables in ways

that suggest contradictory impacts on the overall propensity to invoke exit behaviors. On the one hand, a high-correspondence situation approximating Polar
Scenario I is expected to be associated with enhanced prior satisfaction and
increased investments, factors that serve to depress the exit response. On the
other hand, we have seen that high correspondence between social and political
worlds tends to provide greater alternatives, which should increase propensities
to exit. Similarly, the high-correspondence conditions should lead to high levels
of current dissatisfaction, which, in interaction with the three determinants of
response, should serve to increase exit. The net impact of correspondence on
exit, then, depends on the relative strengths of the determinants in the model.

Similar inconsistencies can be found in efforts to determine the net impacts of
varying levels of correspondence on the remaining two response types. Situations approximating Polar Scenario II, for example, are expected to produce low
prior satisfaction, weak investments, and poor alternatives—all of which are
hypothesized to be associated with greater propensities to invoke neglect
attitudes and behaviors. Yet, high levels of current dissatisfaction—our interaction term which conditions the strength of all other effects—has also been identified as an important trait in the profile of the typical neglect response. However,
as noted above, it is high-correspondence, rather than low-correspondence, situations that are expected to enhance the strength of this interactive term. In short,
level of correspondence should have an impact on mean levels of neglect
through its influence on "levels of current dissatisfaction" that is opposite to that
exercised through the other three terms of the model.

Finally, we also find that high-correspondence types of environments tend to
produce conditions that enhance the likelihood of finding high levels of current
dissatisfaction—the interactive term—and high levels of prior satisfaction along
with strong investments. The model predicts that all three of these traits will be
associated with use of loyalty responses to dissatisfaction. The only inconsistent
factor lies in the impact of varying levels of correspondence on alternatives,
where the model suggests that the typical loyalist has poor alternatives, the
opposite of what we would expect to find in the case of high correspondence like
that in Polar Scenario I. Again, level of correspondence has an inconsistent
impact on the levels of the determinants of response.

For all the response categories but "voice," then, the effects of level of correspondence are mixed and dependent upon the relative strengths of the four determinants
of response. And, as noted in the discussion of the investments term, it is quite
conceivable that the impacts of level of correspondence on the three determinants of
response to dissatisfaction and the current dissatisfaction interaction term are quite
relative in strength. The resulting hypotheses that one might generate about the net
impact of level of correspondence on responses to dissatisfaction will vary, therefore, according to the weight assigned to each of the effects posited by the model.
Ultimately, empirical analysis is essential to unravel the impact of varying levels
of correspondence between the spatial contours of social worlds and jurisdiction

boundaries on dissatisfaction-based political participation.

Given the model developed here, however, it is possible to sketch theoretically sound alternatives to the standard public choice scenario, even if we restrict ourselves to the single response of exit. For instance, if citizens are less than totally mobile, the relative weight of alternatives on the overall propensity to exit would be expected to decline. In such a situation, the impact of level of correspondence would be exercised through its influence on the other three determinants of responses to dissatisfaction, two of which—prior satisfaction and investments—are related to level of correspondence in such a way that propensities to exit would be depressed in the high-correspondence case, a result that is quite inconsistent with the usual Tiebout-type of analysis.[43] Even more fundamentally, as we will see in chapters 5 through 8, if the usual public choice assumptions about the relationships between correspondence and investments, prior satisfaction, and current dissatisfaction—assumptions that greatly informed our theoretical analysis—are invalid, the balance of influences will align in patterns quite different from the hypotheses outlined here.

Conclusion

What we have, then, is a far more elaborate and integrated model for systematically examining various forms of political participation as a response to dissatisfaction. At this point, we believe the model has a number of useful attributes. First, the model theoretically links several formerly disparate and independent behaviors and attitudes associated with local political participation as responses to dissatisfaction. Moreover, the model theoretically links the four responses to dissatisfaction in such a way that a discrete set of variables—ALTERNATIVES, INVESTMENTS, PRIOR SATISFACTION, and CURRENT DISSATISFACTION—can be used to identify how individuals select among them.

Equally important, we have expanded the basic model to include a major contextual variable that has both guided and perplexed urban researchers for decades: the correspondence between the spatial boundaries of neighborhoods as "social worlds" and the boundaries of political jurisdictions. Importantly, the hypotheses generated by this extended model did not combine in such a way that we can unambiguously determine the overall impact of jurisdictional boundaries on political participation as a response to dissatisfaction.

We believe that this finding is an essential strength of the model. The linkages between various patterns of correspondence and noncorrespondence between the boundaries of social and political worlds and various models of local political participation are likely to be far more complex than one is led to believe using essentially unidimensional models such as the much-discussed Tiebout exiting hypothesis. The extended model provides us with a theoretically richer set of propositions with which to explore these complexities empirically, a task we now turn to using the Lexington–Louisville study data.

Notes

1. Lineberry and Masotti (1976).
2. Shevsky and Bell (1955).
3. Tiebout (1956); Ostrom, Tiebout, and Warren (1961); Bish (1971); and Bish and Ostrom (1973).
4. Williams, Herman, Liebman, and Dye (1965); Williams (1971, 1975); and Cox (1973).
5. Goodman (1977).
6. Hirschman (1970).
7. E. Ostrom (1983).
8. See Quigley (1980) for a review of the relevant literature concerning inter- and intraurban residential mobility and local government policies.
9. Sharp (1984a).
10. Orbell and Uno (1972); and Sharp (1984b).
11. Sharp (1984b).
12. E. Ostrom (1983); and Pack and Pack (1978).
13. Guest and Lee (1983).
14. Gans (1962).
15. See Greer (1962); and Janowitz (1967), for a detailed discussion of this term.
16. Guest and Lee (1983, p. 224).
17. Orbell and Uno (1972).
18. Sharp (1984b).
19. Willbern (1966).
20. See Hallman (1974); Fantini and Gittel (1982); and Zimmerman (1972).
21. In some cases, the "outward explosion" of urban populations is served by the county government. In others, massive annexation programs have allowed central cities to embrace large percentages of the diverse, but spatially clustered, populations that would ordinarily be found within more numerous and small political jurisdictions outside a particular core city under the Northeastern or upper Midwestern model.
22. Thibaut and Kelly (1959).
23. Rusbult (1980); Farrell and Rusbult (1981); Farrell and Rusbult (1985); Rusbult and Farrell (1983); Rusbult an Zembrodt (1983); and Rusbult and Lowery (1985).
24. Farrell, Rusbult, Rogers, and Mainous (1985); Farrell (1982); Rusbult and Lowery (1985).
25. Rusbult and Farrell (1983).
26. Berelson, Lazersfeld, and McPhee (1954); Almond and Verba (1963); and Agger, Goldrich, and Swanson (1964).
27. Orbell and Uno, (1972, p. 475).
28. Sharp (1984a); and Zemans (1973).
29. Bachrach and Baratz (1970, pp. 49, 58).
30. Campbell, Converse, Miller, and Stokes (1960).
31. In practice, this means that variables representing the concepts addressed in this larger literature, such as those on predispositions, etc., must be included as controls in empirical tests of the model developed here.
32. Sears and McConahay (1973).
33. For a fairly comprehensive list of such modes of participation coming from the long literature on political participation, see Milbrath and Goel (1977, pp. 18–19); and Verba and Nie (1972).
34. See Milbrath (1968, 1971a, 1971b, 1971c).
35. Finifter (1972).

36. Hirschman (1970).

37. Bachrach and Baratz (1970).

38. Tiebout (1956); Ostrom, Tiebout, and Warren (1961); and Pachon and Lovrich (1977).

39. Pachon and Lovrich (1977).

40. See Pack and Pack (1978).

41. E. Ostrom (1983).

42. Of course, opportunities for or propensities to invent privatization may not be constant across differing levels of correspondence. Quite simply, if, under conditions of low correspondence like that found in Polar Scenario II, there are few neighboring jurisdictions to which the dissatisfied citizen can move, the relative costs of campaigning for or starting up privatized services may be lowered. This situation creates the interesting possibility that one of the major effects of high levels of correspondence will be change in relative reliance on differing forms of "exit" rather than more fundamental shifts in the balance of exit, voice, loyalty, and neglect responses. One specific hypothesis flowing from this speculation is that, all other things being equal, we should find greater privatization in the urban settings similar to those identified as Scenario II than in those approximating conditions in Scenario I. We will explore this topic more fully in chapters 4 and 5.

43. Even if one continues to emphasize the importance of alternatives in the ultimate determination of responses to dissatisfaction, it is possible to posit an alternative set of empirically based hypotheses to those suggested by the Tiebout version of the model developed here. For example, it is possible, based on the literature concerning the effects of such structural variables as district versus at-large representation systems, to argue that noncorrespondence-type situations can be structured to respond to the segmental interests of various spatially defined social worlds, thereby enhancing the prospects of more positive types of responses as "voice" to complement "loyalty." See Karnig (1975); McDonald (1981); and Svara (1977).

4

Testing the EVLN Model

In our introduction to this volume, we observed that one of the primary problems in research on urban politics was the inadequacy of many research designs for simultaneously assessing the competing accounts of responses to dissatisfaction. Given the comprehensive nature of the model outlined in the previous chapter, our research design, as built into the Lexington and Louisville study, must be quite rigorous. Even the most basic features of the EVLN model cannot be adequately tested without gathering detailed and extensive survey data based on independent samples of individuals living in a wide variety of spatially defined communities. These communities, moreover, must be drawn from a variety of different urban settings exhibiting varying levels of correspondence between the boundaries of these various social worlds and the local governmental jurisdictions that serve them. Such a strategy is necessitated by the need not only to control for varying levels of correspondence, but also to ensure that sufficient numbers of citizens will be interviewed within each correspondence and social world condition to control for nonsituational factors that are the focus of the traditional political participation literature, including those arising from individual-level predispositions, social and economic status, and cultural factors. By now, then, the logic underlying the design outlined in chapter 1 and its critical importance to this enterprise should be evident.

Even our unusual research design, however, is not sufficiently developed to test all of the propositions outlined in chapter 3. There are several elements and implications of the model that we cannot directly or adequately confront with even the most elaborate and extensive of cross-sectional survey data. As we will see, many of the propositions concerning the intensification effects of such variables as current dissatisfaction, along with those concerning the net effects of varying levels of correspondence on the relative strengths of the various determinants of the four responses to dissatisfaction, call for longitudinal analyses based on in-depth surveys of the same sets of respondents over time. While we hope that these aspects of the model can be tested in the future using appropriate panel data, many aspects of the EVLN model can be assessed with cross-sectional data. In this chapter, then, we present a partial test of the EVLN model using the rather unique data set based on the Lexington and Louisville surveys described earlier. Other more specific aspects of the model, plus several related questions, will be explored in more detail in subsequent chapters.

Variables and Measures

With the exception of the EXIT-MOVE and privatization (EXIT-PRIV) variables, all of the dependent variables used in our test of the EVLN model are additive indexes.[1] As noted in appendix A, VOICE is constructed with six standard indicators of political participation, with reference to local government (reliability alpha = 0.69). Specifically, the items focus on the respondent's prior activities aimed at solving local problems, including attending meetings, belonging to neighborhood organizations, contacting officials, signing or circulating petitions, and talking to neighbors.

Five items were used to tap feelings of LOYALTY. As noted in appendix A, the five items included feelings of trust; a willingness to defend the local government; faith that problems will work out; a belief in the honesty of local officials; and a feeling that citizens are often too quick to blame local officials when things go wrong (reliability alpha = 0.72).

Four items—believing that you can't fight City Hall; not caring what happens in local government and politics; thinking it is not worth paying attention to local issues; and believing that it is useless to complain to officials—were combined to form our NEGLECT index (alpha = 0.69). In fact, the NEGLECT indicator is simply the inverse of the LOCAL EFFICACY indicator developed in chapter 2, with the inverse scoring necessitated to capture the directionality of the concept of neglect as developed in the previous chapter.

EXIT-MOVE is a dichotomous indicator derived from responses to three questions, which necessitates the use of Probit rather than OLS regression. First, all respondents were asked how likely they were to move in the next two or three years. Those indicating "definitely will move" or "probably will move" were then asked if the move would entail leaving their current local government jurisdiction. Those who answered YES to this question were then asked: "What are the two or three most important reasons you will or might move out of [name of local government]?" Those who made any mention of taxes, local government services, or anything pertaining to local government performance were coded as the "regime-government" type of reasons for moving. All other reasons (e.g., job, divorce, health, retirement, get closer to or further away from relatives, etc.) were coded as "personal-economic" type reasons.

To be coded as an "exiter" for this study, a respondent had to give a YES response to the first two questions *and* a mention of a "regime-government" type of reason in response to the last question. This is admittedly a much more stringent measure of EXIT than used in any other study that we know of, including those by Sharp and by Orbel and Uno.[2] It has the great advantage, however, of tapping precisely the conditions that underlie the notion of exit as set forth in the Tiebout model. Moving for reasons other than what we have called "regime-government" reasons does not satisfy the condition of Tiebout's interpretation that citizens use exit and locational choices to shop for an optimal package of public goods at the lowest possible costs in a competitive "market" of differing tax–service packages within a given urban area. Moving because of a job transfer, to avoid or to be near relatives, or to get closer to one's place of work is not a form of Tiebout exit behavior.

As suggested in the original presentation of the basic model, "some forms of service privatization might be viewed as a more specific or targeted form of exit."[3] To examine this variation on the exit theme, we constructed two indicators to tap the extent to which citizens have considered privatizing some public service they are currently receiving. Respondents were first asked if they had ever considered privately contracting for a *current* service. Those who answered YES were then asked to identify the service. These responses were scored "garbage collection," "private security service," and "other," with virtually all of the responses falling in the first two categories.

The first measure of EXIT-PRIV is simply a dichotomous indicator built on the first question, with values of one indicating a YES response—privatized services had been considered. The second indicator of EXIT-PRIV employed responses from both questions, combined to produce an indicator recording the number of current services the respondent had considered privatizing: zero, one, or two.[4] Given the limited number of values for either measure, Probit, rather than OLS regression, was also used to estimate the model for both indicators of EXIT-PRIV as a form of exit response to dissatisfaction. The empirical estimates using either indicator of the dependent variable were virtually the same. Therefore, we present results only for the more simple dummy variable indicator of EXIT-PRIV.

Two of the three independent variables of substantive interest in the model are also multi-item additive indexes. PRIOR SATISFACTION, as noted in appendix A, is based on two items: a question focusing on evaluations of the performance of city governments in *past years,* and a question focusing on satisfaction with city services in *past years* (alpha = 0.76). The indicator was very similar to the SATISFACTION measure presented in chapter 2, only focused on the past.

Five items were combined to tap the concept of INVESTMENT in the local community, our second independent variable of interest. These five items focused on degree of attachment to the community, how sorry the respondent would be to leave the city, the number of friends that live in the city, the number of relatives that live in the city, and length of residence (alpha = 0.53). It should be noted that renter/homeowner status did not correlate highly with the items included in the INVESTMENT indicator. However, since homeownership has been traditionally viewed as a form of investment in a community, we included a HOMEOWNERSHIP (i.e., rent/own) item as a separate investment variable in the regression equations to be presented.[5]

ALTERNATIVES, the third EVLN independent variable, is an objective measure of whether respondents have a realistic opportunity to find another local governmental jurisdiction within the general urban area. In chapter 3, we conceptualized alternatives in a comparative sense, suggesting that individuals will compare their current tax and service package to others available in the nearby environment. The design of this study and the choices that were made regarding research sites provided a clear opportunity to solicit responses from those who lived in a very fragmented and, thus, alternative-rich political environment (i.e., Louisville–Jefferson County) versus those who lived under an alternative-poor, consolidated form of government (i.e., Lexington–Fayette County). The objective measure assumes, of course, that those in the alternative-rich environment are aware of that richness, while those in the alternative-poor setting will similarly be aware of diminished circumstances for relocation. While we employ this objective measure in our test of the EVLN model, we will explore this underlying assumption of alternative awareness further in chapter 5.

In the original presentation of the model, these three variables—INVESTMENT, PRIOR SATISFACTION, and ALTERNATIVES—were expected to enter the model in interaction with level of Current Dissatisfaction. As seen in appendix A, the measure of CURRENT DISSATISFACTION was constructed with two indicators that are very similar to those used to construct the PRIOR SATISFACTION indicator, but addressing *current,* rather than *past* services (alpha = 0.81). In fact, CURRENT DISSATISFACTION is simply the inverse of the SATISFACTION indicator used in chapter 2, with the inverse scoring a convenience to match the directionality implicit in the concept of current dissatisfaction as presented in chapter 3. This is a somewhat simpler indicator than might be expected, given our discussion in chapter 3 of the concept of current dissatisfaction as a comparative evaluation of one's tax and service package relative to those readily available within the metropolitan environment. The simpler measure is used, however, in order to avoid confounding ALTERNATIVES and CURRENT DISSATISFACTION. We will, though, explore the relationships between these variables more fully in chapter 5.

Finally, we turn to the control variables. The EVLN model explicitly focuses on the situations in which individuals find themselves in accounting for patterns of response to dissatisfying conditions. The traditional participation literature, in contrast, generally has not been attentive to the situational determinants of participation,[6] focusing instead on demographic and psychological factors that predispose individuals to participate. To evaluate the EVLN interpretation, then, we must control for the forces identified in this larger political participation literature that work to encourage or discourage citizen participation behaviors. Initially, four standard items developed by Campbell, Gurin, and Miller were considered for inclusion in an indicator of GENERAL POLITICAL EFFI-CACY.[7] Although there is some controversy over what the traditional four items measure, the two items shown in appendix A produced an alpha of 0.68, and generated nearly the same results as the more standard four-item index. There-fore, we employ the full four-item index as our GENERAL EFFICACY indica-tor.[8] Gender is a straightforward dichotomous measure. The remaining control variables—EDUCATION, INCOME, AGE, and RACE—were coded as indi-cated in notes accompanying Table 1.3.

Testing the Basic EVLN Model

Table 4.1 presents the OLS and Probit estimates for the basic models using all respondents and controlling for EDUCATION, INCOME, AGE, GENDER, RACE, and GENERAL EFFICACY. While we will explore some interesting differences across separate subanalyses of the matched pairs of sites, the results across these sets were, for the most part, very similar. For convenience, then, we initially combine the ten surveys to highlight the general empirical findings on the EVLN model.

One further restriction on this initial model is the exclusion of the CURRENT DISSATISFACTION interaction term as specified in the previous chapter. When this variable was included in the model in interaction with the other EVLN variables, the coefficients became very unstable; the standard errors increased relative to other specifications of the model and the coefficients became very sensitive to even the most minor, further changes in specification. And although regressing the several independent variables on the remaining independent vari-ables did not generate especially large coefficients of determination, the most plausible source of this problem appears to be high collinearity. Since we were unable to increase the size of the sample, we were left with the difficult choice of excluding some of the collinear variables, with the most obvious candidate being the indicator that was entered in interaction with all of the EVLN independent variables. So, for our initial analysis, we dropped the CURRENT DISSATIS-FACTION interaction term and focused on the independent influences of AL-TERNATIVES, PRIOR SATISFACTION, and INVESTMENT. We will return to the issue of how current dissatisfaction can be brought into the model in a more empirically tractable manner shortly.

With a few noteworthy exceptions, the results of the OLS regression and Probit analyses are quite consistent with the hypotheses shown in Table 3.1. This is especially true if we ignore for the moment the coefficients for the homeownership form of the investment measure (HOMEOWNERSHIP) and the results for the privatization form of exit (EXIT-PRIV). In general, the home-owner investment variable generated only weak results relative to the social-psy-chological investment indicator (INVESTMENT) of the concept of investment. And the privatization form of exit is, as we will see, quite distinct from the

Table 4.1

Estimates for Original EVLN Dissatisfaction Model

	Response to Dissatisfaction				
Variable	EXIT-MOVE[a]	EXIT-PRIV[a]	VOICE[b]	LOYALTY[b]	NEGLECT[b]
EVLN Variables:					
PRIOR SATISFACTION	−0.213 (0.194)[c]	−0.386*** (0.094)	−0.782*** (0.103)	1.740*** (0.138)	−0.526*** (0.095
INVESTMENT	−0.169*** (0.051)	0.030 (0.025)	0.153*** (0.026)	0.329*** (0.03)	−0.122*** (0.024)
HOMEOWNERSHIP	−0.201 (0.277)	0.169 (0.180)	0.693*** (0.170)	0.030 (0.228)	−0.045 (0.158)
ALTERNATIVES	0.295 (0.197)	−0.310*** (0.100)	0.130 (0.101)	0.205 (0.136)	−0.084 (0.094)
CONTROL Variables:					
EDUCATION	−0.141** (0.07)	0.039 (0.033)	0.197*** (0.034)	−0.118*** (0.046)	−0.056* (0.031)
INCOME	0.014 (0.056)	0.107*** (0.025)	0.137*** (0.028)	−0.051 (0.037)	−0.011 (0.026)
AGE	0.003 (0.007)	−0.004 (0.003)	0.004 (0.003)	0.017*** (0.005)	−0.003 (0.003)
GENDER	−0.091 (0.188)	−0.074 (0.093)	0.018 (0.098)	0.200 (0.131)	0.141 (0.090)
RACE	0.117 (0.256)	0.191 (0.143)	−0.051 (0.142)	0.576*** (0.191)	−0.409*** (0.132)
GENERAL EFFICACY	0.116 (0.083)	0.046 (0.042)	−0.077* (0.044)	−0.052 (0.060)	0.380*** (0.041)
Constant	4.586	3.557	0.835	2.467	5.023
R^2	—	—	0.158	0.246	0.180
x^2	878.5	1407.1	—	—	—
N	1407	1395	1180	1180	1180

$* = p < 0.10; ** = p < 0.05; *** = p < 0.01.$
[a]Estimated with Probit.
[b]Estimated with OLS regression; coefficients are unstandardized.
[c]Figures in parentheses are standard errors.

traditional Tiebout exit response of voting with one's feet. Thus, ignoring these somewhat special cases in the HOMEOWNERSHIP row and the EXIT-PRIV column for the moment, we are left with twelve coefficients in the upper half of Table 4.1 that correspond to the twelve hypothesized relationships reported in Table 3.1.

Ten of these twelve coefficients are signed as expected and six of these are significant at the 0.05 level or better. Of the three EVLN independent variables, INVESTMENT generated the strongest results; all four of the INVESTMENT coefficients are both signed as expected and meet the 0.01 criterion level; INVESTMENT is positively related to the constructive VOICE and LOYALTY responses and negatively related to the destructive EXIT-MOVE and NEGLECT responses.

In contrast, only three of the four PRIOR SATISFACTION coefficients— those for EXIT-MOVE, LOYALTY, and NEGLECT—are signed as expected and only two of these are significant. PRIOR SATISFACTION is negatively related to the destructive responses of EXIT-MOVE and NEGLECT as expected, but is only statistically discernible in the latter case. The PRIOR SATISFAC- TION coefficient is significant and positive as expected in the passive–construc- tive response of LOYALTY. But in the VOICE model—where, like the constructive response of LOYALTY, we should find a positive PRIOR SATIS- FACTION coefficient—the estimate is instead negative and highly significant (−0.782).

The weakest results were generated for ALTERNATIVES, perhaps the cen- tral variable in the Tiebout exit hypothesis and the public choice perspective. While all but one of the four coefficients (that in the LOYALTY model) are signed as expected, none is discernibly different from zero.

In general, we view these results as offering modestly consistent support for the EVLN model. This is especially true given that the three determinants of response included in the model—PRIOR SATISFACTION, INVESTMENTS, and ALTERNATIVES—generally perform as well or better than the control variables derived from the more traditional political participation literature. There were, however, two noteworthy exceptions to this general pattern of sup- port: two of the twelve coefficients testing the core hypotheses of the model are both incorrectly signed, and one of these was statistically significant.

The first addresses the impact of PRIOR SATISFACTION on VOICE behav- iors. The highly significant coefficient of −0.78 suggests that as prior satisfaction increases, use of voice behaviors declines, a relationship that is fundamentally inconsistent with the model. One possible explanation of this result is misspecification. Specifically, by excluding the CURRENT DISSATISFAC- TION interaction term, we may not be adequately controlling for the need to respond to dissatisfaction with any of the four responses. If those who were satisfied in the past also tend to be satisfied in the present, then those with high prior satisfaction would have less objective need to invoke voice responses; they would have few grievances to redress. If this is the case, the negative coefficient may be assessing the citizen's current grievance level rather than the degree to which they hold experience-based, positive expectations about the city's willingness and ability to respond to problems. Given that this issue is central to the model, we will return to it below by respecifying the model to account for this interpretation of the anomalous finding.

The other anomaly in Table 4.1 concerns the relationship between ALTERNATIVES and LOYALTY. It was originally hypothesized, based on the work by Hirschman and on research on responses to dissatisfaction in job and personal relationship situations, that the presence of alternatives would tend to reduce levels of loyalty.[9] But in the case of responding to dissatisfaction with local government, the opposite seems to be the case. The ALTERNATIVES coefficient in the LOYALTY model is positive, although not significant.

This result might be interpreted in one of three related, but conceptually distinct ways. *First*, it might be viewed as not all that surprising for the case of city services, given that the condition of having numerous locational alternatives is measured by residing in a community with many small, homogeneous political jurisdictions—the Louisville–Jefferson County setting. These types of local jurisdictions, we have been repeatedly told by public choice advocates, are precisely the kinds of political settings that are likely to evidence strong psychological attachments on the part of the citizen for his or her city of residence. If such attachment is systematically higher under the high ALTERNATIVES condition, then ALTERNATIVES may be confounded with our INVEST-SOCIAL variable, with both assessing the higher degree of attachment expected to be found in Tiebout-like arrangements.

To assess this explanation, we conducted difference of means tests on an abbreviated version of the INVESTMENT index across the five pairs of research sites. This shortened index (ATTACHMENT) only included two of the five items in the original index: the first two items on attachment to the city, and the degree to which the respondent would be sorry to leave the city. Only these items were considered because they directly address the psychological-attachment focus of the public choice argument, while having family and friends and long-term residence in a city would seem to be less immediately relevant to this account of our anomalous finding.

As we will see in chapter 8 (especially Table 8.2), where we discuss the issue of attachment much more completely, the public choice expectations were *not* supported. Mean attachment is higher in the Lexington–Fayette neighborhood than it is in the corresponding Louisville–Jefferson cities in all five matched surveys.[10] Moreover, four of those differences are significant at the 0.01 level. It seems that the respondents from the Tiebout-like jurisdictions are considerably *less* attached to their cities than are their counterparts in the consolidated city–county jurisdiction, a relationship that we will explore more closely in the context of urban citizenship in chapter 8. Thus, this first account of the unexpected

ALTERNATIVES coefficient in the LOYALTY model does not seem especially plausible.

A *second* interpretation would suggest that we are again, as in the case of the PRIOR SATISFACTION coefficient in the VOICE model, confounding level of current dissatisfaction with alternatives. That is, if citizens in the Louisville–Jefferson County cases were uniformly more dissatisfied with their local governments than respondents in the corresponding Lexington–Fayette neighborhoods, then the relationship between ALTERNATIVES and LOYALTY might be tapping something other than the hypothesis addressed by the model. Specifically, the model conceptualizes LOYALTY as a response to dissatisfaction: passively and hopefully waiting for conditions to improve. But more generally, loyalty behaviors might also be expected under conditions of high satisfaction. Conventional norms of good citizenship place a high value on passive support of the type measured by our loyalty indicator, norms that would be expected to hold for those citizens who are satisfied. Thus, if citizens under one of our ALTERNATIVE conditions were uniformly more dissatisfied with current services than citizens under the other condition, the relationship between ALTERNATIVES and LOYALTY would be reflecting the high satisfaction, good citizenship interpretation of loyalty, rather than its meaning as a specific form of response to dissatisfaction.

To test this account, and as shown in appendix A, a measure of CURRENT DISSATISFACTION was constructed with two indicators that are very similar to those used to construct the PRIOR SATISFACTION indicator, but addressing *current* services, rather than *past* services (alpha = 0.81). But as we will see in chapter 5 (Table 5.8), there does not seem to be a strong relationship between ALTERNATIVES and CURRENT DISSATISFACTION. Sharp mean differences in dissatisfaction were observed across the jurisdictional types for all five matched sets. But in two cases, dissatisfaction with government services was higher in the consolidated government case than in the fragmented government case, while for the other three matched sets, the opposite pattern was found. ALTERNATIVES do not seem to be related to current dissatisfaction, suggesting that it is likely that local factors account for levels of current dissatisfaction. But, in any case, this particular confound does not seem to account for the unexpected ALTERNATIVE coefficient in the LOYALTY model.

A *third* interpretation would combine part of this last explanation with the added view that we are actually tapping a form of ritualistic response on the part of those who are satisfied with public service quality. This account starts with the assumption that LOYALTY is actually measuring the passive form of citizenship that would be expected from satisfied citizens, rather than a distinct form of response to dissatisfaction. And as seen in Table 4.1, PRIOR SATISFACTION was positively related to response type for only the LOYALTY response. If citizens were highly satisfied with their city services (presuming again that prior satisfaction is correlated with current satisfaction), then they would not need seriously to evaluate the possibility of any form of response to dissatisfaction. Passive loyalty of the good citizenship type would be the normal default response of such satisfied citizens. And reliance on this default response may be especially common for city services. In contrast to previous tests of the model in romantic relationships and job situations, city services are, on their face, considerably less salient; they matter less to most people than their love life or their job. Further, the norm of citizenship is a strong one. Given low salience and a strong, passive citizenship norm, we would expect most people to express attitudes consistent with high values of our LOYALTY measure. And in the absence of somehow controlling for the baseline level of current dissatisfaction, such responses could very well overwhelm the probably fewer cases of LOYALTY as response to dissatisfaction.

So how does this view account for the anomalous finding? The passive loyalty of satisfied citizens may extend to the point of their not seriously evaluating constraints on potential responses were they to become dissatisfied. Thus, someone who has no desire to relocate because he or she is satisfied might not seriously weigh the difficulty of moving; it is all too easy to say that you have alternatives if you do not seriously expect to have to use them. As such, their positive view of availability of alternatives may merely reflect a rosy glow engendered by their satisfaction with the status quo. While we are not able to test this interpretation directly, we will return to it in the conclusion of the analysis.

Beyond the results for the core hypotheses of the EVLN model, we need to comment on our extended interpretation of EXIT to include both the Tiebout response of voting with one's feet and privatization. But before examining the privatization results, we must reiterate that the expectations of the model were largely confirmed for the Tiebout-type of response. Although we found very few respondents who met our test for being classified as a Tiebout type of exiter in the results presented in Table 4.1 (i.e., $n = 21$), a finding that is interesting in its own right given the great faith placed on this response to dissatisfaction by numerous public choice analysts,[11] the size and direction of the Probit coefficients shown for our three determinants in the classic EXIT model are as expected: the prototypical exiter in the Tiebout sense tends to have been dissatisfied in the past, has weak investments in the community, and has numerous alternatives as a consequence of living in an urban environment characterized by high levels of governmental fragmentation.

The privatization (EXIT-PRIV) version of the exit model, however, operates quite differently from the one based on the work of Tiebout. Like Tiebout-type exiters, those who turn to the private sector for some services also tend to have been dissatisfied with local services in the past. But ALTERNATIVES in the Tiebout sense has exactly the opposite effect in the EXIT-PRIV model than it had in the EXIT-MOVE model; the coefficient is negative instead of positive, and is significant at the 0.01 level.

The reasons for these differences seem intuitively clear. Although homeownership can be seen as a constraint on making a decision to move in search of a more satisfactory tax–service package, it can also be viewed as a prerequisite for soliciting such property-oriented services as additional security or trash collection from the private sector. Similarly, it is possible to understand how opting for privatization might prove to be negatively related to the availability of alternatives in the Tiebout sense of that term. Indeed, privatization might be viewed as individual generation of alternatives to current government services that becomes especially important when the dissatisfied citizen has no jurisdictional alternatives to consider.[12]

Respecifying the Model

The Logic of Respecification

While the results presented in Table 4.1 provide support for the EVLN model, they were generated from a misspecified model; the CURRENT DISSATISFACTION interaction term was excluded because of collinearity. This misspecification was necessary to assess several key hypotheses in the original model, but it came at a cost. We have seen that this misspecification may have led to confounding prior satisfaction with current satisfaction, possibly resulting in two key coefficients being incorrectly signed and one of these significant. Further, the exclusion of CURRENT DISSATISFACTION renders the model incapable of more generally clarifying how current feelings of satisfaction or dissatisfaction with local government services and performance will affect the citizen's choice among the four response types.

To better address these issues, then, we considered several other solutions to the collinearity/specification problem. One possibility was to include CURRENT DISSATISFACTION in the model as a separate variable. This reduced the problem, but did not eliminate it. And more importantly, it failed to address the original "intensification effect" interpretation of the role of current dissatisfaction. Therefore, it made more sense, both theoretically and empirically, to include current dissatisfaction in the model by combining it with the PRIOR SATISFACTION indicator. In the absence of being able to ascertain a "baseline propensity to exit, voice, loyalty, and/or neglect,"[13] which was critical to including current dissatisfaction as a simple interactive term in the original model, it seems appropriate to focus on the levels of reported satisfaction and dissatisfaction with city services in the past *relative* to the present.

To capture this notion, we created a RELATIVE DISSATISFACTION (RELDIS) measure that was derived from the responses to the items used to create the original PRIOR SATISFACTION variable included in the model and the two item index of CURRENT DISSATISFACTION. Examination of these two indexes allowed us to identify four sets of respondents. Thus, RELDIS ranges from a low score of one, assigned to those who expressed satisfaction with local government services and performance in both the past and the present, through a score of four, which indicates what turned out to be the most extreme form of dissatisfaction, namely, those who were reasonably well satisfied in the past but who were now dissatisfied. In between are those who were somewhat dissatisfied in the past, but are now satisfied, and those who were chronically dissatisfied both past and present. While this particular measure is less than ideal,[14] it does combine both current dissatisfaction and prior satisfaction by looking at the former *relative* to the latter.

Importantly, though, the substitution of this variable for PRIOR SATISFACTION constitutes a fundamental change in the model. By focusing on RELATIVE DISSATISFACTION from the past to the present, rather than PRIOR SATISFACTION, we are giving primary emphasis to the way in which the current "relative" dissatisfaction shapes citizen behaviors. This has two major implications for the model.

First, we are no longer able to conceptualize LOYALTY as an explicit response to dissatisfaction. Without distinct indicators of both PRIOR SATISFACTION and CURRENT DISSATISFACTION in the model, we are not able to distinguish the two forms of loyalty: loyalty as response to dissatisfaction and loyalty as the default condition of the satisfied citizen. If both measures of satisfaction were included in the model, we would expect high levels of the former type of loyalty to be indicated by high prior satisfaction and high current dissatisfaction. In contrast, high levels of the latter type of loyalty would be associated with low levels of current dissatisfaction. But by combining the measures of PRIOR SATISFACTION and CURRENT DISSATISFACTION, we are inevitably mixing the two responses and giving weight to the latter type of loyalty: loyalty as passive support of satisfied citizens. Therefore, we now expect that there will be a negative relationship between RELDIS and LOYALTY.

This does not mean, however, that we are prepared to abandon LOYALTY as a specific response to dissatisfaction; we strongly suspect that it occurs and is distinct from LOYALTY as the predominant mode of response of the satisfied citizen. But being unable to include both PRIOR SATISFACTION and CURRENT DISSATISFACTION in the model in a more empirically tractable manner, we are essentially forced to focus on only one or the other form of LOYALTY.

Second, because the focus of RELDIS is more heavily weighted toward the current state of dissatisfaction than prior satisfaction, expectations regarding the "satisfaction" term in the model must change for VOICE, EXIT, and NEGLECT. Thus, it is hypothesized that there is a positive relationship between RELATIVE DISSATISFACTION and EXIT, VOICE, and NEGLECT; those who have become more dissatisfied in the present relative to the past should respond by invoking higher levels of the behaviors and attitudes associated with these responses. Such a prediction is quite consistent with the original view of the role of current dissatisfaction in the model and with much of the literature. Individuals must perceive problems or be dissatisfied with the current state of affairs before they are likely to spend the time, energy, and resources to engage in what we have called responses to dissatisfaction.[15] Our respecification, then, addresses the collinearity/specification issue by substituting RELATIVE DISSATISFACTION for PRIOR SATISFACTION, and thereby gives greater weight in the model to the original, but to this point untested, hypotheses about the intensification effect of the current state of dissatisfaction. In effect, we are modifying the theory to be consistent with what we believe to be the underlying message of the previous results, though that message was unclear given that we only suspected that PRIOR SATISFACTION was actually measuring some component of *current dissatisfaction*. Our task, then, is to reestimate the models with the actual indicator of CURRENT DISSATISFACTION to see if those suspicions were valid.

Results for the Respecified Model

The results for this respecified model are presented in Table 4.2. As expected, and remembering that the sign of the RELDIS coefficients should be opposite to those of PRIOR SATISFACTION in Table 4.1, the RELATIVE DISSATISFACTION variable largely resolves both of the two major interpretation conundrums in our previous findings. The coefficient for RELDIS in the VOICE equation is signed as expected and significant at the 0.01 level: people invoke higher levels of VOICE as they become relatively more dissatisfied over time. Such a relationship could not be meaningfully interpreted in the specification including PRIOR SATISFACTION. But in the case of that including RELDIS, it is entirely understandable.

Similarly, the LOYALTY results are more interpretable, if not fundamentally different from those presented in Table 4.1. In the present case, the negative and significant RELDIS coefficient (−1.082) indicates that respondents who became less dissatisfied over time evidence higher levels of LOYALTY. Such a relationship is entirely plausible if our LOYALTY measure is primarily assessing good citizenship under the condition of satisfaction with services, rather than a distinct response to dissatisfaction. If such is the case, the positive and significant ALTERNATIVES coefficient in this equation could be tapping the costless and unconsidered optimism of those who have not had to contemplate actually responding to dissatisfaction by moving.

Beyond these results, the findings reported in Table 4.2 are very similar to those reported in Table 4.1. Again, the results are generally supportive of the EVLN model, all twelve of the core coefficients carry the correct sign expected from our reinterpretation of the RELDIS specification of the model. And of these twelve correctly signed coefficients, nine are statistically significant at the 0.05 level. Beyond the core hypotheses of the model, privatization (EXIT-PRIV) as a form of exit continues to exhibit a significantly different relationship to the EVLN variables from that found for the more traditional Tiebout form of exit.

Table 4.2

Estimates for Respecified EVLN Dissatisfaction Model

Variable	Response to dissatisfaction				
	EXIT-MOVE[a]	EXIT-PRIV[a]	VOICE[b]	LOYALTY[b]	NEGLECT[b]
EVLN Variables:					
RELDIS	0.071 (0.068)[c]	0.147*** (0.040)	0.391*** (0.044)	−1.082*** (0.056)	0.348*** (0.041)
INVESTMENT	−0.169*** (0.047)	0.023 (0.024)	0.151*** (0.025)	0.312*** (0.031)	−0.113*** (0.023)
HOMEOWNERSHIP	−0.038 (0.267)	0.214 (0.171)	0.674*** (0.160)	0.105 (0.203)	−0.071 (0.147)
ALTERNATIVES	0.210 (0.185)	−0.373*** (0.096)	0.001 (0.098)	0.476*** (0.125)	−0.178** (0.087)
CONTROL Variables:					
EDUCATION	−0.108* (0.060)	0.047 (0.031)	0.210*** (0.033)	−0.148*** (0.042)	−0.047*** (0.030)
INCOME	−0.012 (0.053)	0.099*** (0.024)	0.118*** (0.027)	−0.026 (0.034)	−0.024 (0.025)
AGE	0.001 (0.006)	−0.003 (0.003)	0.005 (0.003)	0.015*** (0.004)	−0.003 (0.003)
GENDER	−0.012 (0.177)	−0.083 (0.089)	0.023 (0.094)	0.177 (0.120)	0.183** (0.087)
RACE	0.051 (0.234)	0.140 (0.137)	−0.065 (0.137)	0.492*** (0.175)	−0.409*** (0.127)
GENERAL EFFICACY	0.106 (0.079)	0.046 (0.041)	−0.076* (0.043)	−0.030 (0.055)	0.377*** (0.040)
Constant	4.083	2.736	−1.052	7.224	4.471
R^2	—	—	0.177	0.337	0.210
χ^2	1198.6	1517.8	—	—	—
N	1496	1383	1233	1233	1233

* $= p < 0.10$; ** $= p < 0.05$; *** $= p < 0.01$.
[a]Estimated with Probit.
[b]Estimated with OLS regression; coefficients are unstandardized.
[c]Figures in parentheses are standard errors.

Table 4.3

Estimates for Respecified VOICE Model by Paired Research Sites

Paired research sites[a]

Independent variable	All EVLN respondents	Match 1	Match 2	Match 3	Match 4	Match 5
RELDIS	0.391*** (0.044)[b]	0.429*** (0.096)	0.394*** (0.147)	0.321*** (0.079)	0.496*** (0.123)	0.240** (0.094)
INVESTMENT	0.151*** (0.025)	0.238*** (0.054)	0.203*** (0.060)	0.132*** (0.051)	0.208*** (0.065)	0.076 (0.056)
HOMEOWNERSHIP	0.674*** (0.160)	0.903*** (0.331)	0.322 (0.324)	0.921 (0.631)	0.176 (0.594)	0.226 (0.324)
ALTERNATIVES	0.001 (0.098)	0.908*** (0.230)	0.103 (0.241)	−0.251 (0.194)	0.042 (0.231)	−0.147 (0.256)
R^2	0.177	0.286	0.128	0.172	0.151	0.175
N	1233	258	255	279	234	205

$* = p < 0.10$; $** = p < 0.05$; $*** = p < 0.01$.
[a]These estimates were generated with equations including all of the control variables presented in Tables 4.1 and 4.2. The matched pairs are in the order presented in Table 1.2.
[b]Figures in parentheses are standard errors.

To investigate further the EVLN model, subanalyses of the five pairs of matched surveys were conducted for three of our dependent variables: VOICE, LOYALTY, and NEGLECT. Given the small number of cases reporting Tiebout exit and privatization behaviors, however, subanalyses could not be conducted for these two responses using PROBIT, although we will explore the EXIT-MOVE and EXIT-PRIV variables more completely in the next chapter using somewhat simpler methods. The results of the subanalyses for VOICE, LOY-ALTY and NEGLECT are reported in Tables 4.3 through 4.5. These results were generated from models including all of the controls used in the results presented in Tables 4.1 and 4.2. For convenience, however, we only report the EVLN coefficients in Table 4.3; as would be expected, the coefficients of the control variables were considerably attenuated in these results, since the examination of EVLN variables across sites intentionally matched for socioeconomic similarity significantly reduces the variances of the controls.

While the results of these subanalyses generally support the conclusion drawn from the findings reported for the combined surveys, they also illustrate the weakness of several of the relationships posited by the model. Briefly, there are

Table 4.4

Estimates for Respecified LOYALTY Model by Paired Research Sites

Independent EVLN variable	All Respondents	Match 1	Match 2	Match 3	Match 4	Match 5
		Paired research sites[a]				
RELDIS	−1.082*** (0.056)[b]	−1.052*** (0.129)	−1.107*** (0.154)	−0.980*** (0.114)	−1.060*** (0.138)	−0.954*** (0.140)
INVESTMENT	0.312*** (0.031)	0.415*** (0.072)	0.257*** (0.063)	0.247*** (0.074)	0.407*** (0.073)	0.260*** (0.084)
HOMEOWNERSHIP	0.105 (0.203)	0.087 (0.442	0.360 (0.340)	0.701 (0.916)	−0.050 (0.664)	−0.137 (0.484)
ALTERNATIVES	0.476*** (0.125)	0.443 (0.307)	1.041*** (0.253)	−0.080 (0.281)	0.930*** (0.259)	−0.419 (0.382)
R^2	0.337	0.351	0.394	0.294	0.380	0.313
N	1233	258	255	279	234	205

$* = p < 0.10; ** = p < 0.05; *** = p < 0.01.$
[a]These estimates were generated with equations including all of the control variables presented in Tables 4.1 and 4.2. The matched pairs are in the order presented in Table 1.2.
[b]Figures in parentheses are standard errors.

only four cases in these three tables where a RELDIS, INVESTMENT, or ALTERNATIVES coefficient is *both* correctly signed and significant across all five paired research sites and the full set of respondents. As might be expected given the previous results, the RELDIS coefficients are correctly signed and statistically significant in all five sets of matched sites for all three of the core EVLN independent variables. Similarly, the INVESTMENT coefficients in the LOYALTY models in Table 4.4 are all signed as expected and significant. As seen in Table 4.3, only four of the five matched sets of sites generated significant INVESTMENT coefficients in the VOICE models, although all five are signed as expected, and only three of the five matched pairs generated significant INVESTMENT coefficients in the NEGLECT results in Table 4.5, although, again, all five are signed as expected. By far, the weakest results are for ALTERNATIVES. Of the fifteen subanalyses in Tables 4.3 through 4.5, only four of the ALTERNATIVES coefficients are correctly signed and significant at the 0.10 level, and five are incorrectly signed.

The variables identified by the EVLN model do matter, but clearly, they do not strictly govern responses to dissatisfaction. Thus, while the model is gener-

Table 4.5

Estimates for Respecified NEGLECT Model by Paired Research Sites

Independent EVLN variable	All respondents	Paired research sites[a]				
		Match 1	Match 2	Match 3	Match 4	Match 5
RELDIS	0.348***	0.297***	0.370***	0.410***	0.263**	0.218**
	(0.041)[b]	(0.092)	(0.132)	(0.075)	(0.109)	(0.088)
INVESTMENT	−0.113***	−0.176***	−0.161***	−0.032	−0.164***	−0.067
	(0.023)	(0.051)	(0.054)	(0.048)	(0.057)	(0.053)
HOMEOWNERSHIP	−0.071	0.060	−0.154	−0.739	0.317	0.104
	(0.147)	(0.316)	(0.292)	(0.599)	(0.527)	(0.304)
ALTERNATIVES	−0.178**	−0.024	−0.580***	−0.001	−0.101	0.334
	(0.087)	(0.219)	(0.218)	(0.184)	(0.205)	(0.240)
R^2	0.210	0.196	0.224	0.202	0.126	0.157
N	1233	258	255	279	234	205

$* = p < 0.10;\ ** = p < 0.05;\ *** = p < 0.01.$
[a]These estimates were generated with equations including all of the control variables presented in Tables 4.1 and 4.2. The matched pairs are in the order presented in Table 1.2.
[b]Figures in parentheses are standard errors.

ally supported by these results, we would strongly caution against expecting dramatic and/or inevitable changes in behavior upon natural or manipulated changes in the values of the EVLN independent variables. This is especially true for ALTERNATIVES; improving alternatives by adopting Tiebout-like institutional arrangements may have some positive impact on the use of voice and Tiebout exiting, but the differences would likely be very small and inconsistent, something that we will consider more extensively in the next chapter on the underlying assumptions of the public choice and traditional civic reform models.

Discussion

In sum, the results provide reasonably strong and broadly consistent support for many components of the EVLN model. We would not argue that this constitutes a complete assessment of the EVLN model. More specifically, we were unable to test several elements of the model. Since we were unable to include both current dissatisfaction and prior satisfaction in the model simultaneously, we were unable to isolate both the magnitude of reliance on and the determinants of LOYALTY as a response to dissatisfaction. In general, though, the results com-

Figure 4.1. A Sequential Choice Model of Responses to Dissatisfaction

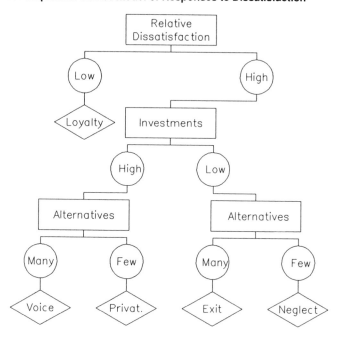

pare quite favorably to those based on the more conventional models of local participation that emphasize individual predispositions arising from psychological and sociodemographic forces. They also compare quite favorably to previous tests of the general EVLN model in employment and romantic situations.

Nevertheless, the system that emerges from this test of the model using cross-sectional data is somewhat different from that suggested in chapter 2. Loyalty as a response to dissatisfaction is missing from the system, if still viable theoretically. Examining this form of loyalty further depends on the availability of sufficient resources to conduct panel studies so that CURRENT DISSATISFAC-TION can be introduced into the empirical analysis as an interaction term as specified in the original model. Moreover, individual contracting as an alternative to current public services must now be viewed as a distinct form of response to dissatisfaction.

To better conceptualize these changes, as well as to highlight the general contributions of this analysis, we can compare the system suggested by these findings to one developed by Orbell and Uno in their innovative first attempt to develop a general model of responses to dissatisfaction.[16] Based on their empirical analysis, they posited a decision tree conceptualization of responses to dissatisfaction, with three response types: exit, voice, and passivity. They then posited several decision points, which focus on the citizen's responses to such questions as "Can voice work for me?" and "Can exit work for me?" In contrast, the analysis presented here suggests a more complex decision tree of the type shown in Figure 4.1.

This alternative decision tree differs from the one presented by Orbell and Uno in two important respects. First, the range of possible response types is more complex. In addition to voice and exit, privatization is added as a viable response to dissatisfaction. Moreover, their passivity response is broken into two components—neglect and loyalty as good citizenship—that have fundamentally different meanings for citizens' relationships with their local government. Missing from even this model, however, is a third form of passive response that is theoretically viable—loyalty as a response to dissatisfaction. The second basic difference is a substitution of a few specific questions about the citizen's situation for Orbell and Uno's less precise queries about whether one of several response types will work. While many of their examples clearly speak to the issues raised in our concepts of investments, prior satisfaction, current dissatisfaction, and alternatives, we believe that our analysis gives more precise meanings to these terms.

The four political responses to dissatisfaction identified at the bottom of Figure 4.1 are defined in the same manner as those shown under the headings of VOICE, EXIT, and NEGLECT in Table 3.1. People who rely on any of these four types of responses to dissatisfaction are characterized by high levels of relative dissatisfaction. What sets those apart in each of these response categories are varying patterns of investments and alternatives. Thus, a typical citizen who relies on *voice* has high investments and many alternatives. In contrast, the typical citizen relying on *neglect* has low investments and few alternatives. Between these two responses are more mixed cases. The typical citizen relying on the classic Tiebout form of *exit* has low investments like those who invoke neglect, but also has many alternatives. And last, the typical citizen relying on *privatization* has a high level of economic investment in the community through homeownership, but few alternatives in the Tiebout sense of the term.[17]

This analysis points also toward at least one rather major methodological implication for the political participation literature. As indicated by the subanalyses discussed in this chapter, survey results from different cities and even different neighborhoods within cities can generate diverse responses to similar questions. There is much about citizens' specific local environment that governs their attitudes and behaviors with respect to local government. We have tried to resolve some of the problems created by this locally induced variation by surveying respondents from a variety of different kinds of neighborhoods located in two quite different government systems. The strategy proved appropriate given the results of the subanalyses. More generally, these results point to the importance of comparative research in understanding local participation, something that is not often the case given the heavy reliance on limited-resource-driven single surveys.

While this test of the EVLN model assesses many of the hypotheses developed in chapter 3, it by no means tests them all. Most importantly, we have addressed only a few of several propositions about the impacts of fragmented versus consolidated government structures developed at the very end of that chapter. In essence, we have focused here only on the direct effects of ALTERNATIVES, when we have already pointed out that the consolidated or fragmented structure of a metropolitan area might also have important indirect effects. To be specific, two indirect effects based on the work of public choice theorists were suggested in chapter three: (i) that investments and levels of correspondence are positively related, and (ii) that satisfaction and levels of correspondence are positively related. Given that the direct effects of correspondence on ALTERNATIVES were unquestionably the weakest of the relationships posited by the EVLN model presented here, it is incumbent upon us to examine these indirect effects further to assess the fragmentation versus consolidation positions fully. We begin consideration of these hypotheses, as well as a number of other assumptions that underlie the public choice theory of local government organization, in the next chapter.

Notes

1. Aside from the measure of Exit-Privatization, which is exclusively related to the governmental arena, all of these measures were designed to provide us with governmentally relevant analogs to the kinds of measures used by other social scientists to capture the notions of Exit, Voice, Loyalty, and Neglect in a variety of other contexts including job and interpersonal relationships (see Farrell, 1982; Rusbult, Zembrodt, and Gunn, 1982). The measures used in these previous efforts had been tested for both reliability and validity using a variety of techniques including multidimensional scaling and construct validity. In addition, the governmental analogs for at least two of our dependent variables look very similar to the items used to construct indices to measure such related political science concepts as political trust and local political efficacy, both of which have been operationalized and tested for reliability using items very close to those included in our measure of Loyalty and Neglect respectively (see Abramson, 1983; and Balch, 1974).

2. Sharp (1984a); and Orbell and Uno (1972).

3. Lyons and Lowery (1986, p. 332).

4. Again, education, which is perhaps the most frequently privatized local service in the United States, was not included in this study because there is no variation in terms of the governmental/institutional format for education in the Lexington and Louisville areas. Since citizens in both of these urban areas are served by consolidated city–county school districts, it would be impossible to sort out the differing effects of being able to exercise the Exit-Move option under conditions of alternative public school systems versus Exit via the Privatization route. It would be most interesting to examine this question with data from appropriate types of fragmented versus consolidated systems affecting education.

5. What is perhaps more curious is that none of the items pertaining to children (e.g., number of children, number of children in school, or number of children in public school) correlated well with the items on the Invest-Social scale. We have no basis for explaining this, but it may indicate that caution should be exercised when using such data to measure the notion of investments.

6. Orbell and Uno (1972, p. 475); and Lyons and Lowery (1986, pp. 328–30).

7. See Campbell, Gurin, and Miller (1954).

8. The two items that are used are the same two items that are consistently found in the literature to be related to the notion of "external efficacy" (see Abramson, 1983, pp. 135–45.)

9. Hirschman (1970); Kenyon (1984); and Oakerson, Parks, and Bell (1987).

10. Indeed, as will be documented in a later chapter, an overwhelming majority (71.8 percent) of respondents in all five Louisville sites claimed that the county government, and not their small incorporated municipality, was the "most important" unit of local government in their "daily lives." This also runs counter to expectations based on the public choice model.

11. V. Ostrom, Tiebout, and Warren (1961); Bish (1971); and Bish and Ostrom (1973).

12. Oakerson, Parks, and Bell (1987); and Lyons and Lowery (1986).

13. Lyons and Lowery (1986, p. 334).

14. The most obvious problem is that the indicator is at best ordinal. We believe, however, that this measure was theoretically superior to its two major alternatives: a simple difference measure and a simple multiplicative interaction term. The former would not have allowed us to distinguish between those who had a mild decline from a previous condition of high satisfaction from those who had a mild decline from a previous condition of low satisfaction. The response hypotheses associated with these two conditions are quite different, but a simple difference measure would have assigned both the same relative dissatisfaction score. A simple multiplicative interaction term would have similarly failed to distinguish those who had low current dissatisfaction, but high prior satisfaction and those who had high current dissatisfaction, but low prior dissatisfaction. Thus, our ordinal measure was considered theoretically superior.

15. Orbell and Uno (1972); Sharp (1984a, 1984c).

16. Orbell and Uno (1972, p. 486).

17. It is interesting to speculate where loyalty as a response to dissatisfaction should be placed in this decision tree. Consistent with our original view of this response, we would place this form of loyalty below or near the privatization response. Like the typical person who privatizes, loyalists of this type would be expected to have high levels of investment and few alternatives. They would differ, however, in terms of their prior satisfaction with the local government, the variable that was dropped from our respecified model. Those who privatize would be expected to have low prior satisfaction, or little expectation that the city would solve the problem, while loyalists would be expected to have high levels of prior satisfaction.

5

A Closer Look at the Tiebout Model

Although comparing government fragmentation and consolidation has been a recurring theme throughout the preceding chapters, it has been but one of several theoretically important elements included in our more comprehensive models on the sources of satisfaction and how citizens respond politically when dissatisfied. It is somewhat surprising, given the substantial attention devoted to this issue by both traditional civic reformers and public choice proponents, that ALTERNATIVES—the fragmented or consolidated structure of a local governmental system—did not generate especially strong results in either of these models. In the SATISFACTION model presented in chapter 2, we found no evidence that government structure directly influenced citizens' evaluations of urban governance, although some interesting indirect effects were observed. And in chapter 4, we saw that ALTERNATIVES generated the weakest results among the EVLN predictor variables. Does structure not matter?

As we will have several occasions to point out in the ensuing chapters, institutions do matter, but often not in the simple manner suggested by either public choice proponents or traditional reformers. In part, we suspect that our failure to find strong effects for the structure variable in our analyses inheres in fundamental flaws in the assumptions underlying many local government institutional analyses. We explore these flaws more thoroughly in this and the following chapters, with special attention to the public choice model's Tiebout exiting hypothesis.

In empirically assessing the veracity of the foundations of the Tiebout model, we carefully draw from the abundant public choice literature in order to identify the assumptions that underlie "voting with one's feet." And in the case of each assumption, we have tried to reflect the thrust and substance of the literature's assertions and propositions with the original language used by the authors whose works were consulted.

Basic Assumptions and Operational Effects of the Tiebout Model

Over the course of the last three decades, the public choice model of local government organization has become much broader than the Tiebout exiting hypothesis. Yet, public choice theory still relies heavily on Tiebout's ideas as originally presented in "A Pure Theory of Local Expenditures" in 1956.[1] Building directly on Tiebout's work, a more complete elaboration of the public choice alternative to the traditional civic reform model emphasizing the need to consolidate or otherwise reduce the number of local governments serving our burgeoning urban areas appeared a few years later in an article entitled "The Organization of Government in Metropolitan Areas: A Theoretical Inquiry" by Ostrom, Tiebout, and Warren.[2]

The central argument of this "new reform tradition," as Bish and Ostrom have dubbed it,[3] stresses the need to create and maintain numerous units of local government offering differing mixes of local services within each urban area in order to maximize opportunities for individual citizens to choose a tax–service package that best suits their needs, including opportunities to "vote with their feet" in the event they become dissatisfied with their current jurisdiction. Such exiting is supposed to produce a more desirable outcome not only for citizens who vote with their feet, but also for those who remain. Exiting may constitute a signal to local officials that service quality has declined or that their tax and service package no longer meets their residents' needs. Thus, locational choice is a demand mechanism to which local governments must respond with the appropriate supply of services if they are to prosper in the quasi-marketplace of the local political system.

In short, a better match between service demand and service supply is expected to result from exiting for those who leave *and* those who stay. Indeed, some supporters of this model have advocated dividing large central city governments into smaller jurisdictions so that those residents might enjoy the same opportunities for choosing from a variety of tax–service packages that many suburban dwellers allegedly have.[4]

Given the importance of the Tiebout model to the public choice paradigm, it is curious that its empirical foundations are not especially well developed. Most empirical investigations only indirectly address many of the model's central assumptions.[5] This is a serious problem given that the model evaluates institutional arrangements on the basis of a number of assumptions *about* individual-level attitudes and behaviors. Yet, most of the purported tests of the model have been conducted at very high levels of aggregation, whether at the state or the metropolitan level.[6] While these analyses usefully test implications of the Tiebout model for public policy, they can only indirectly bear on the many individual-level propositions that provide it with such analytical power. Other studies purporting to address individual-level behaviors unfortunately rely almost exclusively on aggregate data, which effectively precludes more detailed

consideration of the attitudinal foundations of individual political action.
A few studies, primarily within the "citizen contacting" literature, attempt to address some of these individual-level propositions more directly. Especially important in this regard is Elaine Sharp's work, which attempts to assess some of the individual-level propositions of the model with both HUD national survey data and data from individual city surveys of citizens in Wichita and Kansas City.[7] But while Sharp's analysis is an important exception to the general lack of attention to the individual-level assumptions of the model, it too is limited. For example, her necessary reliance on secondary analysis of the HUD survey data precluded consideration of more than a limited range of propositions. And the individual studies of Wichita and Kansas City precluded examination of individual responses under varying levels of fragmented or consolidated institutional arrangements—the key issue in the debate over the design implications of the Tiebout model. In sum, empirical work on the underlying assumptions of the Tiebout model has not matched the theoretical attention it has received.

The Underlying Assumptions of the Tiebout Model

The Tiebout model makes several basic—albeit usually implicit—assumptions about individuals that are central to its institutional design recommendations. *First, it is assumed that individuals living in highly fragmented government settings (e.g., metropolitan areas served by numerous units of local government) are attentive to the tax–service packages offered by the most local unit of government serving their particular neighborhood.* Even under conditions of perfect mobility, as explicitly assumed, citizens cannot make the kinds of initial or subsequent locational choices called for by the Tiebout model if they are not attentive to their most locally provided public goods and services. If, for example, they view the county or some other broader level of local government as the most important in their daily lives, then we might not expect that levels and mixes of services provided by particular subunits of government within the county would play much of a role in locational and exit behaviors.

Second, the Tiebout model implicitly assumes that citizens living under highly fragmented institutional arrangements are aware of alternatives to their present tax–service package. While this is part of the model's general presumption of full information, our specification of this assumption focuses on the essential requirement that not only must there be viable alternatives to an individual's present tax–service package, but consumers of local government services also must be aware of those alternatives. Without such awareness, no Tiebout-like locational choices can be made and no level of dissatisfaction with one's current services can lead to voting with one's feet. And the absence of such awareness on the part of large numbers of citizens would undermine the model's fundamental premise that locational choices are driven primarily by comparative tax–service considerations.

Meeting these two requirements alone would not be enough to make the Tiebout model work. *If citizens are attentive to their most local unit of government and are aware of alternative local governments, it is further required that citizens have a plausibly accurate understanding of both their current tax and service package and that of the alternative under consideration for relocation.* Without such understanding, Tiebout exiting would be essentially random, and could not therefore create meaningful incentives for local officials to meet the tax and service preferences of their constituents. On this score, public choice analysts confidently assert that citizens in fragmented governments are well informed, or at least better informed than their consolidated government counterparts. This belief is implicit in much of the public choice literature, including Tullock's arguments about the loss of information in large organizations.[8] It is made quite explicit, however, in discussions about the alleged effects of "gargantua" (e.g., all larger governmental systems, including consolidated ones) on citizen information by Ostrom, Tiebout, and Warren, and by Bish and Ostrom.[9] While we begin to address some of the implications of these arguments in this chapter, we will examine them much more thoroughly in chapter 6.

Once these preconditions are established and operative, the Tiebout model implies that fragmented institutional settings will influence several of the determinants of responses to dissatisfaction as outlined in the EVLN model presented in chapter 3 and tested in chapter 4. The most obvious is the ALTERNATIVES variable. Fragmentation creates many alternative local units of government with differing tax and service packages from which citizens might choose, *if* they focus on their most local governmental unit in making locational choices, are aware of the alternatives, and can evaluate the respective packages offered by the competitors.

In chapter 3, however, we argued that the public choice literature makes two additional arguments about indirect impacts of ALTERNATIVES, patterns of indirect influences that we have yet to examine. The first of these concerns the INVESTMENT variable in the EVLN model. Put simply, *public choice proponents argue that citizens in smaller communities operating in a fragmented institutional environment will be more highly invested than will be citizens in consolidated governments.* As we saw in chapter 3, public choice proponents have argued that citizens are more likely to be attached to smaller political communities. This assertion is rarely tested in the public choice literature. But even if it is true (a question we will consider more fully in chapter 8), investment in a community, especially as measured by our INVESTMENT index, includes more than psychological attachment. INVESTMENT also includes being embedded in the social life of the community through working and living with friends and family in the same jurisdiction. High levels of social embeddedness, of course, are less likely in very small communities in highly fragmented metropolitan areas where one might work in one jurisdiction, live in another, and visit friends and family in still another city. If this second tie outweighs the psychological attachment that one might have to a smaller community, then we might find that fragmented communities on average have somewhat lower levels of INVESTMENT.

The second hypothesized indirect influence of ALTERNATIVES concerns satisfaction with one's local government. On this issue, though, public choice theory and the Tiebout exiting hypothesis are less than entirely clear. On one hand, and as argued in chapter 3, we might expect that *citizens in fragmented communities will be more dissatisfied on average than their neighbors in a consolidated metropolis.* This expectation is predicated on our comparative conceptualization of satisfaction and dissatisfaction. If a Tiebout citizen is aware of many alternatives and what each offers by way of taxes and services, there is a reasonable chance that some other jurisdiction will offer him or her a somewhat better deal, leading to dissatisfaction with his or her current city. In contrast, the consolidated government citizen has few or no alternatives, thereby eliminating any comparative base on which to become dissatisfied.

On the other hand, though, public choice theory strongly suggests that the *operation of the Tiebout model will lead to higher overall satisfaction with local government.* Consolidated governments with their unified tax–service systems, public choice advocates suggest, cannot respond to the differing tax–service preferences of the many citizens they serve. Smaller units of government operating in a highly fragmented system, in contrast, provide citizens with a variety of choices, each of which can be finely tailored for the needs of a small and homogeneous population. Thus, citizens living in governmentally fragmented urban areas are assumed to have more opportunities to match their own unique needs, desires, and preferences for public goods and services. As stated by Bish and Ostrom, after they note that consolidation implies uniformity of service packages, "the more uniform the output, the less likely that those citizens whose preferences and problems differ from the average will be satisfied with the service product."[10] This strongly implies, of course, that citizens living in fragmented settings will be more satisfied with their city governments than will residents of consolidated governments.

In addition, this thesis implies that mean levels of dissatisfaction across neighborhoods served by their own units of local government within a fragmented system will be quite small, even though the service packages offered by the several jurisdictions will likely be very different. In contrast, most citizens in a consolidated community will be stuck with certain tax–service features that they would not opt for if given a choice. Thus, mean differences in dissatisfaction across neighborhoods in consolidated communities should be large as a result of providing the same tax–service package to neighborhoods with very different preferences.

In chapter 3 we tried to resolve these competing hypotheses about satisfaction by distinguishing between prior satisfaction and current dissatisfaction. But as we saw in chapter 4, we were unable to distinguish clearly between the two concepts empirically using the Lexington and Louisville study data. On balance, however, the public choice literature more explicitly emphasizes a positive relationship between levels of correspondence and satisfaction, leading us to focus on this side of the multifaceted public choice argument on satisfaction in the remainder of this chapter. This is especially justified given the additional public choice assertion that fragmented systems not only offer choice, but stimulate governments to increase service performance because of competition, leading to a "more responsive and efficient public economy in metropolitan areas.[11]

The Operation of the Tiebout Model

Given these preconditions, and both the direct and indirect influence of greater locational alternatives, what is the expected behavioral result of fragmentation? We can consider this question in terms of the behavioral options offered by the EVLN model developed in chapter 3.

   The Tiebout model implies that citizens will be motivated to exit because of dissatisfaction with their current tax–service package. While this is clearly assumed, the point remains ambiguous for many of the same reasons as noted above for the satisfaction hypothesis. On the one hand, the mere existence of Tiebout-like institutional arrangements may lead citizens *initially* to locate in jurisdictions that fully match their preferences. Stein has labeled this interpretation of the dynamics of the Tiebout model the "sorting" hypothesis.[12] If the sorting hypothesis is valid, we would see little *current* dissatisfaction-based exit in Tiebout-like communities because the initial sorting process would have perfectly coordinated citizen preferences with available combinations of local taxes and services.

   An alternative interpretation of the model would suggest that voting with one's feet is instead an ongoing process that never resolves to a static and stable distribution of populations across metropolitan jurisdictions. That is, voter preferences for tax and spending packages might be expected to change as time passes and needs change. Moreover, local jurisdictions may alter their tax–service packages over time in a manner that reduces the level of satisfaction on the part of some citizens. As a result, this interpretation of the Tiebout model suggests that there will nearly always be some level of dissatisfaction-motivated exit within the metropolitan area. Indeed, we would argue that this interpretation of the operation of the model is consistent with Tiebout's original analysis. Tiebout argued that:

> Except when this system is in equilibrium, there will be a subset of consumer-voters who are discontented with the patterns of their community. Another set will be satisfied. Given the assumption about mobility . . . [t]he consumer voter moves to the community that satisfies his preference pattern. The act of moving or failing to move is crucial. Moving or failing to move replaces the usual market test of willingness to buy a good and reveals the consumer-voter's demand for public goods.[13]

And, consistent with this view of movement as a central and ongoing process, most empirical tests of the Tiebout model focus explicitly on mobile subpopulations in searching for evidence of dissatisfaction-based relocation. To these researchers, such movement constitutes evidence of the Tiebout model's operation, not initial sorting into homogeneous and quiescent subpopulations.[14] Given the prevalence of this approach to testing the Tiebout model, we also ascribe to the expectation that effective operation of the Tiebout model necessitates some level of actual exiting behavior in response to dissatisfaction.

This view, however, is in obvious tension with the satisfaction hypotheses discussed earlier. If citizens are highly satisfied with their localities as a result of the Tiebout model's operation, then few will be motivated to exit. We do not feel any great pressure to resolve this tension. To a large degree, it is inherent in the public choice elaboration of the Tiebout model. As originally developed by Tiebout, dissatisfaction-based exit was not a difficult concept to accommodate since the model was a strict analog of market choice that made no further assumptions about the nature of life in small, independent communities. But once grafted into public choice's larger theoretical structure, which does make a number of independent assumptions that highlight the many benefits of living in such communities, certain contradictions began to emerge that have never been adequately resolved. At best, advocates of the model might argue that there must be some equilibrium point that provides just enough exiting as an outlet for citizens and as a signal to local officials, but not so much that the city is transformed into a community of disaffected transients. Unfortunately, the model does not provide clear standards about what minimum level of exiting is needed to make the model work, a point we will return to in the empirical portion of this chapter.

What of the other modes of response? The Tiebout model itself addresses only exit. But some public choice proponents have belatedly come to recognize that exit is costly.[15] Accordingly, they have begun to reconceptualize the behavioral predictions of the Tiebout model, and two of these reinterpretations fit behavioral elements of the EVLN model.

First, *the simple availability of the exit option,* it is argued, *serves to enhance the effectiveness and level of use of "voice" behaviors—complaining to officials and other forms of active-constructive problem solving.*[16] This argument is predicated both on Hirschman's observation that voice will only be effective if the exit option serves as a threat to give meaning to voice, and on the observation that contacting officials should be easier in smaller communities where they are familiar friends and neighbors.[17]

Second, *the fragmented jurisdiction arrangements that are presumed to enhance use of the exit option are also viewed as supportive of other, less extreme forms of severing the relationship between the citizen and his or her government.* These less extreme forms of exit involve remaining in the jurisdiction, but opting out of the municipal service net for a specific service. Particularized forms of exit might include a number of service options, such as relying on volunteers or self-help, that would fall under the general heading of "coproduction" of public services. Tiebout exiting and individual contracting for alternative services are viewed as complementary options within the general framework of public choice theory.[18] That is, all nonbureaucratic service options are viewed as compatible alternatives to traditional forms of service provision. Factors that serve to promote one form of nontraditional response, such as fragmented jurisdictions and the Tiebout exit response, should also promote other forms of responses to dissatisfaction with traditional services. Fragmented jurisdictions, because they are viewed as encouraging citizens to think of tax–service package options more generally, may encourage greater use of this more particularized exit option as well.

An alternative perspective, based on the EVLN model discussed in chapter 3 and, especially, respecified in chapter 4, would suggest a very different result. Because consolidated jurisdictions increase the cost of exit by reducing a citizen's location options, we might find increased reliance on other forms of response to dissatisfaction in precisely these jurisdictions. From this perspective, voice and private contracting for services might become even more important, rather than less, in consolidated jurisdictions simply because the exit option is foreclosed. We might expect, then, to find the opposite of what is generally implied in the public choice literature: the propensity to employ nontraditional responses to dissatisfaction with public services may not be related to jurisdictional boundaries in a one-dimensional manner.[19]

What of the last two EVLN responses to dissatisfaction—loyalty and neglect? As we will argue in chapter 8, loyalty has no special place in the Tiebout model. Passively but optimistically waiting for conditions to improve is the antithesis of the behavior of the Tiebout-like citizen. The same is true for neglect or passive withdrawal from the political system. *In a fragmented system that meets the requirements of the Tiebout model, then, we should see diminished loyalty and infrequent neglect.* Support for these propositions is clearly evident in the discussion by Ostrom, Tiebout, and Warren about how "bureaucratic unresponsiveness in gargantua may produce frustration and cynicism on the part of the local citizen who finds no point of access."[20] It can also be found in the discussion by Ostrom, Bish, and Ostrom concerning the eroding effects of consolidation on the "confidence among citizens about their influence over public policy."[21] Of course, the foregoing discussion of loyalty only refers to that concept as a response to dissatisfaction, not the more generalized and ritualistic response of the satisfied citizens discussed in our respecified model in chapter 4. Given the satisfaction hypotheses developed above, however, we would expect fragmentation to enhance this form of loyalty. That is, if citizens are more satisfied in fragmented communities, then we should observe in these cities more loyalty in the form of ritualistic regime-support on the part of those who are pleased with their tax and service packages.

Testing the Tiebout Model Hypotheses

The Comparative Basis of Our Test

The Tiebout model—or at least the public choice elaboration of it that has developed over time—is ambiguous on a number of points. As we have seen, for instance, it is very unclear about how much exit is needed to make local officials responsive to citizen preferences. Based on partial data and some important assumptions, Sharp estimated that 2.4 percent of Kansas City's population intended to engage in Tiebout exiting over several years.[22] In view of the assumptions involved, this estimate must be regarded with caution. But even if accepted on its face, we do not know if this figure is high or low relative to the requirements of the Tiebout model.

This lack of any built-in evaluative standards is evident in nearly all of the assumptions of the model that we have examined. For example, how many people must be attentive to the local government's tax–service package for the Tiebout quasi-market to come into being? How much must Tiebout citizens know about their tax and service packages to be effective consumers? How many people must be dissatisfied with the tax–service packages of their cities for the model to work? Clearly, some citizens must meet the underlying assumptions of the model, but how many are enough?

Given the lack of absolute standards on the minimum levels of these criteria necessary for the model to be operative, we believe that they can best be studied in a *comparative institutional* setting where responses of those living in fragmented jurisdictions can be compared with those of citizens operating within the essential features of the civic reform model of consolidated government. Thus, we can transform most of the hypotheses into comparative statements about their relative levels across fragmented and nonfragmented jurisdictions. For example, we would expect that since there are objectively more jurisdictions in their environment, citizens in fragmented jurisdictions are likely to be more aware of location alternatives than citizens in consolidated city–county governments. If this objective condition is not recognized by citizens, then fragmentation need not lead to greater exercise of the exit alternative. By shifting to comparative institutional analysis, then, we can better assess the levels of the criterion variables where no absolute standards exist.

Moreover, the use of this comparative jurisdictional strategy will allow us directly to address the important question of the impact of alternative institutional arrangements. That is, what difference do alternative institutional arrangements make in providing for the preconditions essential to the operation of the Tiebout model? If there are no differences in these attitudes between citizens in fragmented and consolidated arrangements, as our regression results in chapter 4 seem to imply, then it would seem that institutional structures would not make a great deal of difference in either facilitating or inhibiting the operation of

Tiebout-like behaviors by citizens, although they may very well still influence other aspects of the local service delivery system.

For the most part, our tests of the underlying assumptions employ many of the same measures as used in the tests presented in chapters 2 and 4. We do not discuss these in detail, but simply refer the reader to the appropriate earlier chapter. The several new indicators that are used, however, are discussed in greater detail here. Importantly, we have already presented tests of several of these hypotheses in previous chapters. Thus, the ALTERNATIVES coefficient in the SATISFACTION models in chapter 2 tests the satisfaction hypotheses outlined above. And the ALTERNATIVES coefficients in the EVLN models in chapter 4 assess the EXIT-MOVE, EXIT-PRIV, VOICE, LOYALTY, and NEGLECT hypotheses developed here as part of our assessment of the Tiebout model. We will note these as appropriate, but we also will present some additional findings that will help us better to interpret the previous results.

Findings

To assess the first underlying assumption of the Tiebout model—that citizens are attentive to their most local unit of government in making and maintaining locational choices—respondents from the five research sites located in the highly fragmented Louisville–Jefferson setting were asked, "What is the most important unit of local government in your daily life—your particular city or the county government?" Respondents living in the five Lexington–Fayette County sites were not asked this question since their city and county governments are merged.

The findings presented in Table 5.1* do not provide much support for the attentiveness assumption implicit in the Tiebout model. Consistently and by rather large margins, respondents from all five incorporated municipalities in the fragmented-government setting pointed to their more inclusive county government as the most important; across the five cities, only 20 to 35 percent of the respondents focused on their particular city government as the most important. Thus, for most respondents, the tax and service packages of their relatively small, Tiebout-like city governments do not seem to play an especially important role in structuring and maintaining their locational decisions. And even this level of attentiveness probably overstates the role of taxes and expenditures in structuring locational choices, given previous findings that public services—whether provided by the city or the county—are of secondary importance when compared to more personal considerations (i.e., income, job, family) in influencing moving decisions.

Beyond attentiveness to local government, we have suggested that some realistic *perception of the availability of alternatives* is a prerequisite of the Tiebout model. To assess this, respondents were asked, "How would you rate your

---

*All the tables for this chapter are found on pages 107–114.

chances of finding another place to live within the [Fayette or Jefferson] County area that has the kind of local tax and service package that you prefer?" The response set included very good, only fair, and poor.

Contrary to expectations, the results were quite mixed across the five matched sets of surveys. As seen in Table 5.2, where the responses are cross-tabulated with jurisdiction type, respondents in the consolidated-government jurisdictions exhibited higher levels of confidence of finding an alternative and preferred tax–service package for three of the matched sets of research sites—Blueberry and Minor Lane Heights, Chinoe and Beechwood Village, and Crest-wood/Shadeland and Windy Hills. Moreover, the difference generated a significant x^2 value in one of these matched sets. For the other two matched sets, however, the respondents in the fragmented institutional arrangement demonstrated higher levels of confidence, a finding that is more consistent with the objective situation in which they find themselves. And in both of these cases, significant x^2 values were generated. Given these mixed results, it appears that perceptions of the availability of alternatives have little relation to the objective presence of alternative jurisdictions.

Are fragmented-government citizens sufficiently informed to make the Tiebout model operative, or at least better informed than their consolidated-government counterparts? We can answer this question in reference to the eleven services outlined in Table 2.1 in chapter 2. Respondents in both research settings were asked to identify if they were provided each of these services by their city government, and, if so, to evaluate the quality of the service. We will have occasion in chapter 7 to examine these evaluations in some detail. Now, however, we focus on just the accuracy of citizens' knowledge about the services they are receiving, or not receiving, from their city governments. If the knowledge base of citizens is limited, then it is hard to imagine how citizens can meaningfully compare the relative advantages and disadvantages of alternative tax and service packages.

In support of the Tiebout assumption, there is at least some basis for arguing that citizens accurately understand the relative service levels of alternative jurisdictions. As seen in Table 5.3, comparisons of the mean perceptions of the number of services received from city government across the two research settings indicate that respondents in all five of the consolidated-government settings believed that they received more services than did their fragmented-government counterparts. This is an accurate perception. As seen in the list of actual services provided to the ten research sites in Table 2.1, the Lexington–Fayette County respondents did receive more services than the residents of their matched Louisville–Jefferson County sites.

Although seemingly promising, this finding provides only the slimmest support for the Tiebout model's information assumption, once we go beyond this simplest kind of comparison. We compare service perceptions with actual services for the ten sites in Table 5.4. As seen in the top third of the table, respondents in four of five consolidated-government settings thought that they were receiving somewhat fewer services than they were actually provided. But while all five of the differences are statistically significant, the magnitudes of the differences between the perceived and actual numbers of services are not very great. On average, the Lexington–Fayette County respondents were "off the mark" by roughly a third of a service. But even if these differences were larger, we must keep in mind that the logic of consolidated-government does not necessarily require that citizens have much knowledge about their service packages since they are rarely called upon to compare their services to those of some other jurisdiction in making a locational choice.

In contrast, the Tiebout model *does* require that citizens in fragmented systems have accurate knowledge about patterns of service provision. And as seen at the bottom of Table 5.4, the residents of the fragmented governments made far more errors in identifying the total number of services they receive from all of their local governments than did the consolidated-government respondents; rather than a third of a service as in the Lexington–Fayette cases, the average errors in the Louisville–Jefferson County sites range from 0.58 to 4.13 services. Even more important, as seen in the middle of the table, the fragmented-government respondents wildly overestimate the numbers of services they receive from their city governments, in one case (Newburg), actually believing that their city provides nearly three times (5.87) the number of services actually provided (2). In short, fragmentation is associated with substantial service attribution error, error that must undermine the effective comparison on one's current tax–service package with that of an alternative jurisdiction. Indeed, we have restricted our attention to just the respondents' own jurisdictions. We can only presume that their knowledge of the tax and service packages provided by the nearly 100 "alternative" jurisdictions in Jefferson County must be even less accurate.

We have also suggested that the Tiebout model implies that citizens in fragmented governments will be less dissatisfied with their local communities than consolidated-government residents. We found little support for this in the tests offered in chapter 2 in Table 2.4. But did those results tell the whole story? To answer this question, we employ the CURRENT DISSATISFACTION measure developed in chapter 4. Differences in the mean responses across the five matched sets of cases are presented in Table 5.5. Sharp differences in CURRENT DISSATISFACTION were observed across the jurisdictional types for all five matched sets. But in two matches—Chinoe and Beechwood Village and Crestwood/Shadeland and Windy Hills—dissatisfaction with local governance was higher in the consolidated-government case than in the matched fragmented-government case. For the other three matched sets of surveys, the opposite pattern was found, with the fragmented-government condition exhibiting higher levels of dissatisfaction. Although there are rather sharp differences across the matched research sites, jurisdiction structure does not have any strong relation to CURRENT DISSATISFACTION. It seems likely that localized factors are more important than this variable, as indicated in chapter 2. If dissatisfaction is what drives individuals to invoke the exit response, there would seem to be no inherently higher or lower motivation to leave either the fragmented or consolidated jurisdictions. Also, it is worth noting that the difference of means results reported in Table 5.5 are very similar to the regression results presented in Table 2.4, indicating that our matching procedures were quite effective in controlling for many of the individual-level influences that were separately controlled for in the former analyses.

Importantly, we need to consider one other implication of the Tiebout model's satisfaction hypotheses—that despite differences in mixes of services, satisfaction levels should be more similar across the five Louisville–Jefferson County sites than across the Lexington–Fayette County sites. Yet, as seen in Table 5.6, we find nearly the opposite. The differences in the mean levels of CURRENT DISSATISFACTION among the five fragmented-government sites are much more pronounced than those among the consolidated-government sites. And four of the ten possible differences of means for the Lexington–Fayette sites are not statistically discernible, while all ten of those for the Louisville–Jefferson County sites are. In short, and despite offering a supposedly common batch of services to several very diverse neighborhoods with presumably very different service preferences, the consolidated-government respondents exhibited far greater uniformity in CURRENT DISSATISFACTION than did the fragmented-government respondents.

The other indirect effect of ALTERNATIVES concerns INVESTMENT. The Tiebout model implies that citizens in fragmented-government settings will be more invested in their communities than will their consolidated-government counterparts. We noted, however, that very different expectations might be generated for the psychological attachment and social investment components of our INVESTMENT measure. While we will have occasion to discuss more disaggregated results in chapter 8, preliminary findings for the full INVESTMENT indicator are presented in Table 5.7. And contrary to the expectations of public choice theorists, INVESTMENT was found to be uniformly higher in the consolidated-government settings, with all five of the differences in means across the matched research sites being highly significant.

To this point it seems that the assumptive base of the Tiebout model is in some trouble. But what of the actual play of behaviors that this assumptive base is supposed to produce? We saw in the last chapter that the ALTERNATIVES coefficient in the EXIT-MOVE model was positive, as expected by both the Tiebout and EVLN models, although not significant. We can better interpret the meaning of this finding by examining the results presented in Table 5.8, which cross-tabulates the EXIT responses with the fragmented/consolidated structure of the local government for the five matched sets of surveys. As expected, higher levels of actual intentions to exit were found for the fragmented-government cases, with more exiters found in the fragmented-government condition in all five matched sets of cases. Only one of these contrasts, however, produced a significant x^2 value.

The most important implication of Table 5.8, however, is the across-the-board, low-level use of the exit response. The actual number of exiters is extremely small—ten or fewer—in each of the ten survey sites. So, while the differences between the fragmented and consolidated cases follow a pattern that might be expected based on the logic of the Tiebout model, both the differences between the levels of exit found in the matched cases, as well as the absolute levels of intentions to exit, are so small that they raise serious doubt about the viability of the exit threat seriously to influence the decisions made by local government officials.

If actual exit through moving is not the manner in which institutional fragmentation or consolidation primarily influences political behavior, what of the other forms of response to dissatisfaction? In our discussion of the theoretical interpretation of the Tiebout model, we noted that recently theorists have suggested that the primary manner in which fragmentation will alter patterns of political behavior is not exit, but voice, and, perhaps, privately contracting for services already provided by government. Based on the respecified EVLN model, we also indicated that the opposite might be plausibly expected, at least in regard to EXIT-PRIV.

As seen in chapter 4, the ALTERNATIVES coefficient in the VOICE model was positive, as expected by both the Tiebout and EVLN models, albeit nonsignificant. To shed further light on this finding, we can examine the results presented in Table 5.9, which highlight differences of means on the VOICE index across the five matched sets of survey responses. Contrary to all expectations, greater availability of the exit option in the form of high ALTERNATIVES seems to have a very inconsistent impact on voice behaviors. That is, higher levels of VOICE were found in consolidated-government settings for three of the five matched sets, and two of these differences—for Stonewall and Barbourmeade and Crestwood/Shadeland and Windy Hills—were significant at the 0.10 level or better. But the differences in VOICE ran in the opposite direction for the two remaining matched sets of research sites, although these were not statistically significant. If anything, then, relative lack of a viable exit alternative seems to enhance the exercise of voice behaviors.

The ALTERNATIVES coefficient was highly significant and negative in the EXIT-PRIV results presented in the last chapter, or exactly opposite of what recent elaborations of the Tiebout model might lead us to expect. This strong finding is reinforced by the results in Table 5.10, which cross-tabulate the EXIT-PRIV responses with jurisdictional fragmentation/consolidation. In four of the five matched survey sets, respondents in the fragmented-government exhibited lower levels of private contracting behavior than respondents in their matched consolidated-governmental setting, and three of these differences generated significant x^2 values. The expected difference was observed only for the Green

Acres/Newburg case, and it generated a significant x^2 value as well. On balance, it seems that diminished prospects of exit in the consolidated-government setting enhance use of the private contracting option.

The final two responses to dissatisfaction are LOYALTY and NEGLECT, and in chapter 4 we saw that the ALTERNATIVES coefficients were small and nonsignificant in the models addressing each. But it would be wrong to conclude from this that there were no differences between the matched sites on these variables. Actually, some rather sharp differences appeared between several of our matched research sites on these two responses to dissatisfaction, but they do not add up to the predicted pattern of public choice proponents.

We can see this more clearly, for example, in Table 5.11, which presents the difference of means tests for NEGLECT for the five matched sets of sites. Three of the Lexington–Fayette County sites exhibited statistically significant, lower levels of neglect than their counterparts in the fragmented-government setting. In contrast, two of our Jefferson County cities—Beechwood Village and Windy Hills—evidenced lower levels of neglect than the respondents in their matched Lexington–Fayette County neighborhoods, although only one of these was statistically discernible.

In addition, virtually the same overall pattern was found for the LOYALTY results presented in Table 5.12, although the specific order of positive and negative differences is somewhat different across the pairs in this case than in the NEGLECT results. Again, in three of the five comparisons, we find that the consolidated-government site produced higher mean LOYALTY responses than their matched fragmented site, and two of the three were significant. In contrast, however, the two sets of comparisons showing higher mean LOYALTY in the fragmented setting were also significant. Taken together with the satisfaction results presented in Table 5.5, these findings suggest that local factors are probably far more important in determining satisfaction and responses to dissatisfaction than the kinds of institutional features addressed by both the Tiebout exiting hypothesis and traditional civic reformers.

Discussion

The findings in this chapter are noteworthy in two respects. Perhaps most obvious is that they point to a fairly consistent set of conclusions regarding most of the individual-level assumptions and operational propositions of the Tiebout model as elaborated over the last three decades by public choice theorists. Contrary to their expectations, citizens in small, rather homogeneous governmental jurisdictions operating in highly fragmented systems are not very attentive to their most local unit of government. Nor are they significantly or systematically more aware of opportunities for finding other places with equally satisfactory tax and service packages within the same urban area than are their counterparts in a more consolidated-government setting. Moreover, despite the robust information requirements of the Tiebout model, the residents in our consolidated-government sites were far better informed about their local government services than their fragmented-government counterparts. The consolidated-government respondents were also found to be more highly invested in their communities. Further, no consistent patterns of differences were found across the two types of governmental arrangement on CURRENT DISSATISFACTION, LOYALTY, or NEGLECT. And the consistent patterns that were found for VOICE and EXIT-PRIV ran opposite to public choice expectations. In short, we found almost no support for the Tiebout model.

Nearly the only positive result for that model is our finding on intentions to exit (EXIT-MOVE). As expected, the fragmented-government respondents were marginally more likely to consider leaving their jurisdiction for regime-based reasons than their consolidated-government counterparts. But the number of exiters was so small as to raise serious doubts about the importance of "voting with one's feet" as a political behavior in response to dissatisfaction.

The second reason for giving serious consideration to these findings is that they are based on data generated from a research design that was specifically constructed to allow direct empirical evaluation of the Tiebout model's underlying assumptions and propositions. For the first time, these important and longstanding hypotheses were tested using survey data from respondents living in precisely the kinds of small-scale units of government that are so highly touted by public choice theorists, compared to residents of a textbook example of the consolidated system of metropolitan government. Moreover, the analysis included comparisons across an array of socioeconomic communities, rather than simply a comparison of one fragmented and one consolidated-government sample. If there were real differences between these two research settings of the kinds hypothesized by the Tiebout exiting hypothesis and proponents of the public choice model, we should have found them.

It is possible, of course, that there is something unique about the Lexington and Louisville settings, or even the particular research sites drawn from each, that might account for the findings presented in this chapter. After all, the public choice model is quite dynamic and quite capable of accommodating such aberrant findings on the basis of either: (i) temporary mismatches between median voter preferences and short-term responses by local governments, or (ii) widespread but temporary disequilibriums in the constant game of citizens "voting with their feet." But given the consistency of our findings, we would view interpretation of our results on either basis as placing a bit too much faith in the power of coincidence.

A far more persuasive explanation of why the public choice model fares so poorly lies in several faulty assumptions it makes, not only about the nature of fragmented governments, which we have explored, but about the nature of consolidated governments as well. Most important on this score is the assumption that consolidated governments present their citizens with a uniform tax and service package tailored to the median-voter preference of the entire urban population. In the Lexington–Fayette County case, and in virtually all other consolidated-government systems, this assumption is simply not true. At a minimum, consolidated governments commonly offer at least two basic sets of tax and service packages by providing general and full urban-service districts that are tied to differing levels and/or kinds of taxes. In our case, the charter of the consolidated Lexington–Fayette Urban County Government provides for even more variation in tax and service packages through its creation of "Partial Service Districts," each with its own tax base.[23] Thus, as shown in Table 2.1, the total service package actually received by residents in the five Lexington neighborhoods varied considerably, if not quite as much as the total packages received by the Louisville respondents when county and municipal services are taken together.

This may help to explain why respondents from the five research sites in the fragmented greater-Louisville setting were not significantly or consistently more aware of alternative tax and service packages than their counterparts from the consolidated-government setting. It may also help to explain why they were also not systematically more dissatisfied. Residents of Lexington have opportunities to choose from among several tax and service packages under the charter of their local government. And by offering various tax and service packages, consolidated governments can do much to meet the many different preferences of their citizens. Indeed, the results in Table 5.6 on the within-system differences in CURRENT DISSATISFACTION suggest that Lexington–Fayette County has done a far better job on this score than the independent cities in the Tiebout-like world of Louisville–Jefferson County.

Although the evidence is much more impressionistic, a similar argument can be made regarding a second and related public choice assumption that consolidated governments are inherently larger and, therefore, more remote from citizen influence than are fragmented governments. It is certainly possible—and many consolidated governments have done this—to create legal and institutional arrangements that offset some of the alleged negative effects of very large and comprehensive units of local government. Emphasizing district as opposed to at-large representation, providing legal and administrative channels to involve citizens in key decision-making processes, and insuring informal avenues for voicing, hearing, and redressing grievances, for example, can go a long way toward creating conditions similar to those advocated by supporters of the public choice model of local governmental organization.

If coupled with some of the other advantages of consolidated governments to be considered in the next three chapters, these complex structures can create a governmental system that looks very different from the "gargantua" of public choice theory. Indeed, it seems that gargantua is more of a caricature than an accurate description of government in metropolitan America. Once this caricature is exposed, the prospects for consolidated-government meeting the varied preferences of its citizens become more plausible.

Notes

1. Tiebout (1956).
2. V. Ostrom, Tiebout, and Warren (1961).
3. Bish and Ostrom (1973, pp. 11–12).
4. For examples of this position, see Kotler, (1969); Hallman (1974).
5. Sharp (1986, pp. 136–37); Schneider and Logan (1982a, p. 97).
6. See Pack and Pack (1978); Parks (1985); Stein (1987); Cebula (1974, 1976, 1977, 1978); Cebula and Avery (1983); Wagner and Weber (1975); Zodrow (1983); DiLorenzo (1983); Broder and Schmid (1983); Lowery (1982); Schneider and Logan (1982a); and Parks and Ostrom (1981).
7. Sharp (1980, 1984a, 1984b, 1984c, 1986).
8. See, for example, E. Ostrom (1972).
9. See V. Ostrom, Tiebout, and Warren (1961, pp. 837–38); and Bish and Ostrom (1973, pp. 88–89).
10. Bish and Ostrom (1973, p. 27).
11. Bish and Ostrom (1973, p. 11).
12. Stein (1987).
13. Tiebout (1956, p. 420).
14. Cebula (1974, 1976, 1977, 1978).
15. Oakerson, Parks, and Bell (1987); Orbell and Uno (1972).
16. Oakerson, Parks, and Bell (1987); Kenyon (1984); Sharp (1986, pp. 138–39); Orbell and Uno (1972); and Hirschman (1970).
17. The proposition concerning the effects of fragmentation versus consolidation on citizen participation can be found in E. Ostrom (1972, p. 486); Bish and Ostrom (1973, p. 24); V. Ostrom, Bish, and Ostrom (1988, pp. 92–93).
18. Savas (1983); V. Ostrom, Tiebout, and Warren (1961); Bish and Ostrom (1973); Bish (1971).
19. Generally, however, the propensity to use private contracting, as one form of particularized exit, or voice is not analyzed in terms of jurisdictional boundaries. Rather, wealth is usually identified as the key variable determining a citizen's likelihood of invoking the contracting option. Miller (1981), for example, in his analysis of contracting in the Los Angeles metropolitan area, concluded that the formation and operation of "minimal cities" that rely on extensive private provision of public services was based on a desire of property owners to avoid funding of redistributional services. Wealth is clearly important in facilitating voice and private contracting, probably far more important than jurisdictional boundaries. To assess the independent impact of jurisdictional boundaries, then, we need to control for differences in wealth across jurisdictions. And once again, the use of a comparative jurisdictional design is critical; by comparing jurisdictions that are similar in all important respects but the framing of jurisdictional boundaries, we should be able to assess the specific role of boundaries in facilitating or inhibiting voice and private contracting for services.
20. See V. Ostrom, Tiebout, and Warren (1961, p. 837).
21. See V. Ostrom, Bish, and Ostrom (1988, pp. 92–93).
22. Sharp (1986, p. 153).
23. For an extended discussion of variations in tax–service packages as they are revealed in consolidated government charters, see Lyons (1977).

Table 5.1

Primary Governmental Jurisdiction Orientation of Fragmented Arrangement (Louisville) Case Respondents

City	Percent oriented to city government	Percent oriented to county government	n
Minor Lane Heights	30.76%	69.23%	143
Beechwood Village	35.06	64.94	174
Barbourmeade	28.31	71.69	166
Windy Hills	26.54	73.46	162
Newburg	20.13	79.87	154

Table 5.2

Perceptions of Alternatives by Institutional Arrangement—Matched Lexington and Louisville Sites

Perceptions of alternatives	Consolidated government	Fragmented government	n	x^2
	Blueberry	Minor Lane Heights		
Poor	10.62%	17.98%	47	
Fair	40.09	41.00	140	
Good	49.27	41.00	159	
	100.00	100.00		
n	207	139	346	4.568
	Chinoe	Beechwood Village		
Poor	11.76	18.58	51	
Fair	31.01	44.23	127	
Good	57.21	37.17	165	
	100.00	100.00		
n	187	156	343	13.776***
	Stonewall	Barbourmeade		
Poor	17.12	11.92	55	
Fair	33.33	23.84	108	
Good	49.53	64.23	204	
	100.00	100.00		
n	216	151	367	7.786**

(continued)

Table 5.2 *(continued)*

Perceptions of alternatives	Consolidated government	Fragmented government	n	x^2
	Crestwood/Shadeland	Windy Hills		
Poor	10.64	14.89	43	
Fair	32.87	31.20	115	
Good	56.48	54.60	199	
	100.00	100.00		
n	216	141	357	1.013
	Green Acres	Newburg		
Poor	21.87	13.28	61	
Fair	43.22	39.86	140	
Good	34.89	46.85	134	
	100.00	100.00		
n	192	143	335	6.472*

$* = p < 0.10;$ $** = p < 0.05;$ $*** = p < 0.01.$

Table 5.3

Service Level Perceptions: Difference-of-Means Tests across Institutional Arrangements—Matched Lexington and Louisville Sites

Consolidated/fragmented government matched sets		Mean no. services	Standard deviation	n	Difference of means	t-value
LEX:	Blueberry	9.42	(1.39)	219		
LOU:	Minor Lane Heights	7.80	(1.80)	157	1.62***	9.47
LEX:	Chinoe	10.95	(0.26)	224		
LOU:	Beechwood Village	7.64	(1.65)	188	3.31***	27.26
LEX:	Stonewall	8.89	(1.35)	253		
LOU:	Barbourmeade	6.42	(1.86)	175	2.47***	15.00
LEX:	Crestwood/Shadeland	9.66	(1.05)	253		
LOU:	Windy Hills	6.01	(2.54)	181	3.65***	18.25
LEX:	Green Acres	10.95	(0.28)	208		
LOU:	Newburg	5.87	(4.19)	165	5.08***	15.53

$* = p < 0.10;$ $** = p < 0.05;$ $*** = p < 0.01.$

Table 5.4

Differences in Number of Services Perceived to be Provided from Actual Number of Total and Most Local Services

Cities/ neighborhoods	No. of perceived services	Standard deviation	Actual no. of services	Difference	t-value
Lexington–Fayette neighborhoods (total urban county gov't services)					
Blueberry	9.42	1.39	10.00	−0.58***	−6.19
Chinoe	10.95	0.26	11.00	−0.05***	−2.88
Stonewall	8.89	1.35	8.50	0.39***	4.55
Crestwood/Shadeland	9.66	1.05	10.00	−0.34***	−5.22
Green Acres	10.95	0.28	11.00	−0.05***	−2.71
Louisville–Jefferson Cities (total city gov't services)					
Minor Lane Heights	7.80	1.80	4.00	3.80***	26.42
Beechwood Village	7.64	1.65	5.00	2.64***	22.01
Barbourmeade	6.42	1.86	4.00	2.42***	17.21
Windy Hills	6.01	2.54	4.00	2.01***	11.04
Newburg	5.87	4.19	2.00	3.87***	11.85
Louisville–Jefferson Cities (total city, county, and district gov't services)					
Minor Lane Heights	7.80	1.80	9.00	−1.20***	−8.35
Beechwood Village	7.64	1.65	9.00	−1.36***	−11.30
Barbourmeade	6.42	1.86	7.00	−0.58***	−4.10
Windy Hills	6.01	2.54	7.00	−0.99***	−5.25
Newburg	5.87	4.19	10.00	−4.13***	−12.66

$* = p < 0.10;$ $** = p < 0.05;$ $*** = p < 0.01.$

Table 5.5

CURRENT DISSATISFACTION Difference-of-Means Tests across Alternative Institutional Arrangements—Matched Lexington and Louisville Sites

Consolidated/fragmented government matched sets	Mean dissatis- faction	Standard deviation	n	Difference of means	t-value
LEX: Blueberry	2.53	(0.99)	210		
LOU: Minor Lane Heights	2.78	(1.25)	153	−0.25**	−2.06
LEX: Chinoe	2.00	(1.09)	220		
LOU: Beechwood Village	1.29	(1.15)	185	0.71***	6.38
LEX: Stonewall	2.43	(1.08)	247		
LOU: Barbourmeade	3.76	(1.54)	169	−1.33***	−9.76
LEX: Crestwood/Shadeland	2.14	(1.08)	242		
LOU: Windy Hills	1.79	(1.35)	167	0.35***	2.76
LEX: Green Acres	2.60	(1.28)	199		
LOU: Newburg	4.22	(1.62)	139	−1.62***	−9.86

$* = p < 0.10;$ $** = p < 0.05;$ $*** = p < 0.01.$

Table 5.6

CURRENT DISSATISFACTION Difference of Means Tests across Neighborhoods/Cities within Alternative Institutional Arrangements

The Lexington–Fayette Sites[a]

	Blueberry	Chinoe	Stonewall	Crestwood/Shadeland
Chinoe	0.53*** (5.31)			
Stonewall	0.11 (1.12)	–0.43*** (–4.23)		
Crestwood/ Shadeland	0.40*** (4.08)	–0.14 (–1.35)	0.29*** (2.97)	
Green Acres	–0.07 (–0.62)	–0.60*** (–5.17)	–0.18 (–1.57)	–0.47*** (–4.09)

The Louisville–Jefferson Sites

	Minor Lane Heights	Beechwood	Barbourmeade	Windy Hills
Beechwood Village	1.50*** (11.37)			
Barbourmeade	–0.98*** (–6.28)	–2.48*** (–17.00)		
Windy Hills	0.99*** (6.28)	–0.50*** (–3.74)	1.97*** (12.46)	
Newburg	–1.44*** (–8.45)	–2.94*** (–18.26)	–0.46** (–2.54)	–2.43*** (–14.11)

* $= p < 0.10$; ** $= p < 0.05$; *** $= p < 0.01$.

[a]The actual means and their standard deviations for the individual sites are reported in Table 5.5. These differences are calculated by subtracting the column site mean from the row site mean as these are reported in 5.5.

Table 5.7

INVESTMENT Difference-of-Means Tests across Alternative Institutional Arrangements—Matched Lexington and Louisville Sites

Consolidated/fragmented government matched sets	Mean investment	Standard deviation	n	Difference of means	t-value
LEX: Blueberry	7.27	(1.70)	214		
LOU: Minor Lane Heights	6.56	(2.44)	152	0.71***	3.10
LEX: Chinoe	8.63	(2.06)	217		
LOU: Beechwood Village	7.87	(1.84)	181	0.85***	3.91
LEX: Stonewall	7.99	(1.79)	249		
LOU: Barbourmeade	7.04	(1.97)	170	0.95***	5.06
LEX: Crestwood/Shadeland	8.45	(1.72)	241		
LOU: Windy Hills	7.61	(1.87)	161	0.84***	4.54
LEX: Green Acres	8.21	(1.83)	200		
LOU: Newburg	7.72	(2.52)	154	0.49**	2.03

* = $p < 0.10$; ** = $p < 0.05$; *** = $p < 0.01$.

Table 5.8

Likelihood of Moving for Regime/Government Reason (EXIT-MOVE) by Institutional Arrangement—Matched Lexington and Louisville Sites

Likelihood of moving	Consolidated government	Fragmented government	n	x^2
	Blueberry	Minor Lane Heights		
Low	98.17%	95.54%	365	
High	1.82	4.45	11	
	100.00	100.00		
n	219	157	376	5.243**
	Chinoe	Beechwood Village		
Low	99.55	99.46	410	
High	0.44	0.53	2	
	100.00	100.00		
n	224	188	412	0.000
	Stonewall	Barbourmeade		
Low	98.81	98.28	422	
High	1.18	1.71	6	
	100.00	100.00		
n	253	175	428	0.174

(continued)

Table 5.8 *(continued)*

Likelihood of moving	Consolidated government	Fragmented government	n	x^2
	Crestwood/ Shadeland	Windy Hills		
Low	99.20	98.89	430	
High	0.79	1.10	4	
	100.00	100.00		
n	253	181	434	0.00
	Green Acres	Newburg		
Low	97.59	93.93	358	
High	2.40	6.06	15	
	100.00	100.00		
n	208	165	373	0.989

* $= p < 0.10$; ** $= p < 0.05$; *** $= p < 0.01$.

Table 5.9

VOICE Difference-of-Means Tests for Alternative Institutional Arrangements—Matched Lexington and Louisville Sites

Consolidated/fragmented government matched sets	Mean voice	Standard deviation	n	Difference of means	t-value
LEX: Blueberry	2.30	(1.86)	217		
LOU: Minor Lane Heights	2.52	(1.70)	155	0.22	0.20
LEX: Chinoe	2.44	(1.89)	218		
LOU: Beechwood Village	2.24	(1.67)	155	−0.20	−1.14
LEX: Stonewall	3.55	(1.63)	252		
LOU: Barbourmeade	3.22	(1.45)	173	−0.33**	−2.20
LEX: Crestwood/Shadeland	3.14	(1.73)	248		
LOU: Windy Hills	2.85	(1.77)	176	−0.29*	−1.77
LEX: Green Acres	2.45	(1.83)	206		
LOU: Newburg	2.49	(1.93)	163	0.04	0.20

* $= p < 0.10$; ** $= p < 0.05$; *** $= p < 0.01$.

Table 5.10

Considered Privatized Services (EXIT-PRIV) by Institutional Arrangement—Matched Lexington and Louisville Sites

Considered privatization	Consolidated government	Fragmented government	n	x^2
	Blueberry	Minor Lane Heights		
No	86.17%	93.58%	333	
Yes	13.82	6.41	40	
	100.00	100.00		
n	217	156	373	4.466**
	Chinoe	Beechwood Village		
No	95.04	97.31	392	
Yes	4.95	2.68	16	
	100.00	100.00		
n	222	186	408	.844
	Stonewall	Barbourmeade		
No	60.95	88.88	345	
Yes	23.10	11.11	77	
	100.00	100.00		
n	251	171	422	9.025***
	Crestwood/Shadeland	Windy Hills		
No	75.40	92.00	348	
Yes	24.59	8.00	75	
	100.00	100.00		
n	248	175	423	18.254***
	Green Acres	Newburg		
No	96.11	85.09	335	
Yes	3.88	14.90	32	
	100.00	100.00		
n	206	161	367	12.447***

$* = p < 0.10; ** = p < 0.05; *** = p < 0.01.$

Table 5.11

NEGLECT Difference-of-Means Tests across Alternative Institutional Arrangements—Matched Lexington and Louisville Sites

Consolidated/fragmented government matched sets		Mean neglect	Standard deviation	n	Difference of means	t-value
LEX:	Blueberry	4.10	(1.49)	204		
LOU:	Minor Lane Heights	4.46	(1.95)	131	−0.36*	−1.80
LEX:	Chinoe	3.60	(1.57)	200		
LOU:	Beechwood Village	3.15	(1.75)	172	0.45***	2.62
LEX:	Stonewall	3.72	(1.39)	235		
LOU:	Barbourmeade	4.08	(1.61)	155	−0.36**	−2.29
LEX:	Crestwood/Shadeland	3.84	(1.49)	228		
LOU:	Windy Hills	3.78	(1.49)	146	0.06	0.39
LEX:	Green Acres	4.68	(1.51)	188		
LOU:	Newburg	5.12	(1.86)	131	−0.44**	−2.28

$* = p < 0.10; ** = p < 0.05; *** = p < 0.01.$

Table 5.12

LOYALTY Difference-of-Means Tests across Alternative Institutional Arrangements—Matched Lexington and Louisville Sites

Consolidated/fragmented government matched sets		Mean loyalty	Standard deviation	n	Difference of means	t-value
LEX:	Blueberry	8.42	(2.08)	189		
LOU:	Minor Lane Heights	8.23	(3.07)	136	0.19	0.63
LEX:	Chinoe	8.73	(2.33)	187		
LOU:	Beechwood Village	10.01	(1.81)	149	−1.28***	−5.67
LEX:	Stonewall	8.47	(2.02)	221		
LOU:	Barbourmeade	7.37	(3.13)	147	1.10***	3.75
LEX:	Crestwood/Shadeland	8.66	(2.25)	193		
LOU:	Windy Hills	9.24	(2.20)	123	−0.58**	−2.26
LEX:	Green Acres	8.18	(2.76)	171		
LOU:	Newburg	6.73	(3.17)	123	1.45***	4.06

$* = p < 0.10; ** = p < 0.05; *** = p < 0.01.$

6

Institutions and Citizen Attribution Error

We have seen in the last two chapters that the fragmented or consolidated governmental structures of metropolitan areas do not seem to have a great deal of impact on local political behavior. The results for ALTERNATIVES in our assessment of the EVLN model presented in chapter 4 were the weakest of the core explanatory variables examined. And in chapter 5, we saw that for the most part it is idiosyncratic and particular neighborhood and city factors that distinguish the Lexington–Fayette and Louisville–Jefferson County respondents, not their very different local governmental systems. Do institutions not matter in determining how citizens react to local public services and the governments that provide them? Or are both public choice proponents and traditional civic reformers wrong in their near-exclusive attention to institutional structure, especially the issue of fragmentation versus consolidation?

We believe that institutions matter, but that their influence on the play of political behavior can be far more subtle and—to tell the truth—more interesting than is commonly indicated in the literature on urban government and politics. In this and the following two chapters, then, we examine three such subtle and, we hope, interesting ways in which institutions matter. The chapters examine collectively the two sides of the analytic coin that has been our focus. In this chapter, we examine an indirect but important way in which urban institutions influence citizen evaluations of government services or *satisfaction* with local governance. In the next chapter, we take a closer look at our two predominantly black research sites to see how government structures influence minority assessments of the quality of local services. And in chapter 8, we examine another indirect influence of local institutions on *responses to dissatisfaction* and the nature of citizenship, again using the EVLN model.

Metropolitan Institutional Structure and Evaluation Errors

An electorate's evaluation of the quality of public services, and, thus, the need to sanction or reward public officials is one of the central elements of democratic government. It is also a decision that is subject to error. On one hand, citizens might incorrectly conclude that service quality is inadequate, and, in response to their dissatisfaction, inappropriately punish their local officials. On the other hand, citizens might incorrectly conclude that service quality is adequate, and, in failing to recognize that they should be dissatisfied, reward an official when he or she really is a rascal in need of a timely toss. Either type of error would diminish the prospects for effective democratic government. A series of overly harsh judgments, for example, could unnecessarily create a revolving-door government where lack of continuity undermines effective policy making and management. Alternatively, a series of excessively lenient evaluations would mean that officials were not being held accountable for poor performance.

It is hardly surprising, then, that much of our attention in the design of democratic institutions is devoted to analyzing the impact of governmental structures on balancing these two types of error. But institutions may affect such errors in judgment in at least two ways. First, given the public's collective judgment that the quality of public services is not up to snuff, institutions can make it more or less difficult to implement available sanctions. This is the aspect of institutional influence on errors that we have been most attentive to in debates over such varied issues as the frequency of elections, recall, and structures of bureaucratic oversight.

Institutional arrangements, however, may also influence the public's *perception* of the quality of public services in the first place. That is, the citizen's evaluation of service quality may itself be biased by institutions, thereby altering judgments about whether punishment or reward is merited. Our attention to open meetings and access to official information reflects some level of concern for this aspect of institutional design. But it is also clear that from the founding fathers to modern public choice theory and neo-institutionalism, those who are attentive to the implications of institutional structure have been more concerned with the former impact.

In part, this imbalance is understandable. Unlike analyses of the impact of institutions on the likelihood that a well-deserved penalty will be imposed, consideration of the impact of institutions on the *perceived need for punishment* requires us to consider how citizens evaluate the quality of public services, a task that is difficult. Even more importantly, it requires a theoretical model of how citizens make errors in evaluating service quality, including specification of the types of errors that might be committed and how each relates to specific aspects of institutional structure. To date, the literature contains little theoretical consideration of how institutions influence the content of service evaluations.

The urban politics literature, we have seen, offers two very different theoretical perspectives on the link between structure and errors in evaluation. The oldest of these two perspectives is the *traditional reform theory,* which posits that citizen control is best exercised when services are consolidated in a metropolitan area under a single set of elected officials or an executive whom the public then holds politically responsible for the efficient and effective operation of the government.

One justification for this theme is found in the argument that centralization and consolidation promote a better informed citizenry. Ostrom, Bish, and Ostrom, longtime critics of the traditional reform model, provided probably the best summary of the logic underlying this argument on the relationship between structure and evaluation error when they wrote:

> The existence of multiple jurisdictions in the metropolitan area is presumed [by the civic reformers] to cause confusion among citizens about what jurisdictions should perform what functions and about who is held responsible for the conditions prevailing within the community. If citizens do not know whom to hold responsible, they cannot exercise their electoral responsibility in choosing among differing candidates for governmental office.[1]

Thus, a central concern from the perspective of the traditional reform theory is the presumed loss of accountability when institutional fragmentation obscures responsibilities for the delivery of services.

More recently, this emphasis on the relationship between institutional fragmentation and citizen confusion has been augmented with a corollary argument that confusion breeds citizen apathy. As Dagger has noted in his analysis of the decline of urban citizenship:

> For the inhabitants of metropolis the consequences of this fragmentation are often confusion, disorientation, and a sense of impotence. It is easy to lose one's bearings, and one's interest, when there is no central political authority to provide a focal point. As jurisdictions proliferate, overlap, and cut across each other in an increasingly confusing manner, the individual can come to believe that charting a course through the maze that confronts him is neither within his capacities nor worth his effort.[2]

Thus, not only is a given level of citizen effort hypothesized to lead to greater confusion about government service provision under fragmented institutional conditions than under consolidated and centralized governments, but the level of effort the citizen is likely to devote to becoming informed is also hypothesized to decline under fragmented institutional conditions.

The second theoretical perspective is provided by *public choice theory*. Unfortunately, the beliefs underlying the traditional reform view of the relationship between consolidation/fragmentation and citizen evaluations have not been fully addressed by public choice scholars. While these beliefs are never clearly articulated, however, Ostrom, Bish, and Ostrom seem to react to the two basic strains of the traditional reform theory hypothesis in quite different ways. They never directly challenge the core argument that, all other things being equal, fragmentation generates confusion on the part of the citizen over which government is providing which services. But they vigorously, albeit implicitly, reject the notion that all other things are equal, and argue that citizen interest in, and therefore information about, government will be enhanced by fragmented institutional arrangements. *First,* and in direct conflict with Dagger's analysis, they assert that fragmented institutional arrangements are conducive to developing a sense of community that, in turn, is assumed to enhance interest in public affairs.[3] *Second,* this perspective suggests that fragmentation promotes higher levels of political participation, through which citizens are assumed to become more educated about governmental issues.[4] And *third,* fragmentation is thought to promote more complex electoral arrangements, and thereby a greater number of more specialized political entrepreneurs with an interest in both educating their constituents and soliciting their views on public issues. In sum, the public choice perspective suggests that fragmentation enhances the citizen's interest in government and implies that this will more than offset any confusion inherent in having a multiplicity of governments.

We have, then, two sharply contrasting prescriptions on the optimal design of urban governmental structures for enhancing citizen information about public services, and, thereby, citizen efforts to ensure accountability on the basis of accurate appraisal of government performance. Unfortunately, we have no firm basis for accepting either set of prescriptions. Neither approach's hypothesis on the link between structure and accuracy in evaluations has been subject to empirical scrutiny.[5] More importantly, neither of the competing perspectives offers a well-articulated typology of citizen information errors, or an interpretation of the impacts of such errors on citizen evaluations. It is to this issue that we now turn as a necessary prelude to empirical analysis.

Types of Errors in Evaluation and Their Decomposition

For effective democratic control of government, citizen evaluations must be founded on an accurate appraisal of what the government is actually doing. Given this definition, two very different types of errors are possible. First, citizens might incorrectly evaluate the quality of a service the government is providing, a type of error that can be identified as an *assessment error.* Alternatively— and this is our concern in this chapter—a citizen may base his or her judgments on an incorrect understanding of just what services the government is responsible for. That is, appropriate evaluation would hold government responsible for all of the things it is doing, but none of the things it is not doing. Errors of this second type can be identified as *errors in attribution,* which can occur in three different ways.

The *first* type of attribution error occurs when the citizen fails to recognize that a government is providing a particular service. His or her evaluation of government services is based on a subset of the true set of services provided by the government. For brevity, we will refer to this type of error as a *SUBSET*

ERROR, or the citizen's evaluating overall government service performance on the basis of a subset of the full service set.

The *second* type of attribution error obtains when the citizen holds a government responsible for the performance of a service that is not being provided by any of several local governments that might provide it. It is important to stress that we do not mean by this that the citizen is holding a government responsible for nonprovision of the service, or that the citizen believes that a specific government should provide a given service, knows that it does not, and is willing to punish the elected officials of that government for its failure to provide the service. This would be an evaluative judgment that is based on an accurate understanding of what the government actually does in terms of service provision. Rather, we mean that the service in question is not provided at all, but the citizen believes that it is, makes some evaluation of the government's performance in providing this nonexistent service, and then proceeds to punish local elected officials on the basis of that judgment. We might call this a *NONSET ERROR,* in that the citizen is basing his or her evaluation of governmental performance on at least some items that are not included in the government's service set.

The *third* type of attribution error occurs when the citizen holds one government responsible for the performance of a service that is actually provided by another government. This is a form of political externality where service performance of one government "spills over" into the citizen's performance evaluation of another government. Since this type of error occurs when the citizen misassigns responsibility for different services that several governments provide, we will refer to this form of error as *MISSET ERROR.*

Importantly, these three types of errors relate differently to the various arguments of the traditional reform and public choice perspectives on the relationship between evaluative errors and institutional structure. SUBSET and NONSET errors, for example, occur when the citizen lacks basic knowledge about what services he or she is receiving. Consolidated or fragmented institutional structures are only indirectly related to such errors insofar as they enhance or diminish citizen interest in or information about governmental affairs. In contrast, MISSET errors are more directly a function of the confusion that, all other things being equal, is inherent in complex institutional arrangements. If the public choice perspective is correct, all other things will not be equal, and fragmented structures will sufficiently enhance the level of the citizen's knowledge and information that this confusion-based type of error will be overcome.

Beyond noting that several different types of errors are possible, it is also important to realize that each might have two very different effects on both the *individual* citizen's judgment and the electorate's *collective* assessment of government performance. On one hand, and starting at the individual level, the impact may be in the form of *random* error. Evaluative judgments about performance of specific services that are not provided (NONSET error) or are provided by another government (MISSET error), or lack of evaluative judgment on services that are actually provided (SUBSET error) may only render a citizen's judgment of the government's performance unreliable rather than invalid. Some services, or nonservices, would be judged too harshly or too leniently, but the citizen's mean judgment of the government's service performance would accurately represent his or her perception of how well the government is doing its job. Alternatively, the errors might be *systematic*. That is, the errors in evaluating specific services or nonservices may combine to bias the citizen's overall judgment of the government. And this systematic bias might be positive, so that the citizen fails to punish the government for poor performance, or negative, in that the citizen unfairly punishes the government.

While troubling, systematic error or bias at the individual-level need not necessarily lead to systematic bias at the aggregate or collective level. The individual-level systematic errors in judgment could cancel out at the aggregate level, transforming systematic individual-level error into random aggregate-level error. Some citizens would judge the government's overall performance too harshly, while others would be excessively lenient, but the mean judgment of the electorate would not be biased by the cumulative errors.

This distinction between random and systematic aggregate error is important for two reasons. First, they have different implications for our understanding of *effective citizenship* on one hand, and the possibility of *democratic control* on the other. Individual-level systematic error due to misattribution of responsibility that is transformed into random error at the aggregate level would still constitute evidence of ineffective citizenship for those citizens making the overly harsh or overly generous assessments of governmental performance. This is because *effective citizenship* is an inherently individual concept; being a good citizen is more than having your wild evaluations of public services canceled out or balanced by someone else's equally wild but divergent judgments. While such error might attenuate democratic control of government, it would not undermine it. The judgment of the electorate in any given election would be less sharp than desired perhaps, but the winners would still be winners and the losers would still be on the outside of the City Hall doors. But if systematic individual-level errors are translated into systematic aggregate-level errors, the prospects for effective *democratic control* become problematic. Excessively sharp judgments in the form of always turning the rascals out could be as damaging to effective government as failures to hold government accountable for service quality.

Second, this distinction is also important because the three types of error identified above, SUBSET, NONSET, and MISSET, would, on their face, seem more or less likely to generate systematic or random error in citizen evaluations. For instance, barring for the moment the empirical possibility that NONSET errors are actually accurate criticisms of the government for failure to provide a service that the citizen wishes to receive, NONSET errors, because they are performance judgments about nonservices, would seem *likely* to be random in terms of their impact on our overall judgment of service quality. Judgments about nonservices cannot be very precise by their very nature.

In contrast, SUBSET and MISSET errors are more likely to have a systematic effect at the individual and, perhaps, aggregate level. Bias is possible as long as the mean level of the performance evaluation for the set of services being combined to form the citizen's overall judgment is systematically different from the mean of service evaluations for the service set actually provided by a government. This would seem likely if citizens are systematically excluding some of their government's services from their evaluation set or wrongly including evaluations of services provided by other governments. But the case for such systematic bias appears especially strong for MISSET errors. If a citizen fails to credit government for something it is doing—a SUBSET error—it is likely that that service is not especially salient to the citizen, and, thus, would not be all that important to the citizen in forming his or her overall impression of governmental performance. It is more difficult to dismiss the importance of MISSET errors on the basis of low salience. Still, we must note that even if systematic error exists, it may still have no general political effect. Systematic individual-level error may, as we have pointed out, be translated into random aggregate-level error.

We can specify the direction and size of the bias introduced by the three sources of error. The direction of the bias is indicated by the difference between the mean of the invalid service evaluations and the mean of the valid service evaluations. And the total impact of the bias would be the product of this difference and the proportion of services incorrectly included in the service set upon which the citizen forms his or her overall evaluation and the size of the observed service set upon which that assessment is based. Thus, the three biases introduced by errors in attribution can be identified as:

$$\text{SUBSET BIAS} = [N_{\text{sub}} * (\text{Mean}_{\text{sub}} - \text{Mean}_{\text{true}})] / N_{\text{obs}} \qquad [1]$$
$$\text{MISSET BIAS} = [N_{\text{mis}} * (\text{Mean}_{\text{mis}} - \text{Mean}_{\text{true}})] / N_{\text{obs}} \qquad [2]$$
$$\text{NONSET BIAS} = [N_{\text{non}} * (\text{Mean}_{\text{non}} - \text{Mean}_{\text{true}})] / N_{\text{obs}} \qquad [3]$$

where N_{sub}, N_{mis}, N_{non} are, respectively, the number of SUBSET, MISSET, and NONSET errors in attribution made by the citizen; Mean_{sub}, Mean_{mis}, Mean_{non} are, respectively, the mean evaluations of SUBSET, MISSET, and NONSET services; $\text{Mean}_{\text{true}}$ is the citizen's unobserved mean evaluation of the true service set; and N_{obs} is the number of services the citizen believes that the government provides and upon which his or her observed evaluation is based.

We can combine these errors with the citizen's initial or *observed evaluation* of governmental performance to determine his or her *true evaluation* in the following identity:

$$\text{Mean}_{\text{true}} = \text{Mean}_{\text{obs}} + \text{SUBSET BIAS} - \text{MISSET BIAS} - \text{NONSET BIAS} \quad [4]$$

which we can then use to assess the impact of alternative institutional arrangements on citizen evaluations of government performance. That is, we can begin to assess the impact of alternative institutional arrangements on the size and direction of the components of the identity, and, thus, their role in influencing citizens' attribution errors in their evaluations of the quality of local public services.

This process of decomposing the errors in a citizen's evaluation of governmental services can be understood best through the example presented in Table 6.1. The citizen's task in this example is to evaluate his or her city government's service performance, and, as seen at the top of the table, nine services might potentially be included in the evaluation: five actually provided by the city; two provided by the county that the citizen might misidentify as city services; and two services that are not provided by either government but that the citizen might think are being provided by the city. Each service is evaluated on a seven-point scale. The citizen's unobserved true evaluation of the city's services would be represented by the calculations in the first row, where the citizen's summary evaluation is the mean evaluation for the five services actually provided by the city, or 3.10.

In our case, however, the citizen makes a number of errors in his or her evaluation. The *observed evaluation* of the city's services, as seen in the second row of the table, contains three different sets of errors. First, the citizen makes a SUBSET error by not including service number four and service number five in the evaluation. Second, the citizen makes a MISSET error by wrongly holding the city government responsible for the two county-provided services: services six and seven. And third, a NONSET error is committed via the citizen's inclusion in the service set of two services neither government provides: services eight and nine. Instead of having a mean evaluation of 3.10, these errors combine to produce a mean observed evaluation of only 3.03.

Our task, then, is to decompose these errors in evaluation and determine their impact on the citizen's summary judgment of the quality of city service provision. This is done at the bottom of Table 6.1 using the SUBSET, MISSET, and NONSET equations. The citizen's observed mean evaluation of 3.30 is biased by 0.41 due to SUBSET error, by 0.74 from MISSET error, and by −0.40 due to NONSET error. When the observed mean is adjusted for these biases, as seen in the last row and last equation in the table, the corrected mean evaluation of 3.10 is, as expected, the same as that found for the unobserved true evaluation presented in the first row of the table.

It is also worth noting that the directions of the three biases in the example are not uniform. Therefore, simply observing the difference in the means of the *true evaluation* (3.10 in row one) and the *observed evaluation* (3.03 in row two) would not have provided a sufficient guide to the level of error our citizen made in evaluating his or her city's services. That total level of error of 0.07 confounds three distinct sources of error, each of which is substantially greater in magnitude

Table 6.1

Decomposition of Attribution Errors in Service Evaluations

Type of service evaluation	Services of city being evaluated					County services		Nonexistent services		Sum	Mean	n
	1	2	3	4	5	6	7	8	9			
TRUE evaluation	2.2	1.1	3.1	4.4	4.7					15.50	3.10	5
OBSERVED evaluation	2.2	1.1	3.1			6.3	5.1	1.5	1.9	21.20	3.03	7
SUBSET evaluation				4.4	4.7					9.10	4.55	2
MISSET Evaluation						6.3	5.1			11.40	5.70	2
NONSET evaluation								1.5	1.9	3.40	1.70	2
OBS. + SUBSET − MISSET + NONSET	2.2	1.1	3.1	4.4	4.7					15.50	3.10	5

SUBSET BIAS $= [N_{sub} * (Mean_{sub} - Mean_{true})] / N_{obs}$
$= [2*(4.55 - 3.10)] / 7 = 0.41$

MISSET BIAS $= [N_{mis} * (Mean_{mis} - Mean_{true})] / N_{obs}$
$= [2*(5.70 - 3.10)] / 7 = 0.74$

NONSET BIAS $= [N_{non} * (Mean_{non} - Mean_{true})] / N_{obs}$
$= [2*(1.70 - 3.10)] / 7 = -0.40$

TOTAL BIAS $=$ SUBSET BIAS − MISSET BIAS − NONSET BIAS
$= 0.41 - 0.74 + 0.40$
$= 0.07$

TRUE EVALU $= Mean_{obs} +$ TOTAL BIAS
$= 3.03 + 0.07$
$= 3.10$

than their combined impact given their contrary signs. Thus, if the three types of errors relate differently to the various arguments of the traditional reform and public choice perspectives, as we have indicated they might, or if the separate biases differ in the degree to which they are random or systematic, it becomes essential to decompose the total error to understand the real impact of consolidation/fragmentation on evaluations of government performance.

Having presented the sources of error, their likely impacts on citizen evaluations, and a method for decomposing that error, we must now discuss several troubling aspects of the analysis. First, while the method of decomposing the sources of error in evaluations is straightforward, one of its elements is not directly observable. Specifically, SUBSET error involves the citizen not evaluating a service because he or she believes that it is not provided by the government. Thus, the values of row three of Table 6.1 are unobserved, as is, therefore, the true evaluation outlined in the first row. This is a problem we will tackle in the empirical portion of this chapter.

Second, we have begged the question of whether evaluations of performance on an array of specific services is an appropriate characterization of how citizens judge their governments. This characterization is problematic in several respects. It is certainly possible that specific service evaluations reflect a common, underlying, global assessment of government, rather than reflective assessment about the quality of individual local services. It is also unlikely that citizens weigh all services equally, or even consider all services, instead focusing on a few specific services that are controversial. Also, it is legitimate for citizens to evaluate critically the performance of cities in terms of nonprovision of services that the citizen believes should be provided, but realizes are not currently provided. And other variables certainly enter into a citizen's summative assessment of the government's job performance, including the tax cost of services. Even more generally, the judgments we make about our governments may not be based on services at all, but on more symbolic attributes or policy stances of officials. If our characterization of the evaluation process is incorrect, we may be able to decompose errors in evaluation, but find that ultimately they have little impact on how citizens relate to their government.

We believe that each of these criticisms has some validity, although we would argue that our characterization of the evaluation process also is at least partially correct. As many mayors who have not gotten the snow cleared in a timely manner have learned, service quality does matter. But the process we have outlined is probably only one part of the larger evaluation enterprise that citizens undertake in making judgments about elected officials.

The issue becomes, then, how important is service evaluation, and its possible biases, to the citizen's overall satisfaction with the quality of government? Answering this question is essential to validate the substantive importance of any differences we find in biases in service evaluations across different types of institutional designs. We can make such an assessment by testing the following model:

$$\text{SATISFACTION} = a + b_1\text{Mean}_{true} + b_2\text{SUBSET BIAS} +$$
$$b_3\text{MISSET BIAS} + b_4\text{NONSET BIAS}$$

where SATISFACTION is the general measure of satisfaction with government used as our dependent variable in the analysis in chapter 2, and does not make reference to the specific array of services that it provides. If evaluations, and biases in service evaluations, do matter, the coefficients should be different from zero. And while we cannot give an a priori ranking of the services in the array the citizen is considering, we can, through the model, empirically weigh the impacts of the different biases on the citizens' overall satisfaction with his or her government.

Testing the Level and Impact of Institutionally Induced Errors

Defining the Service Universe

Given the definitions of the types of errors offered above, it is essential that we define a universe of services against which citizens' evaluations can be compared. That is, there is no limit to the range of MISSET and NONSET errors that a citizen might make. He or she could, for instance, mistakenly credit city officials for national-level policymaking. To set some reasonable bounds for the analysis, we identified eleven services, as seen in chapter 2 in Table 2.1, that are commonly provided by local government as the reference service universe. This provides the base against which we define SUBSET, MISSET, and NONSET errors. Therefore, when we refer below to "bias" in evaluations induced by these errors, we mean *bias with respect to the service universe* identified in Table 2.1. Admittedly, this is not a complete specification of evaluative errors a citizen might make. But it does delimit the analysis in such a way that we can reasonably compare the impact of local governmental structures on service evaluations.

Errors were determined by checking the responses of citizens on a series of service evaluation questions against the actual service patterns outlined in the table. Respondents were asked, "I'm going to read you a short list of services that local of governments often provide. Please tell me how you would rate the performance of [name of city government] when it comes to providing each of the following services. Would you say that the service provided is EXCELLENT, GOOD, FAIR, POOR, or IS NOT PROVIDED by [name of city government]?" Those responding with one of the first four categories were coded as having evaluated the service as a city service, and their one to four ranking of service was then used to develop an observed mean ranking of city services. Those responding that the service was not provided by the city government were coded as not evaluating the service.

Of the three sources of error, MISSET error is the most clearly discernible from the results. Identification of a service actually provided by the county or sewer district as a city service would constitute a MISSET error, and the selection of the matched Jefferson and Fayette County sites was designed to provide a clear contrast on this source of error. Respondents in the Fayette County sites, because they reside within a consolidated urban county governmental arrangement, cannot misattribute responsibility for the eleven local services; each of the eleven services is provided or not provided by the urban county government. In contrast, substantial opportunity exists for MISSET error in the fragmented Jefferson County cases. As seen in Table 2.1, the county and sewer district provide a number of services, responsibility for which respondents might misattribute to their city officials. Critically, this is not loading the deck against the fragmented-government respondents. It is simply a class of error that is not operative for consolidated-government respondents. And since we are ultimately interested in the total number of errors in evaluation that are made, we must consider this type as well as NONSET and SUBSET errors.

A NONSET error occurs if a respondent evaluated a service not being provided by any local government. NONSET errors were, for the most part, easily interpretable based on comparisons of the respondent's evaluation to the list of provided services in Table 2.1. However, there is some potential for ambiguity in some of the consolidated Fayette County responses. Two of the Fayette County sites, the Chinoe and Green Acres neighborhoods, are full-service districts, and receive all eleven services from the urban county government. Thus, there is no possibility for a NONSET error by respondents from these research sites with reference to our defined service universe. But the remaining three Fayette County sites are not full service districts, and thus, as seen in Table 2.1, receive a subset of the full eleven-item service package. These respondents might have answered the evaluation questions by making a judgment about how the city provides the service in the other service districts, even though the service is not provided in their neighborhood. These cases were coded as NONSET errors, although some form of reasonable evaluation may underlie the respondent's answers. Also, only half of the Stonewall neighborhood was provided street lighting by the urban county government. We coded all of these cases as not receiving the service and identified any service evaluations as NONSET errors. Importantly, in both of these interpretations, we have made coding decisions that will probably serve to inflate the numbers of errors recorded for the consolidated government. If anything, we have loaded the deck *against* consolidated government.

Of the three types of errors, the most problematic is SUBSET error—the failure of a citizen to evaluate a service that is actually provided by his or her city government. The problem here, of course, is that we need the evaluation of such services to calculate how much bias the failure to evaluate the service introduces into summary judgments about overall service performance, but the needed evaluation is unobserved.

Three approaches to developing proxies for such unobserved evaluations might be taken. The *first,* using the average of the evaluations for services the citizen did think were being provided by the city, is clearly inappropriate, because the method of decomposition we have outlined draws our attention to the difference between these two values. If the individual's mean observed evaluation is used as the proxy, we will have guaranteed that there will be no difference. A *second* approach is to use the average evaluation of a given service by those in the jurisdiction who did make a judgment about it as an estimate of the missing evaluation for those who did not think the service was provided. And a *third* approach entails developing a model using demographic and attitudinal variables to predict the value of the missing evaluations. A combination of the second and third methods was used to develop the proxy evaluations. That is, eleven models were estimated, one for each of the eleven types of services, using cases for which complete information was available. In each model, the dependent variable was the evaluation of the service and the independent variables were a number of demographic and attitudinal indicators and nine dummy variables representing nine of the research sites to capture the mean level of the service evaluation for those sites relative to the reference site.[6] The coefficients from these models were then combined with data on the demographic, attitudinal, and site dummy variables to estimate the missing service evaluations.

Several of these models generated reasonably strong results, with the coefficients of determination for two services *(parks and recreation* and *public health)* falling in the range from 0.60 to 0.69, and for three others *(police, trash and garbage,* and *social services)* between 0.50 and 0.59. The *transportation* and *sanitary sewer* coefficients ranged from 0.40 to 0.49. Unfortunately, the remaining four models produced less robust results, with the *street lighting* and *road and street maintenance* coefficients falling in the 0.30 to 0.39 range, and the *planning and zoning* and *storm sewer* coefficients in the 0.20 to 0.29 range. However, only 5.2 percent of the SUBSET errors were made on planning and zoning or storm sewer services, the two services with the weakest prediction models. And by far the largest percentage of SUBSET errors (38.7 percent) were made for parks and recreation services, which produced the second strongest prediction model $(R^2 = 0.61)$.

A frequency distribution of the three types of errors and the total number of errors for the two major research settings, the consolidated and fragmented governments, is presented in Table 6.2. As seen in the second and third columns of the table, SUBSET errors were relatively infrequent in both the consolidated and fragmented settings; nearly 77 percent of the Fayette County respondents and just over 70 percent of the Jefferson County respondents made no SUBSET errors. And in both cases, only a handful of respondents made more than one error. This is especially surprising for the Fayette County respondents. As noted in Table 2.1, the urban county government provided all eleven services to two of the five research sites in that community and at least eight services to all of the

Table 6.2

Frequency Distribution of Numbers of Errors in Evaluations Made by Fragmented- and Consolidated-Government Respondents

Percent of respondents making errors

Number of errors	SUBSET errors Consol.	Frag.	MISSET errors Consol.	Frag.	NONSET errors Consol.	Frag.	TOTAL errors Consol.	Frag.
0	76.8%	70.1%	100.0%	25.3%	71.7%	41.5%	53.1%	7.9%
1	16.7	23.3	—	28.6	21.5	37.9	29.9	16.1
2	4.2	6.2	—	20.3	3.9	15.8	11.5	19.4
3	1.6	0.3	—	9.8	2.9	3.7	4.5	17.8
4	0.3	—	—	5.8	—	1.2	0.7	15.2
5	0.3	—	—	2.9	—	—	0.3	9.3
6	—	—	—	2.1	—	—	0.1	5.1
7	—	—	—	1.3	—	—	—	4.0
8	—	—	—	3.9	—	—	—	1.7
9	—	—	—	—	—	—	—	3.3
10	—	—	—	—	—	—	—	0.2
%	100.0	100.0	100.0	100.0	100.0	100.0	100.0	100.0
n	1157	866	1157	886	1157	886	1157	886

consolidated-government respondents. Thus, these respondents could have made a large number of SUBSET errors, but did not relative to the fragmented-government respondents.

As expected, and by design, there were no MISSET errors among the Fayette County respondents. In contrast, only 25 percent of the Jefferson County respondents failed to make at least one MISSET error. And the frequencies do not decline sharply as the number of errors increases; over 25 percent of the respondents misidentified at least three special district or county services as city services. This suggests that fragmentation does generate some confusion over service delivery patterns.

The number of NONSET errors committed by the consolidated respondents was somewhat lower than that for those in the fragmented-institutional setting, even though we have noted that our coding strategy probably inflates the number of NONSET errors for three of the five Fayette County research sites. Over 71 percent of the former did not commit a NONSET error, compared to only 41 percent for the Jefferson County respondents. However, the opportunity for NONSET errors is, to some extent, the mirror image of the opportunity for SUBSET errors. That is, because the Fayette County respondents received all or most of the eleven services, they have a greater opportunity to commit a SUBSET error, but reduced opportunities for NONSET errors. And since the opposite is true for the fragmented cases, we should not be too surprised about the somewhat higher level of NONSET errors in that setting.

The last two columns of Table 6.2 combine all of the errors, and a great many misevaluations were made. This is especially true since the calculations excluded the "don't know" responses from the count of errors; for the purposes of this table, they were treated as accurate responses, although they are dropped from most of the analyses that follow. Thus, the actual level of error is probably understated by these results. But for these results, it appears that the level of error is considerably higher for the fragmented-government respondents. Less than 8 percent made no attribution errors in evaluating the eleven services, while fewer than 50 percent of the consolidated-government respondents made even one error.

Importantly, this difference in the total number of errors is not a function of our design, which by intention precluded the Fayette County respondents from making MISSET errors. All of the respondents could have made a maximum of eleven errors. The only impact of our unusual design is in terms of how those potential eleven errors are distributed. For the respondents in the three full-service districts sites in Fayette County, for example, all eleven potential errors would have to have been in the form of SUBSET errors, rather than distributed across SUBSET, MISSET, and NONSET errors.

The Impact of Evaluative Errors

In assessing the impact of institutional arrangements of metropolitan government on biases in citizen evaluations of public services, we have three tasks. First, we must assess the differences in the number of evaluation errors between the respondents living in the consolidated and fragmented research sites, a task we have already begun with Table 6.2. Second, we must determine if and how the several types of errors bias mean service evaluations. And third, we must see if these differences influence the citizen's overall satisfaction with the quality of city government.

We can address the first question more completely than we have to this point by examining difference-of-means and difference-of-differences tests in the numbers of errors made by consolidated- and fragmented-government respondents. These results are presented in Table 6.3 for the five matched sets of research sites. Starting with the first column of the table, the number of SUBSET errors was different from zero in all ten research sites. More importantly, the difference of differences tests in column two indicate that the number of SUBSET errors was greater in two of the fragmented-government communities—Beechwood Village and Newburg—in comparison to their matched consolidated-government site, and that both of these differences were significant. But in the remaining three matched comparisons, a higher rate of error is observed in the consolidated-government site, although only two of these differences were statistically discernible. Thus, it seems that the two types of institutions are equally

Table 6.3

Difference of Means on Numbers of Errors by Matched Consolidated/Fragmented Institutional Arrangements

Matched Consol.frag. cases	Mean no. SUBSET errors	Diff-erence	Mean no. MISSET errors	Diff-erence	Mean no. NONSET errors	Diff-erence	Mean no. TOTAL errors	Diff-erence
Blueberry	0.858*** (1.089)[a] 219[b]		0.000 (0.000) 219		0.420*** (0.496) 219		1.279*** (1.032) 219	
		−0.807***		0.247***		0.077		1.734***
Minor Lane Heights	0.051*** (0.221) 157		0.247*** (0.130) 157		0.497*** (0.713) 157		3.013*** (1.743) 157	
Chinoe	0.022* (0.176) 224		0.000 (0.000) 224		0.000 (0.000) 224		0.022* (0.176) 224	
		0.606***		1.814***		1.090***		3.312***
Beechwood Village	0.628*** (0.517) 118		1.814*** (0.944) 188		1.090*** (0.601) 188		3.532*** (1.412) 188	
Stonewall	0.182*** (0.503) 253		0.000 (0.000) 253		1.028*** (1.067) 253		1.210*** (1.069) 253	
		−0.108***		0.789***		0.275***		0.956***
Barbourmeade	0.074*** (0.284) 175		0.789*** (0.821) 175		1.303*** (1.025) 175		2.166*** (1.591) 175	
Crestwood/ Shadeland	0.518*** (0.705) 253		0.000 (0.000) 253		0.352*** (0.478) 253		0.870*** (0.698) 253	
		−0.076		0.746***		0.670***		1.340***
Windy Hills	0.442*** (0.694) 181		0.746*** (0.761) 181		1.022*** (1.070) 181		2.210*** (1.581) 181	
Green Acres	0.048** (0.274) 208		0.000 (0.000) 208		0.000 (0.000) 208		0.048** (0.274) 208	
		0.558***		3.855***		0.315***		4.728***
Newburg	0.606*** (0.839) 165		3.855*** (3.143) 165		0.315*** (0.466) 165		4.776*** (3.128) 165	

$* = p < 0.10; ** = p < 0.05; *** = p < 0.01.$
[a]The figures in parentheses are standard deviations.
[b]Italics are number of cases.

likely to produce SUBSET errors, even though citizens in consolidated settings have more chances to make such errors.

Similar comparisons on the number of MISSET errors are provided in the next two columns of the table, although these tests are somewhat artificial in that the design insures that the values of the consolidated-government cases will be zero. Thus, the t-tests in this case devolve to tests of the difference between the mean number of errors and the null of zero. Nevertheless, the null of zero does have substantive meaning in this case and the MISSET results are, therefore, quite straightforward. As seen in the fourth column of the table, the mean number of MISSET errors is discernibly greater than zero in all five fragmented-government research settings.

Virtually the same pattern is observed for NONSET errors in the fifth and sixth columns of Table 6.3. Again, the pattern of differences between the matched consolidated and fragmented research sites in the table suggests that the number of NONSET errors is systematically higher in the latter; all of the difference-of-differences values in the sixth column are positive and four are significant at the 0.01 level.

Given that the greater proportion of total errors is made up of NONSET and MISSET errors, the pattern of results for TOTAL errors in the last two columns of the table should not be surprising. Again, the number of errors is related to consolidated/fragmented institutional structures. Across all five sets of comparisons, the fragmented Jefferson County respondents evidenced discernibly higher mean numbers of errors. In answer to our first question, then, we can conclude that there are differences in the level of errors across the two types of institutional structures. Both forms of institutional arrangement generate SUBSET errors, while fragmented governments are associated with greater numbers of MISSET, NONSET, and TOTAL evaluation errors.

Do systematic differences in the numbers of evaluative errors that citizens make translate into systematic differences in biases of their mean evaluation of governmental service performance? Errors need not lead to bias. We have seen that errors may cancel out at the individual or the aggregate level, so that no bias would be evident. More generally, we may not even be measuring real judgments about service quality. As noted above, the eleven specific service evaluations could all be reflecting a common, underlying, global impression of service quality, or could be essentially random judgments designed to please the interviewers. If such were the case, bias would be zero given the structure of equations [1] through [3], which highlight the difference in the means of the appropriately evaluated and the inappropriately evaluated services as well as the proportion of errors to total judgments made in the evaluation. If there is no difference in the means, for any of the reasons noted above, no bias will be evident in our findings.

As seen in Table 6.4, however, bias introduced by the several types of error is statistically discernible in a number of cases.[7] The first column shows significant

Table 6.4

Difference of Means on Biases in Evaluations by Matched Consolidated/Fragmented Institutional Arrangements

Matched Consol.frag. cases	Mean SUBSET bias	Diff-erence	Mean MISSET bias	Diff-erence	Mean NONSET bias	Diff-erence	Mean TOTAL bias	Diff-erence
Blueberry	-0.045*** (0.087)[a] *160[b]*		0.000 (0.000) *219*		0.008** (0.045) *179*		-0.064*** (0.105) *133*	
		0.046***		0.114* **		-0.052***		0.248***
Minor Lane Heights	0.001 (0.016) *153*		-0.114*** (0.204) *89*		-0.044*** (0.103) *130*		0.184*** (0.265) *86*	
Chinoe	0.001 (0.007) *223*		0.000 (0.000) *224*		0.000 (0.000) *224*		0.001 (0.007) *223*	
		-0.175***		0.065***		-0.001		-0.307***
Beechwood Village	-0.174*** (0.171) *158*		0.065*** (0.153) *119*		-0.001 (0.098) *124*		-0.306*** (0.308) *115*	
Stonewall	-0.002** (0.015) *226*		0.000 (0.000) *253*		0.008 (0.058) *160*		-0.013** (0.066) *140*	
		0.001		0.032***		-0.004		-0.030
Barbourmeade	-0.001 (0.037) *172*		0.032*** (0.105) *147*		0.004 (0.173) *129*		-0.043* (0.245) *126*	
Crestwood/ Shadeland	-0.013*** (0.042) *175*		0.000 (0.000) *253*		0.001 (0.030) *201*		-0.018*** (0.060) *135*	
		-0.103***		0.013		-0.022		-0.163***
Windy Hills	-0.116*** (0.216) *164*		0.013 (0.125) *128*		-0.021 (0.151) *124*		-0.181*** (0.363) *100*	
Green Acres	0.001 (0.018) *206*		0.000 (0.000) *208*		0.000 (0.000) *208*		0.001 (0.018) *206*	
		-0.022		0.254***		0.014***		-0.387***
Newburg	-0.021 (0.156) *126*		0.254*** (0.451) *115*		0.014*** (0.051) *151*		-0.386*** (0.522) *88*	

$* = p < 0.10; ** = p < 0.05; *** = p < 0.01.$
[a]The figures in parentheses are standard deviations.
[b]Italics are number of cases.

SUBSET bias for five of the ten research sites—three for the consolidated sites and two for the fragmented sites. In all of these cases, the bias was negative, indicating that the citizen's observed mean evaluation of service quality is inflated by SUBSET error. That is, not giving the city credit for services that it is actually providing tends to lead citizens to think the city is doing a better job than it really is.

The third and fourth columns assess bias due to MISSET error. Again, these tests are somewhat artificial in that the design insures that the values of the consolidated-government cases will be zero. Thus, the t-tests in this case devolve to tests of the difference between mean bias and the null of zero. Four of the five values in the fourth column are positive, indicating that MISSET bias, attributing county or special district services to city government, like SUBSET bias, tends to lead citizens to think the city is doing a better job than it really is. And three of these differences are significant. However, the Minor Lane Heights value for MISSET bias is negative and significant, indicating that misattribution leads to a poorer impression of the quality of city services in that community. Thus, MISSET bias does not have a necessary impact on citizen evaluations in terms of direction. This, of course, would be expected given that the direction of the bias effect depends on the difference between the citizen's mean assessment of the quality of services actually received and his or her mean assessment of the quality of services he or she incorrectly thinks are being provided, a difference that might take on negative or positive values.

As seen in the fifth and sixth columns of Table 6.4, NONSET error seems to be the least important in the creation of bias of the three types of error, something that should not be surprising given that we have pointed out that NONSET errors would seem, by their very nature, to be nonattitudes. Only three of the research sites—Blueberry, Minor Lane Heights, and Newburg—produced evidence of significant NONSET bias. Yet, as seen in column six, two of the paired comparisons found evidence of greater NONSET bias in the fragmented-government site than in its matched consolidated-government site. In one of these comparisons, Blueberry and Minor Lane Heights, the relative bias operates to deflate the fragmented-government citizen's appreciation of the quality of local government services, while in the other, Green Acres and Newburg, it tends inappropriately to inflate the fragmented-government citizen's view of the quality of services.

The final two columns of Table 6.4 present difference-of-means and difference-of-differences tests for TOTAL BIAS (calculated as SUBSET BIAS − MISSET BIAS − NONSET BIAS). As seen in column seven, eight of the research sites produced evidence of statistically discernible bias in their overall mean evaluation of the quality of local government services. In only two consolidated-government sites—Chinoe and Green Acres—does it appear that attribution errors generate little or no overall bias. The final column presents the difference-of-differences tests, where evidence of statistically significant relative bias is found across four of the five comparisons. In one case, Blueberry and Minor Lane Heights, that bias serves to deflate the fragmented-government citizen's perception of the quality of services relative to that of his or her consolidated-government counterpart. In the remaining three contrasts with significant differences, the effect is the opposite.

This is better seen in Table 6.5, which presents the observed mean evaluation of the citizens of each community, their corrected or true mean evaluation, which is purged of bias, and the difference between the two sets of evaluations, or TOTAL BIAS. As seen in the fourth column of the table, evidence of statistically significant bias was found for eight of the ten research sites, or all but two of the consolidated-government sites. Of these eight sites, the bias operates in seven of them, all but Minor Lane Heights, to inflate citizens' true mean evaluation or to make them less critical of the quality of local government services than they should be.

But how substantively important are these differences? After all, the bias values reported in the fourth column do not seem very large in terms of the four point evaluation scale. Despite the small apparent magnitudes of the bias values, their impact is considerable. One way to assess this is to compare the relative rankings of the observed and true mean evaluations reported in columns two and three of Table 6.5. Moving from the observed scores to the true, unbiased scores changes the relative rankings of two of the five consolidated neighborhoods. And four of the five relative rankings of fragmented Jefferson County sites change when we shift from the observed to the true, unbiased evaluation scores.

Alternatively, we can assess these differences by expressing the bias values in column four as a proportion of the standard deviations of the observed mean evaluations. This is done in the last column of the table. Reported in this manner, the impact of bias on evaluations does not seem very great for four of the five consolidated-government sites. Only the Blueberry's observed mean evaluation of 2.478 is shifted very much (up to -0.176 of a standard deviation) by attribution error. In contrast, the impact of bias is considerable for four of the five fragmented-government sites, all but Barbourmeade. Bias serves to alter the observed mean evaluation of these four cities by a third of a standard deviation (Minor Lane Heights) to more than three-fifths of a standard deviation (Newburg).

How does this bias then influence the citizen's general satisfaction with city government? As noted earlier, mean values of service evaluations may not be a valid indicator of citizen perceptions of the quality of government services, although the fact that we have found evidence of bias, given the structure of the BIAS equations, strongly discounts this possibility. But even if we are tapping service assessments, as we believe we are, it is also true that satisfaction with government is determined by more than satisfaction with services. To assess the full impact of bias, then, we need to examine how bias in mean service evaluations influences a more general indicator of citizen evaluations of government as

Table 6.5

Difference (Bias) in Observed Mean Evaluation and True Mean Evaluation

Research site	n	Observed mean evaluation	True mean evaluation	Bias	Bias divided by observed mean s.d.,
Consolidated, Lexington–Fayette sites					
Blueberry	106	2.578	2.498	−0.081***	−0.176
Chinoe	88	2.744	2.746	0.001	0.003
Stonewall	82	2.520	2.498	−0.022**	−0.049
Crestwood/Shadeland	72	2.646	2.612	−0.034***	−0.063
Green Acres	121	2.544	2.546	0.002	0.003
Fragmented, Louisville–Jefferson Sites					
Minor Lane Heights	81	2.542	2.737	0.196***	0.326
Beechwood Village	109	3.092	2.769	−0.322***	−0.658
Barbourmeade	116	2.281	2.235	−0.046*	−0.076
Windy Hills	75	2.898	2.658	−0.241***	−0.467
Newburg	70	2.382	1.897	−0.485***	−0.781

outlined in the SATISFACTION reaction function presented earlier.

The dependent variable, SATISFACTION with urban service delivery, is the same measure used in chapter 2. The index taps both a very general impression of the effectiveness of city government as well as a general impression of service quality. While we use the combined measure because we have seen in chapters 3 and 4 that it is related to a number of measures of political behavior, separate analyses of each component of the SATISFACTION index generated substantively identical findings.

The SATISFACTION indicator was regressed on the true or corrected mean evaluation of service quality, the measures of the three types of biases resulting from evaluative errors as outlined in Table 6.4, and a number of demographic and attitudinal control variables used in chapter 2.[8] Superficially, this model appears similar to that presented in chapter 2, but there are important differences. In that chapter, we examined *jurisdiction level* or mean levels of these service evaluations as a proxy for objective quality of a city's services. And the mean site bias figures were included in that model only as a correction factor for our proxy indicator. In this case, we are examining the individual impact of evaluations and evaluative attribution error using the individual-level information from the Lexington and Louisville study. If the individual-level biases introduced by evaluative errors ultimately do not matter, then only the real or corrected mean evaluation of service quality should be related to SATISFACTION and the three bias coefficients should be negligible and nonsignificant. Alternatively, if the biases introduced by evaluative errors do matter, the three bias coefficients should be different from zero.

The results from the OLS regression analyses are presented in Table 6.6 for the consolidated-government sites and Table 6.7 for the fragmented-government sites. Starting with Table 6.6, evaluation biases seem to have some impact on the consolidated-government settings. Two SUBSET bias and two NONSET bias coefficients are significant, and the signs of all four of these significant coefficients indicate that when the real mean level of perceived service quality is inflated by either of these biases, the citizen's general satisfaction with government is also biased upward. In the case of the NONSET bias, however, we have noted that there is a unique ambiguity of the service evaluations in the consolidated Lexington sites. That is, for the three less-than-full service districts, the wording of the service evaluation questions creates a special opportunity for citizens' legitimate evaluations of "a lack of provision" of some service to be identified as an illegitimate NONSET error. Thus, also keeping in mind the likely "nonattitude" character of NONSET errors, we should be cautious about the findings of significant NONSET effects in the consolidated-government settings.

Turning to the fragmented-government sites in Table 6.7, we again find evidence of some impact of attribution error bias on overall satisfaction with government service provision. In these cases, none of the NONSET coefficients is significant. But like the consolidated-government settings, two cases of significant SUBSET bias are found for the five fragmented-government sites. More importantly, MISSET bias was found to have a statistically discernible impact on SATISFACTION in three of the five fragmented-government sites.

Again, we need to go beyond statistical significance and examine the substantive meaning of these findings. The results presented in Table 6.8 can help us do this. The table presents two sets of predicted SATISFACTION scores based on the regression coefficients presented in Tables 6.6 and 6.7. For both, mean community values on all of the independent variables but the bias scores were used to generate the prediction. In the first set of results, the mean levels of biases were included in the prediction equation, while in the second, the bias values were set to zero. That is, the two predictions and the difference between them compare how overall SATISFACTION with government would change if BIAS shifted from its mean community value to zero. And clearly, this is not an extreme scenario given that two of our research sites evidenced bias levels of essentially zero.

As in Table 6.5, the difference between these two predictions is represented in the last column of the table as a proportion of the standard deviation of the mean bias predicted value of SATISFACTION. As seen in that column, evidence of a sizable impact of attribution bias on SATISFACTION was found for one of the consolidated-government sites; bias shifts the predicted SATISFACTION score of Blueberry by almost a quarter of a standard deviation. But, the impact of

Table 6.6

OLS Regression of Satisfaction with Government on Real Service Evaluation, Evaluation Biases, and Controls—Consolidated Cases

Independent variable	Consolidated, Lexington–Fayette Sites				
	Blueberry	Chinoe	Stonewall	Crestwood/ Shadeland	Green Acres
TRUEMEAN	0.956*** (0.178)[a]	0.933*** (0.325)	1.380*** (0.226)	1.238*** (0.256)	1.311*** (0.205)
SUBBIAS	−2.206*** (0.720)	−3.480 (7.851)	0.938 (3.422)	2.327 (2.127)	−6.914* (4.123)
MISBIAS	—	—	—	—	—
NONBIAS	2.642* (1.195)	—	1.940* (1.033)	−0.106 (2.403)	—
GENDER	0.106 (0.138)	−0.310 (0.213)	−0.366* (0.194)	−0.666** (0.279)	0.168 (0.196)
HOMEOWNERSHIP	−0.008 (0.211)	0.046 (0.295)	0.331 (0.512)	0.405 (0.401)	0.203 (0.260)
RACE	0.021 (0.246)	—	—	—	0.914** (0.377)
INCOME	0.010 (0.050)	0.028 (0.052)	0.005 (0.052)	−0.011 (0.065)	−0.004 (0.072)
EDUCATION	0.093** (0.046)	0.061 (0.078)	0.057 (0.077)	−0.006 (0.086)	−0.031 (0.080)
LOCAL EFFICACY	0.144*** (0.050)	0.213*** (0.079)	0.127* (0.067)	0.053 (0.090)	0.191*** (0.066)
INVESTMENT	−0.034 (0.045)	0.044 (0.057)	0.057 (0.055)	0.099 (0.079)	0.078 (0.057)
AGE	−0.000 (0.007)	0.009 (0.007)	−0.002 (0.007)	0.001 (0.008)	0.016 (0.010)
Constant	1.327	1.163	−0.219	0.016	−0.343
R^2	0.50	0.33	0.54	0.48	0.56
n	94	70	69	63	89

* = $p < 0.10$; ** = $p < 0.05$; *** = $p < 0.01$.
[a]Figures in parentheses are standard errors.

Table 6.7

OLS Regression of Satisfaction with Government on Real Service Evaluation, Evaluation Biases, and Controls—Fragmented Cases

Fragmented, Louisville–Jefferson Sites

Independent variable	Minor Lane Heights	Beechwood Village	Barbour-meade	Windy Hills	Newburg
TRUEMEAN	0.986*** (0.258)[a]	1.315*** (0.214)	2.063*** (0.278)	1.301*** (0.324)	1.527*** (0.398)
SUBBIAS	−10.692** (4.896)	−0.380 (0.644)	1.343 (2.476)	−1.355*** (0.453)	0.903 (0.760)
MISBIAS	0.032 (0.617)	2.883*** (0.664)	1.088 (1.093)	2.903*** (0.755)	0.921* (0.485)
NONBIAS	−1.182 (0.924)	0.037 (0.998)	0.313 (0.756)	0.148 (0.676)	2.582 (2.475)
GENDER	0.142 (0.236)	−0.103 (0.187)	0.332 (0.265)	−0.145 (0.251)	0.013 (0.417)
HOMEOWNERSHIP	−0.535 (0.553)	0.116 (0.512)	−0.410 (1.170)	—	−0.069 (0.459)
RACE	−1.042 (0.899)	—	−0.580 (0.786)	—	1.340* (0.745)
INCOME	0.126 (0.100)	−0.088 (0.068)	−0.111* (0.066)	0.003 (0.065)	−0.263 (0.180)
EDUCATION	0.001 (0.091)	0.033 (0.067)	−0.107 (0.097)	−0.209** (0.090)	0.091 (0.140)
LOCAL EFFICACY	0.184** (0.069)	0.143** (0.059)	0.080 (0.080)	0.135 (0.109)	0.039 (0.101)
INVESTMENT	0.151** (0.060)	0.027 (0.056)	0.008 (0.095)	0.157* (0.080)	0.065 (0.074)
AGE	−0.004 (0.011)	−0.003 (0.007)	−0.019 (0.012)	0.020 (0.065)	−0.046*** (0.016)
Constant	1.513	1.173	0.780	−0.050	2.582
R^2	0.66	0.57	0.63	0.63	0.64
n	65	91	82	57	49

$* = p < 0.10; ** = p < 0.05; *** = p < 0.01.$
[a]Figures in parentheses are standard errors.

Table 6.8

Predicted Satisfaction with Government with No Biases and with Mean Level of Biases

Research site	Pred. SATIS, mean bias	Pred. SATIS, no bias	Difference	Difference divided by SATIS S.D.
	Consolidated, Lexington–Fayette Sites			
Blueberry	3.620	3.426	0.194	0.233
Chinoe	4.129	4.132	–0.003	–0.004
Stonewall	3.610	3.586	0.024	0.025
Crestwood/Shadeland	2.594	2.671	–0.077	–0.069
Green Acres	3.654	3.667	–0.014	–0.011
	Fragmented, Louisville–Jefferson Sites			
Minor Lane Heights	3.157	3.083	0.074	0.055
Beechwood Village	4.661	4.353	0.309	0.262
Barbourmeade	2.301	2.257	0.044	0.027
Windy Hills	4.265	3.812	0.453	0.355
Newburg	2.134	1.688	0.446	0.278

BIAS on the other four consolidated sites is negligible—never more than 0.07 of a standard deviation. In contrast, evidence of a significant impact of BIAS on SATISFACTION is found for three of the five fragmented-government sites. The predicted SATISFACTION scores of Beechwood Village, Windy Hill, and Newburg shift by more than a quarter of a standard deviation when bias is set at zero compared to when it is held at its mean level for the three communities. In all four of the communities where sizable effects were observed, the impact of bias is such that it acts to inflate citizens' perceptions of the quality of government services.

To construct a comparative base from which to assess the substantive meaning of these changes, several other predictions based on the regression results in Tables 6.6 and 6.7 were developed. Two sets of predictions were generated involving manipulation of the GENDER variable. The first held all of the other variables at their mean community values, but set the value of GENDER at one, indicating an all-male community. This was compared to a similar prediction for an all-female community, and the difference between these two predictions was again expressed as a proportion of the standard deviation of SATISFACTION. Another prediction was generated based on the mean values of all of the variables except EDUCATION, which was set at a value of one, indicating that no one in the several communities had more than an eighth grade education. The difference between the predictions generated from this model and the "mean bias" predictions in the first column of Table 6.8 was also expressed as a proportion of the standard deviation of SATISFACTION. These are obviously implausible manipulations, especially so in that our manipulation of BIAS to a value of zero actually represents a state that was realized for two of the ten communities in the study. Still, while both GENDER and SATISFACTION did not generate especially sizable coefficients in the regression models, both have been found previously to be associated with SATISFACTION. Thus, such manipulations can serve as a base against which to assess the comparative substantive importance of the impact of BIAS on our predicted values of SATISFACTION.

In all four cases where sizable bias effects were observed in Table 6.8 (Blueberry, Beechwood Village, Windy Hills, and Newburg), the difference in standard deviation units between predicted SATISFACTION with an observed mean level of attribution error bias and predicted SATISFACTION with no bias (0.23, 0.26, 0.36, and 0.28, respectively) was at least twice the size of that between the all-female and all-male predictions (0.12, 0.09, 0.11, and 0.01, respectively). Similarly, the difference in standard deviation units between predicted SATISFACTION with all values set at their mean and the manipulated prediction where EDUCATION was set at a value of one was not overly sizable when compared to scores presented in the last column of Table 6.8. The EDUCATION manipulation difference was less than the BIAS manipulation difference for two of the communities: Beechwood Village (0.12 and 0.26, respectively) and Newburg (0.25 and 0.28, respectively). In the other two communities, the EDUCATION manipulation difference was approximately twice the size of the BIAS manipulation difference: Blueberry (0.41 and 0.23, respectively) and Windy Hills (0.77 and 0.36, respectively). The implication of these manipulations is, of course, that the impact of BIAS on SATISFACTION is substantially sizable, even when compared to the range of implausible changes in the values of other variables often thought to influence SATISFACTION.

Discussion

In sum, we have found that biases in service evaluations of government resulting from errors in evaluative judgments induced by institutional structure are real, sometimes systematic with respect to the direction of their impact, and often statistically discernible. This evidence of bias, and its relation to institutional structure, however, must be interpreted cautiously. We have only considered bias introduced by attribution errors, not total bias, which would include assessment error bias as well. The attribution error bias we have found is bias *relative* to only the service universe as we have defined it. While the services we have examined cover a broad array of those typically provided by city governments, they are by no means all of the services that citizens might include in their evaluations of city government. Moreover, we were unable to balance these

Figure 6.1. **Average Bias in Satisfaction by Average Number of Attribution Errors—Five Consolidated and Five Fragmented Communities**

Number of errors

Absolute bias in satisfaction

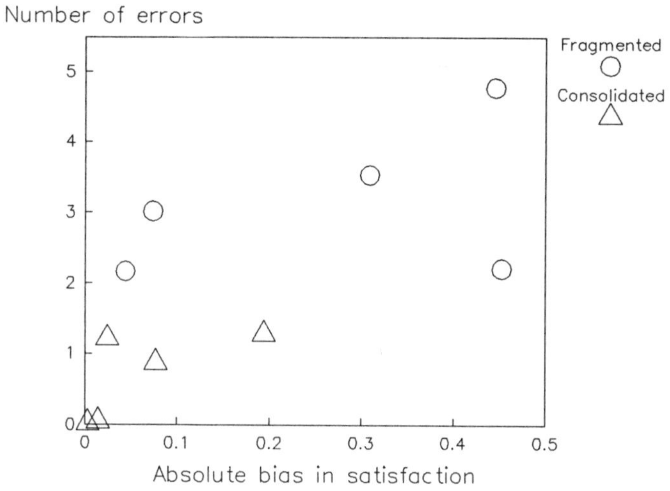

evaluations against the costs of city services, a balance that is presumably critical in the citizen's ultimate evaluation of local governmental performance.

Even so, we believe that these results bear heavily on the debate between public choice theory and the traditional reform theory. The latter was correct in suggesting that fragmentation leads to confusion in attribution of service responsibility; citizens of fragmented governments make more attribution errors, suggesting that individual-level *effective citizenship* is more difficult in fragmented communities. Contrary to the public choice school, any impact that fragmentation has on enhancing citizen interest in local government does not seem to overcome the confusion that inevitably arises when citizens confront multiple service providers. And our results suggest that it is this greater number of errors committed by citizens in fragmented communities that creates the potential for greater evaluation bias, potentially undermining aggregate-level *democratic control.*

The interaction between the number of errors committed and bias in overall satisfaction with government can better be understood by examining the results presented in Figure 6.1. The y axis in the figure is the mean number of total attribution errors committed by citizens, with the values of the ten communities examined in this study taken from column seven of Table 6.3. The x axis is the absolute value of the bias introduced in SATISFACTION with government as a proportion of the standard deviation of SATISFACTION, with the values for the ten communities taken from the third column of Table 6.8.

As the figure demonstrates, fewer attribution errors are made by citizens in the consolidated communities; all five consolidated communities are in the lower half of the figure, despite the fact that citizens in both types of communities had an equal number of chances to make attribution errors. Quite simply, it would seem that MISSET errors are easier to make than SUBSET errors. Thus, citizens in fragmented communities, where MISSET errors are uniquely possible, will tend to make more errors. But just because they tend to make more attribution errors does not mean that their satisfaction with services will be biased, only that there is greater potential for such bias. Whether bias develops, given equations [1] through [3], depends on a divergence between the mean evaluations of services actually provided by the city and those the citizen only thinks are being provided. If the difference is not great, then even a large number of errors will not produce bias. Thus, we find the fragmented communities arrayed quite widely in the figure in terms of *bias in satisfaction*. In contrast, when fewer are made, even large differences in the mean evaluations of appropriately and inappropriately judged services cannot translate into especially large biases in satisfaction. As a result of this interaction, the distribution of the ten cases in the figure takes on a distinctive funnel shape; as we move up the scale in *number of errors,* the potential range of values that bias can take on expands.

In sum, fragmentation does not inevitably generate more evaluative bias. Fragmentation does, however, create the potential for greater bias. Thus, at a minimum, officials in fragmented governments may have a heightened need to inform citizens about what the government is doing and what it is not doing. But there may be reason to expect that they will not so respond, at least in some cases. Of the four cases where sizable bias was found in Table 6.8, all four evidenced *positive* bias—i.e., bias served to inflate the perceived quality of city services. While we do not have a sample of cities, and, thus, cannot generalize too broadly, we suspect this asymmetrical finding may not be an accident. That is, if bias were negative and served to reduce the perceived quality of city services, then city officials would have a strong incentive to provide more information about what services are provided by various levels of government. But if the bias is positive, those officials would have no incentive to correct the attribution errors made by citizens. The officials would be benefiting from a positive externality; the positive evaluations that citizens have about county services, for example, "spill over" to benefit the city official. If such an asymmetry of incentives is plausible, then our pattern of positive bias results is both understandable and even more troubling because it would mean that there is no incentive for officials to correct such misattributions. Indeed, they may even have an incentive to create such errors.[9]

Finally, we should note that the implications of this analysis go beyond issues associated with metropolitan reform and local political behavior in the form of contacting officials, participation, and alienation. More generally, attribution errors can develop whenever responsibility is divided. Evaluative errors of the type we have examined here may be important in considering such varied and traditional issues as the relative merits of federal and unitary political systems, the impacts of separation of powers, and the implications of responsible party government. In discussions of each of these issues, we find some concern for whether and how fragmented responsibility creates opportunities for attribution errors and, thus, evaluative bias. Defining the relevant "service" set, however, would be far more difficult for these issue areas than in the present case. Still, such extensions of the present analysis would seem a fruitful avenue for further understanding the links between individual political behavior and institutional structure.

Notes

1. V. Ostrom, Bish, and Ostrom (1988, p. 66).
2. Dagger (1981, p. 752).
3. V. Ostrom, Bish, and Ostrom (1988, p. 96).
4. V. Ostrom, Bish, and Ostrom (1988, p. 26).
5. The traditional reform theory has long been justly criticized for resting its prescriptions for institutional reform on "self-evident" propositions. All too often, these self-evident propositions did not survive when eventually confronted with data. And while public choice analysts have a strong record of assessing many of their propositions about institutional reform, the fragmentation–information hypothesis has yet to be tested.
6. The demographic variables included all of the independent variables in the EVLN models in chapter 4 and the LOYALTY and VOICE indices.
7. The n values change as we move through this table and the following tables because cases were lost as more instances of "don't know" responses were encountered on the service evaluation questions. To see if this loss of cases was influencing the pattern of results, these analyses were run for a minimum reduced number of cases where complete data were available for every step in the analysis. The substantive pattern of results for these additional analyses did not differ from those presented in the rest of the chapter.
8. The demographic variables are identified in chapter 1. The LOCAL EFFICACY and INVESTMENT indices are those used in chapter 2. Examination of the coefficients of determination generated from regressing each of the independent variables on the remaining independent variables produced no evidence of even moderately strong collinearity in the regression results.
9. For another example of such "positive externalities" generated from institutional complexity, see Lowery (1985).

7

Fragmentation and Suburban Ghettos

In the long-standing disagreement between traditional urban reformers—those advocating consolidated urban-county governments—and the proponents of a public choice model based on governmental fragmentation, there is no more sensitive issue than the relationship between institutional structure and racial inequality. Do fragmented metropolitan institutions promote or diminish equity in service provision? While the basic elements that might be used to develop an answer to this question are fully contained in the issues we have examined in chapter 5, the special importance of this topic to our multiracial urban society has generated a separate literature that is largely independent of the research reviewed until now. For this reason, we think it important to consider the issue of metropolitan government structure and racial equality in the provision of public services as a distinct topic, although the answers offered here are highly consistent with the larger account we have been developing about satisfaction and responses to dissatisfaction in urban communities.

The question of whether or not governmental fragmentation and suburbanization encourage inequality in public service provision seems on its face to be a simple one that would be readily amenable to empirical inquiry. But such has not been the case. As on several of the other issues we have examined, our failure to resolve what seems a straightforward issue is due to the use of inappropriate research designs and excessive reliance on aggregate data to address individual-level hypotheses. We examine these issues in the course of outlining the evolving dialog between reformers and those supporting fragmentation. In particular, we focus on public services and citizen satisfaction levels. We then use the Lexington and Louisville study data to test several hypotheses at the individual level, comparing several communities both within and across institutional forms. The implications of our findings are discussed in the final section of this chapter.

The Unsettled Controversy over Institutions and Race

While there has been a steady evolution in the arguments of both proponents of consolidation and supporters of fragmentation in regard to racial inequality, the starting point of the debate is the urban social stratification literature. Although not concerned with consolidation per se, this literature viewed postwar suburbanization as a vehicle for perpetuating segregation. Norton Long summarized this orientation when he noted: "The suburb is the Northern way to insure separate and unequal."[1] This argument was most forcefully presented by Richard Child Hill, who employed aggregate data on median income to examine the sources of intrametropolitan social stratification. His most important conclusion was that the number of governments in a metropolitan area is directly related to the level of income inequality in the area.[2] This finding added fuel to the fragmentation/consolidation controversy by suggesting that under fragmented arrangements, the poor and blacks are segregated in central city and suburban ghettos primarily due to zoning restrictions and land-use controls employed by autonomous, suburban governmental jurisdictions, an argument that has echoed through a generation of scholarly work.[3]

The nascent public choice view was quick to respond to Hill's argument with a number of counterclaims. The initial attacks were more narrow, focusing on Hill's measure of inequality,[4] and the causal link between fragmentation and inequality.[5] But very rapidly the debate moved beyond these narrow issues to focus on several competing claims.

The *first* of these claims challenged the assumption of the stratification theorists that suburbanization in a fragmented metropolitan area will lead to segregation and inequality, with poor blacks left in central cities while the suburbs develop into exclusive enclaves of upper- and middle-class whites. Analysts pointed to the development of black suburbs and black suburbanization during the 1960s and 1970s, which on its face challenges the key assumption underlying Hill's argument.[6] Many of these same authors noted, however, that these demographic patterns only altered, rather than fundamentally undermined Hill's argument. That is, in Schneider and Logan's summary of this literature, "these suburbs were more similar to central cities than they were to white suburbs, especially with regard to their low socio-economic status, age, employment base, and emerging fiscal problems."[7] Although modified, this view still supports Hill's claim that fragmentation promotes racial inequity. Indeed, it could compound the problem of inequity by the reghettoization of blacks in municipalities with even weaker fiscal foundations than those of central cities. Although these black majority suburbs are uncommon and cannot be characterized as having identical demographic patterns, of particular concern is the growth in suburban areas of what Lake terms "spillover" communities[8] adjacent to central cities and quasi-rural, low-income "slums" on the periphery of metropolitan areas.[9]

The *second* contentious issue concerns the initial level of discrimination suburbanization is presumed to enhance. If blacks are discriminated against and receive inadequate public services in central cities, then increased fragmentation/suburbanization would not act to increase the overall level of inequality, contrary to Hill's argument. And numerous studies of minority satisfaction with public service provision have generally found that under most conditions—fragmented or consolidated, central city or suburb—blacks are more dissatisfied with public services than are whites.[10] Indeed, supporters of fragmentation have at times implied that consolidation could further undermine black control of services and their evaluations of them by diluting the emerging black voting strength in central cities resulting from white flight. With the addition of white suburban areas, services of consolidated governments would more likely be designed to meet white citizens' demands and, thus, risk increased dissatisfaction on the part of black citizens.[11]

Presentations of this argument, however, fail to document fully why blacks are more dissatisfied with services. Indeed, more recent studies, including the results presented in chapter 2, have not found racial differences in levels of service dissatisfaction when better-specified models have been employed,[12] nor have systematic social-class and racial biases been found in most of the research on actual service distribution patterns in central cities.[13] If true, suburbanization attendant with fragmentation may still generate greater inequity by leaving central city minorities and black suburbs with an inadequate tax base from which to finance services. Services within these cities may still be distributed equitably, but inequity in services across the metropolitan area could be exacerbated due to the separation of needs and resources.

The *third* argument plays off the previous two by suggesting that, if blacks and the poor do have access to suburbs (however segregated they might be), and if blacks are discriminated against in central cities, then black majority suburbs within the context of fragmentation offer certain efficiency and empowerment gains for poor and minority suburbanites. As Elinor Ostrom has summarized this position, "suburbs often enable poor families to receive higher services for lower costs and to participate with greater effect in local political life."[14] In effect, accepting racism as a regrettable constant, they argue that for minorities who can establish majority suburban enclaves, fragmentation offers comparative advantages—higher-*quality services*,[15] reduced *dissatisfaction*,[16] *reduced disaffection*,[17] and enhanced *participation*.[18] The notion of the sense of community being fostered by small-scale, grass-roots government has also been promoted by communitarians and neighborhood control advocates,[19] who argue that the government boundaries should be coterminous with each distinct social community. Indeed, this position has found strong support among some segments of the civil rights community as an alternative to integration to achieve black empowerment.[20]

Thus far our study of the Lexington and greater-Louisville communities has raised serious questions about the veracity of each of these propositions in regard to the general citizenry. But more to the point, very few studies have focused on the responses of black citizens to fragmentation or consolidation. Using aggregate data, Schneider and Logan found that despite systematically weaker tax bases, black suburbs tend to spend more than white suburbs.[21] If one is willing to assume that black citizens favor higher levels of spending, then this suggests that black suburbs provide better opportunities to implement black spending preferences than do central cities within which blacks are a minority. Unfortunately, this study made no comparisons between black central city and black suburban spending rates, which is the more important question. And Schneider has elsewhere found that suburban fragmentation depresses spending in general, suggesting that despite the expenditure difference between black and white suburbs, blacks may be no better off in terms of spending in suburbs than in central cities.[22]

Two other studies have made comparisons between suburban and central city minorities. Using survey data to compare responses to police services in a black suburb of Chicago and a matched black neighborhood in the central city, Ostrom and Whitaker found higher levels of efficacy, greater participation, and greater satisfaction in the former.[23] And in a study based on survey data from a large number of central cities and their suburbs, McDougall and Bunce note that the racial differences in satisfaction found in the central cities are replicated in the suburbs for most services, except that suburbanites, white or black, report higher satisfaction with education, police, and fire services.[24] Interestingly, the one exception in the replication of inner-city racial differences in the suburban responses was for police services, the focus of Ostrom and Whitaker's analysis, where McDougall and Bunce found a sharp improvement in satisfaction scores among suburban blacks. Both studies, because they compare survey responses of suburban and central city blacks, are used prominently to support the public choice assertion that fragmentation benefits blacks even if under the condition of suburban discrimination.

There are, however, reasons to view these findings as inadequate. First, as pointed out by McDougall and Bunce, police services, because of their coercive character and special concern to minorities, may be especially responsive to the purported benefits of fragmentation and, thus, these results may not generalize to all local services. Indeed, for some other services—most notably transportation and street services—suburban satisfaction rates were lower than those of central city respondents.[25] Given the potential exceptionalism of police services and the mixed results on the remaining services, these findings provide, at best, less than complete support for the public choice assertions. What is needed is some assessment of *overall efficacy, overall satisfaction, and overall participation rates* if we are to assess these claims fully.

Yet, even if they employed more comprehensive measures, these studies are largely inadequate in directly addressing the consolidation–fragmentation debate.[26] None of these studies compared truly consolidated government with fragmented systems, a problem that we discussed in chapter 2. They instead generally examine large and small cities within a single metropolitan setting. Thus, their findings apply more to judging the relative merits of large and small governments under fragmentation rather than to the merits of consolidation versus fragmentation.

Unfortunately, then, our question remains unanswered: are black citizens better off with public services provided via consolidated government (where blacks are in the minority) or when they control municipal government in a autonomous, suburban setting? We explore this question by investigating the following four hypotheses using the Lexington and Louisville study data: that blacks in predominantly black suburbs in a fragmented environment enjoy more and better services, evidence less dissatisfaction with services, are less disaffected, and participate more than blacks living within a consolidated government within which they are a minority.

Testing the Hypotheses

The Black Majority Research Sites and Measures

While numerous comparisons can be made between black and white communities within both the consolidated and fragmented settings, our primary focus will be on our two black communities. Our selection of these two research sites was largely predicated on the limited number of predominantly black cities in Jefferson County. Despite the noted trend of black suburbanization,[27] most of the incorporated municipalities in Jefferson County outside of the core City of Louisville had only a handful of black residents. Only three suburban cities had significant black populations at the time the surveys were completed in late 1986, and only Newburg, where 93 percent of our respondents were black, represented the kind of predominantly black city at issue.

Newburg was incorporated only a few years before our survey, and race played a key role in its founding. An interview with James Jones,[28] the former city clerk and treasurer, indicated that a group of residents sought incorporation as a wholly residential municipality following considerable discussion and an agreement with the nearby business community. In exchange for removing them from the incorporation petition, the businesses promised to help fund a library for the new city and provide jobs for its residents. As a result, Newburg was born as an entirely residential city.[29]

This outcome in itself is not unusual given the many wholly residential cities in Jefferson County, including all of our predominantly white research sites. But it was to be a source of continuing fiscal problems for Newburg. The residential petitioners were apparently willing to exclude the businesses and thereby limit the tax base exclusively to modest residential housing because they wanted to create a black city. Their pride in the claim that it would be the largest black suburban city east of the Mississippi led them to proceed despite the new city's inability to provide much in the way of independent services. After five years, however, harsh fiscal realities, including declining tax collections and a $30,000 legal fee resulting from the initial incorporation effort, resulted in Newburg's disincorporation in 1988.

At the time of our surveys, then, Newburg was midway through its existence. Thus, the responses of the citizens of Newburg are based on their recent experience of founding a new city. If anything, however, we expect the unique time frame to bias our results in favor of the public choice expectations. That is, this was a new city established in some controversy by its largely black residents. We would expect a honeymoon period to be operative in their evaluation of their new government, and for the experience of incorporation itself to heighten their levels of political participation and civic attachment. Perhaps an even better justification for our examination of Newburg is that it effectively constitutes the universe of black independent cities in the fragmented setting of Jefferson County. And both the excitement and difficulties of establishing a low- to moderate-income, residential city with a limited fiscal base, do not seem especially unique when compared to other efforts to establish predominantly black suburban cities.[30]

The Green Acres neighborhood was selected as our matched consolidated government site, and is a majority black community—88 percent of our respondents—somewhat removed from the center of Lexington. Before consolidation, Green Acres was located near the periphery of the old city of Lexington. Like Newburg, Green Acres is a newer subdivision adjacent to older, black, low-income neighborhoods in the central city. As such, both of these communities could be considered central city "spillover" suburbs.[31] There were no statistically significant differences between the two sites in age, education, income, racial makeup, occupation, homeownership, or numbers of children, as seen in Table 1.3.

Our hypotheses address questions of the number and quality of public services, satisfaction or dissatisfaction with public services, political disaffection, and political participation. As in the last chapter, our objective indicators of service provision will provide our indicator of the number and quality of public services. And for the three attitudinal dependent variables, we will again rely, respectively, on our CURRENT DISSATISFACTION, NEGLECT, and VOICE indicators.

Findings

The issue of numbers of services and differences in patterns of service delivery is addressed with data provided earlier in chapter 2 in Table 2.1, which outlines the service packages provided by the Urban County Government (UCG), in the case of Fayette County, and the Cities, County, and Sewer District in the Jefferson

County cases. The fifth neighborhoods/cities in the set are Green Acres and Newburg, the two predominantly black research sites. There are only small differences in the total number of services received by the two black communities. Green Acres, the consolidated government site, has one more service than does Newburg: trash collection. Otherwise, it appears that both sets of citizens receive the full range of services. Nor do the black communities, taken together, seem disadvantaged relative to the eight predominantly white sites. Green Acres is one of only two of the five consolidated research sites receiving the full eleven services. And similarly, Newburg was the fragmented government city receiving the highest level of service, with ten of the total eleven being provided by some government, whether city, county, or district. Thus, no sharp differences appear between the fragmented black community and its consolidated counterpart, nor was there overt discrimination against the two black communities in the form of reduced number of services.

The most striking result in Table 2.1, however, is the large number of services for Newburg residents provided by the county, rather than the municipality, in comparison to the predominantly white fragmented cities; only street lighting and road maintenance were city services in Newburg, only half the number of city services provided by the other Jefferson County cities. This result is not surprising from a public choice perspective. As can be seen on the municipal service row of the table, all the Jefferson County suburbs receive some county services, and each has a different array of service providers. This conforms to the ideal fragmented model in that a combination of services at different governmental levels is presumed to promote greater efficiency in service delivery.[32] In addition, county provision of many services may facilitate the incorporation of poorer areas like Newburg without having to provide the full range of services themselves, as occurred in the Lakewood Plan in Los Angeles County.[33]

This does not mean, however, that Newburg received the level of services desired by the community. With heavy reliance on the county, Newburg residents had little control over many local services. This is especially true for police services, which continued to be provided by Jefferson County. This is the one service, given the findings of McDougall and Bunce, and Ostrom and Whitaker,[34] for which we would expect incorporation as an independent black city to produce the most dramatic improvement in citizen evaluations. Yet, the weak fiscal base of Newburg did not allow it to accrue this advantage. And more generally, it seems unlikely that all county services are equally substitutable for city provision. That the four majority white cities in Jefferson County established some level of municipal police service when the option of continued county service was equally available to them, for example, suggests that city provision provides enhanced policing. Yet Newburg, with its limited tax base, lacked the same opportunity to secure this higher level of service.

In contrast, the black neighborhood of Green Acres was one of the two full-service districts of the five Lexington–Fayette County sites. Barring discriminatory provision of such services, for which we have noted the literature has found little supporting evidence, this suggests that minority neighborhoods in the consolidated government had full access to the highest level of services. In sum, while reliance on multiple service providers in a fragmented setting does allow poor, predominantly black suburbs to provide some level of access across most of the service universe examined here, fragmentation can produce inequities. By segregating tax bases, fragmentation creates differential opportunities to substitute city for county services, an outcome that produces inequity when such substitution implies enhanced service levels.

Given these service patterns, are there differences across the two sets of communities in CURRENT DISSATISFACTION, disaffection (NEGLECT), and political participation (VOICE)? In exploring these issues, we need to make two sets of comparisons. First, we must compare the two predominantly black communities of Green Acres and Newburg directly on these variables. This comparison is provided in Table 7.1, which reports the mean levels of each community on these three variables and presents tests of the differences of these means. As seen in the first set of results in the table, and contrary to public choice expectations, the fragmented site of Newburg produced a substantially higher mean DISSATISFACTION score (4.22) than did the matched consolidated-government neighborhood of Green Acres (2.60), a difference that was significant at the 0.01 level.

While dissatisfaction provides one basis for comparing the jurisdictions, the more general phenomenon of political disaffection from local government provides perhaps a broader frame for comparison. While recent research suggests that an underlying source of higher service dissatisfaction, especially for blacks, is community disaffection,[35] the two may not be necessarily linked for residents of smaller, black-controlled governments. While their services may not be viewed favorably, it is reasonable to think that they still may find the smaller government to be more responsive. Yet, as seen in the second set of results presented in Table 7.1, this is not the case; Newburg residents reported higher levels of disaffection or NEGLECT (5.12) than those of Green Acres (4.68), the consolidated-government case. The direction of this difference, which is significant at the 0.05 level, again runs counter to the claims of supporters of fragmented government.

Poor government performance and disaffection may spur citizens to action to remedy problems. If so, we would expect to find higher levels of political participation in Newburg than in Green Acres. Moreover, Newburg was a newly incorporated community, which implies that more than a few citizens must have been involved in its founding. And, of course, the public choice approach would lead us to expect higher levels of participation in the Newburg setting, because its citizens reside in a small, homogeneous jurisdiction, which presumably enhances both the motivation and opportunity to participate more frequently in municipal affairs. Yet none of these expectations is met, as seen in the last set of results in

Table 7.1

Dissatisfaction, Disaffection, and Political Participation Difference-of-Means Tests across Alternative Institutional Arrangements—Green Acres and Newburg

Consolidated/fragmented government matched sets	Mean	Standard deviation	n	Difference of means	t-value
		CURRENT DISSATISFACTION			
LEX: Green Acres	2.60	(1.28)	199		
LOU: Newburg	4.22	(1.62)	139	−1.62***	−9.86
		NEGLECT			
LEX: Green Acres	4.68	(1.51)	188		
LOU: Newburg	5.12	(1.86)	131	−0.44**	−2.28
		VOICE			
LEX: Green Acres	2.45	(1.83)	206		
LOU: Newburg	2.49	(1.93)	163	−0.04	0.20

* = $p < 0.10$; ** = $p < 0.05$; *** = $p < 0.01$.

Table 7.1. While Newburg did evidence slightly higher levels of political participation in the form of VOICE behaviors (2.49–2.45 for Green Acres), the difference between them produced a tiny t-value of only 0.20, a result that is especially striking given all the reasons to expect higher levels of political participation in the fragmented-government setting.

Comparisons of the two black communities only constitute the first means of assessing racial inequality associated with metropolitan institutional structure. Importantly, the absolute differences we have observed between black consolidated and fragmented respondents may tell us only part of the story. It also is possible that the relative positions of black vis-à-vis white respondents is improved under fragmentation. Thus, our second approach focuses on the differences across the consolidated and fragmented settings between the predominantly black and white research sites on our dependent variables.

As a first step in a two-stage approach to assessing such relative differences, Table 7.2 compares the two black communities to their white, generally more advantaged, neighbors. The first, third, and fifth columns report mean levels of CURRENT DISSATISFACTION, disaffection (NEGLECT), and participation (VOICE) in the same manner as in Table 7.1, but for the four largely white communities in the two institutional settings. The second, fourth, and sixth columns report the difference between those scores and those of the respective

Table 7.2

Dissatisfaction, Disaffection, Participation Difference-of-Means Tests for Neighborhoods/Cities within Alternative Institutional Arrangements

Predominantly white neighbor- hoods/cities	Mean CURRENT DISSATISFACTION		Mean NEGLECT		Mean VOICE	
	White comm.	Difference	White comm.	Difference	White comm.	Difference
	Lexington–Fayette Consolidated Sites					
Blueberry	2.53 (0.99)[a] 210[c]	−0.07 [−0.62][b]	4.10 (1.49) 204	−0.58*** [−3.82]	2.30 (1.86) 217	−0.15 [−0.84]
Chinoe	2.00 (1.09) 220	−0.60*** [−5.17]	3.60 (1.57) 200	−1.08*** [−6.91]	2.44 (1.89) 218	−0.01 [−0.06]
Stonewall	2.43 (1.08) 247	−0.18 [−1.57]	3.72 (1.39) 235	−0.93*** [−6.52]	3.55 (1.63) 252	1.01*** [6.72]
Crestwood/ Shadeland	2.14 (1.08) 242	−0.47*** [−4.09]	3.84 (1.49) 228	−0.84*** [−5.68]	3.14 (1.73) 248	0.69*** [4.10]
	Louisville–Jefferson Fragmented Sites					
Minor Lane Heights	2.78 (1.25) 153	−1.44*** [−8.45]	4.46 (1.95) 131	−0.66*** [−2.80]	4.46 (1.95) 155	1.97*** [9.05]
Beechwood Village	1.29 (1.15) 185	−2.94*** [−18.26]	3.15 (1.75) 172	−1.97*** [−9.37]	3.15 (1.75) 155	0.66*** [3.20]
Barbourmeade	3.76 (1.54) 169	−0.46** [−2.54]	4.08 (1.61) 155	−1.04*** [−5.01]	4.08 (1.61) 173	1.59*** [8.17]
Windy Hills	1.79 (1.35) 167	−2.43*** [−14.11]	3.78 (1.49) 146	−1.34*** [−6.57]	3.78 (1.49) 176	1.29*** [6.85]

* = $p < 0.10$; ** = $p < 0.05$; *** = $p < 0.01$.
[a]The figures in parentheses are standard deviations.
[b]The figures in brackets are t-values.
[c]The figures in italics are number of cases.

black communities as reported in Table 7.1. Importantly, significant differences in means would be expected here since we are now comparing across socioeconomic classes and service districts, and therefore are not controlling for the influence of these factors on the three variables of interest. The key to analyzing the table is to see if there are any differences in patterns across the differences in the two research sites.

As can be seen by the uniformly negative signs of the differences reported in the second column of Table 7.2, the two black communities consistently evidence higher levels of DISSATISFACTION than their four respective white neighboring sites. This, of course, is what previous research would lead us to expect. But the differences in the levels of DISSATISFACTION among black and white sites is much greater in the Jefferson County comparisons. All four of the Jefferson County differences are significant at the 0.05 level or better, and all are considerably larger than their counterpart Lexington–Fayette County difference-of-means values. Indeed, two of the four differences in the consolidated-government case are not significant at even the 0.10 level.

In the same manner, the results in the fourth column of Table 7.2 compare reported disaffection (NEGLECT) in the two black communities to that of their respective white counterparts. The differences were statistically significant in all of the comparisons, with the black sites uniformly more disaffected. More importantly, the differences are modestly greater in the Jefferson County setting.

The last column of Table 7.2 compares the two black neighborhoods to their white, generally more economically advantaged, counterparts on levels of political participation, or VOICE. The magnitudes of the differences in levels of participation are substantially greater in the four Jefferson County comparisons than in those of the consolidated-government setting. And the differences are not statistically significant in two of the Lexington–Fayette County comparisons— the two where Green Acres respondents actually showed somewhat higher levels of participation then their predominantly white neighbors. In all of the Jefferson County contrasts, Newburg had lower levels of participation than its neighbors and these differences were highly significant.

In sum, differences between black and white respondents in dissatisfaction, disaffection, and participation are smaller in the consolidated than in the fragmented setting. But the results in Table 7.2 only suggest this because they are somewhat clouded by expected differences due to comparing across quite different socioeconomic settings. We can make the comparisons sharper by examining the *difference of differences* tests presented in Table 7.3, which control for these underlying socioeconomic relationships.

The findings in Table 7.3 indicate that fragmentation heightens the relative differences between blacks and whites, the exact opposite of what is generally suggested by proponents of the public choice approach. The signs of the differences indicate that the differences between blacks and whites on DISSATISFACTION and disaffection (NEGLECT) are greater in the fragmented-

Table 7.3

Dissatisfaction, Disaffection, Participation Difference between Consolidated and Fragmented Black Communities' Differences from Corresponding White Communities

Matched predominantly white neighborhoods/cities	Difference mean CURRENT DISSATISFACTION	Difference mean NEGLECT	Difference mean VOICE
LEX: Blueberry and	1.37***	0.08	−2.12***
LOU: Minor Lane Heights	(7.06)[a]	(0.29)	(−7.49)
LEX: Chinoe and	2.34***	0.89***	−0.67**
LOU: Beechwood Village	(11.71)	(3.39)	(−2.44)
LEX: Stonewall and	0.28	0.11	−0.49*
LOU: Barbourmeade	(1.30)	(0.44)	(−1.92)
LEX: Crestwood/Shadeland and	1.96***	0.50**	−0.60**
LOU: Windy Hills	(9.44)	(1.98)	(−2.37)

* $= p < 0.10$; ** $= p < 0.05$; *** $= p < 0.01$.
[a]The figures in parentheses are t-values.

government comparisons. And three of the DISSATISFACTION differences are highly significant, while only two of the disaffection (NEGLECT) differences were statistically discernible. Most interestingly, despite the fact that we found no sharp absolute differences in participation across the two black communities, the uniformly negative and significant differences in the last column of Table 7.3 indicate that the difference between black and white participation rates in use of VOICE behaviors is far greater in the fragmented-government settings than in the consolidated-government settings.

Summary and Caveats

In both absolute and relative terms, then, blacks fared worse in Newburg than in Green Acres, our neighborhood in the consolidated setting, both in objective numbers of services and the more subjective perceptions of services and government. Our concern, however, was not with the specific cases of Newburg and Green Acres, but how these cases shed light on the larger question of the role of metropolitan institutional structure in reducing or fostering racial inequity. To what extent can these results be used to comment on this larger issue? For several reasons, we need to be cautious in generalizing from these results.

First, our cases are selected from a border state, where racial discrimination in both consolidated and fragmented governments might be expected to be operative. If this analysis were conducted in another state in another region, different results might obtain. But while we cannot present firm evidence on this issue, we suspect that Kentucky is not all that unusual. Indeed, as noted in the Long quote presented at the beginning of this chapter, metropolitan fragmentation is usually viewed as the North's tool of racial segregation given the extensive use of formal governmental consolidation and/or annexation by the major cities of the Sun Belt.

Second, our results say little about the quality of specific services under consolidated or fragmented governmental structures. As we have noted, it is quite reasonable to expect that police services, for example, might be more efficiently and responsively provided by city governments under a fragmented institutional arrangement. Therefore, just as one cannot infer that overall service satisfaction is higher under conditions of fragmentation from evidence on just police services, we cannot make valid inferences from our general results to individual services. Our results apply only at the level of general dissatisfaction, disaffection, and participation. Related to this, the conclusions of this study rely on two major data sources—numbers of services provided in the respective jurisdictions and the perceptions and attitudes of citizens. Since we have not attempted to measure directly the objective quality of services delivered in the two types of governments, we cannot make firm evaluations about service efficiency, effectiveness, or overall quality, although some proxies of these variables were developed in chapter 2 and we addressed the issue of service quality more deeply in the previous chapter.

And third, our majority black sites were purposively selected. In the Newburg case, we were highly constrained by the limited universe of predominantly black cities in Jefferson County in selecting our research site. And our comparison group design then constrained us to select Green Acres as our consolidated-government research site. While many public choice scholars have shown little reticence in drawing wide-ranging conclusions from such limited comparisons,[36] it is possible that Lexington–Fayette County may be an unusually successful case of consolidation, although we see no reason to believe so. Or, more likely, Newburg may have been an unusually dismal experiment in fragmented government. But was it unexpectedly dismal? We believe that while somewhat unusual in the brevity of its life-span and the degree of problems it faced, Newburg was not unrepresentative of the experience of suburbs populated by economically disadvantaged minorities within the kinds of fragmented systems proposed by proponents of the public choice model. Whether these Kentucky suburban areas are representative of those in other, larger metropolitan areas is not clear, although Newburg and Green Acres appear to have many characteristics in common with cases and types of black suburbs previously discussed in the literature.[37]

Rather than dismissing problems of segregation and racial inequality as issues that are at best only indirectly related to the structure of metropolitan government, as Ostrom does,[38] we believe that Newburg's problems illustrate the direct role of fragmentation in perpetuating inequality. As we have noted, very few of the suburbs in Jefferson County have sizable black populations. This is not an accident. Even without recourse to illegal forms of housing discrimination, fragmentation provides the largely white suburbs the necessary tools of zoning restrictions and land-use controls to enforce de facto economic segregation.[39] Indeed, many observers have concluded that the suburban enclaves of fragmented metropolitan areas exhibit a "politics of exclusion."[40] To these analysts, such de facto segregation is not a separate problem, but one that is vitally and inherently dependent for its means of enforcement on the fragmentation of governmental power.

Given the reality of substantial housing segregation on economic and/or racial criteria, Newburg then illustrates the limited range of options for economically disadvantaged minorities. Their two major options are to live in the core city of the metropolitan area or to live in an unincorporated area in the county. The third option found in Elinor Ostrom's hope that racial discrimination will be overcome by offering minorities the same benefits flowing from small, localized government now available to whites is quite limited.[41] In this regard, the fact that Newburg was the only predominantly black city of Jefferson County and one of only three with sizable minority populations may be as telling a claim against the public choice model as its specific history. Such areas lack the tax base to take advantage of Ostrom's option. Thus, the ultimate failure of Newburg fully illustrates the difficulties minority low-income residents have in establishing municipalities in a fragmented setting. And its failure suggests that blacks may become ghettoized in the suburbs, locked in unincorporated areas in which they receive few municipal-type services, continuing to be a small minority within a mainly white suburban area, and yet unable to form their own governments. Nor are they likely to be seen as an annexation prospect by any of the cities around them, including Louisville, given their weak tax base and high service needs.

Proponents of fragmentation might finally argue that if such problems are real, fragmentation allows for higher levels of metropolitan government such as Councils of Governments (COGs) to address such metropolitan wide issues.[42] But because of fragmentation, COGs generally employ a constituent-unit form of representation. As a result, COGs have proven largely incapable of overcoming the veto power of wealthier, predominantly white suburbs in addressing issues of redistribution.[43] It is hardly surprising, therefore, that Minneapolis–St. Paul's tax-base-sharing experiment remains unemulated after nearly two decades. Again, the empowerment of localities within the metropolitan area that is the hallmark of fragmentation effectively precludes this "fragmented" response to racial disparities.

In sum, if fragmentation provides white middle- and upper-class-dominated local governments the tools to exclude lower-income minorities, creates constituent-unit vetoes on COG efforts to redistribute resources across cities, and thereby undermines prospects of building independent, lower-income, predominantly minority cities on a viable tax base,[44] minorities will be penalized in reaching the threshold level of organization needed to secure the purported benefits of fragmentation. Thus, simply establishing a quasi-market of local public services cannot in and of itself overcome inequities in the provision of public services, and, indeed, may institutionalize the kinds of difficulties encountered by the citizens of Newburg. In contrast, the Green Acres results suggest that consolidated governments can lead to less absolute and relative dissatisfaction and disaffection, and greater relative participation on the part of minority citizens.

Notes

1. Long (1967, p. 254).
2. Hill (1974).
3. Danielson (1976); Hamilton, Mills, and Puryear (1975); and Mills and Oates (1975a).
4. Neiman (1976); E. Ostrom (1983).
5. Logan and Schneider (1982).
6. Farley (1970); Connolly (1970); Guest (1978); and Rose (1976).
7. Logan and Schneider (e.g., 1982) systematically excluded all SMSAs with fewer than ten suburban political jurisdictions. And E. Ostrom and Whitaker's analysis (1974) implies that any consolidated government's services would mirror those of downtown Chicago in 1970, ignoring the implications of fragmenting Cook County into hundreds of jurisdictions and the unique character of Mayor Daley's police services.
8. Lake (1981, p. 51).
9. Rose (1976).
10. Aberbach and Walker (1970); Schuman and Gruenberg (1972); Durand (1976); Brown and Coulter (1983); and McDougall and Bunce (1986).
11. Zimmerman (1970).
12. Beck, Rainey, Nicholls, and Traut (1987).
13. Lineberry (1977); Boyle and Jacobs (1982); Cingranelli (1981); Jones et al. (1978); Mladenka and Hill (1977); B. Jones (1980); and Mladenka (1981).
14. E. Ostrom (1983, p. 92).
15. V. Ostrom, Bish, and Ostrom (1988).
16. Bish and Ostrom (1973, p. 27).
17. V. Ostrom, Bish, and Ostrom (1988, pp. 80–81).
18. V. Ostrom, Bish, and Ostrom (1988, pp. 92–93).
19. Elkin (1987); Kotler (1969); and Barber (1984).
20. Goel, Lovett, Patten, and Wilkens (1988).
21. Schneider and Logan (1982b).
22. Schneider (1989).
23. E. Ostrom and Whitaker (1974).
24. McDougall and Bunce (1986).
25. McDougall and Bunce (1986, p. 601).
26. Logan and Schneider (1982) also challenged the belief in income segregation in suburbs by finding substantial income diversity in suburbia. Although this finding has been used frequently (e.g., E. Ostrom, 1983, pp. 96–98) to dispute the view of suburbanization as an instrument of segregation, the authors also found that income segregation increased as the proportion of the black population of metropolitan areas increased.
27. Clark (1979); and Farley (1970); and Lake (1981).

28. Telephone interview with Mr. Jones, Newburg City Clerk and Treasurer, by W. E. Lyons.

29. There had been two competing incorporation petitions in the works at the time Newburg was created. The one filed by local business owners sought to create a city to be named Newburg encompassing only the business district. The other, filed by the residents of the predominantly black area outside the City of Louisville, sought to incorporate both the residential and business areas into a city to be named Petersburg, after they were told that the name of Newburg had already been used in another petition. Following considerable discussion, a compromise was reached in which the business owners' petition was withdrawn in exchange for removing the business district from the residents' petition. In addition, the residents got to use the name Newburg.

30. Goel, Lovett, Patten, and Wilkins (1988).

31. Lake (1981).

32. Parks and Oakerson (1989).

33. Miller (1981).

34. McDougall and Bunce (1986); and E. Ostrom and Whitaker (1974).

35. Beck, Rainey, Nicholls, and Traut (1987).

36. Rogers and Lipsey (1974).

37. For example, Goel et al., (1988); Lake (1981); and Rose (1976).

38. E. Ostrom (1983, p. 107).

39. Clark (1979); Danielson (1976); Hamilton, Mills, and Puryear (1975); and Mills and Oates (1975a).

40. Harrigan (1989, pp. 284–302); and Fainstein and Fainstein (1980, p. 259).

41. E. Ostrom (1983, p. 92).

42. Advisory Commission on Intergovernmental Relations (1987, pp. 43–47).

43. Harrigan (1989, pp. 345–47).

44. Danielson (1976); Hill (1974); Hamilton, Mills, and Puryear (1975); and Mills and Oates (1975a).

8

Citizenship in the Metropolis

In the last chapter, we saw that minority communities are better served by consolidated rather than fragmented government. This conclusion, in combination with our findings in chapter 6 that institutions influence citizens' evaluations of public service and, therefore, their satisfaction with urban governance, provides us a strong basis for arguing that the fragmented or consolidated structure of local government influences urban political behavior as responses to dissatisfaction. For, as we saw in the test of the EVLN model in chapter 4, satisfaction—or rather, CURRENT DISSATISFACTION as represented in RELATIVE DISSATISFACTION—is our most consistent and stable predictor of EXIT, VOICE, LOYALTY, and NEGLECT behaviors. But do metropolitan institutions matter in any other way? We believe that they do, and that the character of that influence strikes to the heart of the nature of citizenship in the urban community.

In "The City and the Future of Democracy," Robert Dahl discusses the appropriate locus of democratic citizenship as a problem of Chinese boxes, showing that any unit thought to have special legitimacy is but one box nested in others of equal legitimacy. Dahl then concludes that "there is not necessarily a single kind of unit, whether it be the city-state or the nation-state, in which majorities have some specially sacred quality."[1] But in the end, Dahl, like Tocqueville, identifies the city as the primary locus of democratic citizenship. Because cities provide for direct participation on issues of vital concern to citizens, and thereby offer numerous opportunities for "educating citizens in civic virtue,"[2] cities are the most important box in an interlocking arrangement of democratic boxes. Yet, there is substantial disagreement about the meaning of such primacy, with two questions standing out. *First*, just what does urban citizenship entail? And *second*, if we can forge some agreement over the meaning of citizenship, how shall the Chinese boxes of the city be constituted to best promote it?

Two Interpretations of Urban Citizenship

The *liberal* and *communitarian* interpretations of citizenship, as seen at the top of Table 8.1, offer sharply different answers to the first question, a divergence that inheres in their respective understandings of the foundations of the civic community and its relation to the social community. Citizenship in the liberal tradition is founded on individual and property rights which enable citizens to address problems of interdependence via exchange.[3] Thus, citizenship entails contracting to establish a civil entity both to provide agreed-upon public goods and services and to enforce the contractual arrangement.[4] Given the prior status of rights and the contingent nature of the contract, liberals insist upon a sharp delineation of public and private spheres, with the latter having priority.[5] Accordingly, citizenship does not require active participation, although citizens must be alert to potential infringements of their rights via close monitoring of the representative process.

Communitarians reject this "thin" conception of citizenship, as Benjamin Barber terms it.[6] Instead, they start with the Greek understanding of citizenship as "the prideful participation of the free citizen in a community whose life is fashioned to achieve the ethical self-realization of its citizens."[7] Democratic citizenship, they claim, must be more "thickly" rooted in empathy, affect, and common struggle over common problems.[8] Thus, they argue that there can be no independent constitution of the social and political communities. As Barber notes, "to be a citizen *is* to participate in a certain conscious fashion that presumes awareness of and engagement in activity with others . . . . Indeed, from the perspective of strong democracy, the two terms *participation* and *community* are aspects of a single mode of social being: citizenship."[9] Participation both defines and is the product of community.

Surprisingly, these very different views are sometimes used to promote similar answers to our second question of how to promote urban citizenship. The liberal understanding of citizenship has been related to a host of institutional forms, usually those associated with representative democracy. But the set of local institutional analyses most conducive to liberalism's aims is the *public choice literature on local government structure* that we have been examining.[10] By contrast, the communitarian alternative seems to fit best with the set of institutional analyses found in the *neighborhood movement literature* of the 1960s and early 1970s.[11] Yet, both of these sets of institutional analyses reject the city of the progressives and argue that the consolidation, professionalization, and centralization of the reformed city undermines meaningful citizenship by substituting managerial governance for popular control.[12] Moreover, they also often agree on the alternative to the reformed city.[13]

The liberal view of citizenship, as noted above, is flexible in terms of the kinds of institutional reforms with which it may be compatible. Even to public choice scholars, those ascribing to the most extreme liberal interpretation of citizenship, there is no one best institutional arrangement. There should be as many different boxes for as many scales of problems facing a community. But in such complex arrangements, there are inevitably variations in the degree of democratic control. That is, one could arrange the boxes so that the citizen

Table 8.1

Summary of Conceptual, Behavioral, and Structural Implications of Liberal and Communitarian Notions of Citizenship as Applied to Metropolitan Governance

Major theoretical conceptions of citizenship	Liberal		Communitarian	
Basic conception of citizenship	Rooted in social contract theory viewing government as a contractual entity to provide goods and services and to enforce terms of contract.		Rooted in Greek conception of prideful participation in community to achieve self-realization.	
	Stresses notion of individual and property rights.		Stresses notions of empathy, affect, and common good.	
Variations on the themes	Watchdog Liberalism	Virtuous Liberalism	Strong Demo Communitarian	Representative Communitarian
Preferred behavior in problem solving	EXIT	LOYALTY	VOICE	VOICE
Secondary behaviors in problem solving	VOICE to make exit credible.	EXIT as a last resort. VOICE has a positive role but not essential.	—	LOYALTY is expected when voice is not feasible.
Undesirable behaviors in problem solving	LOYALTY NEGLECT	NEGLECT	EXIT LOYALTY NEGLECT	EXIT NEGLECT
Metropolitan structural/ institutional impications	Classic Tiebout model	A range of institutions from fragmented to metropolitan justifiable depending on their efficiency in service provision.	Classic Neighborhood Government model	2 Competing Scenarios: Metropolitan Federation with strong emphasis on neighborhood empowerment or Metro Government to create Metro Communiatrian Citizens.

exercises direct democratic control over the largest-scale government and only indirect control over the subordinate units addressing smaller-scale problems, as is done in consolidated governments. Or, the boxes can be arranged so that direct democratic control is exercised at the lowest scale, and broader-scale issues are addressed by "Councils of Governments" or "special districts" over which the citizen generally exercises less direct control.[14] In their consistent preference for the latter,[15] it is clear that public choice scholars view the basic unit of democratic control to be the independent towns found in governmentally fragmented metropolitan areas.

While some view such fragmentation as troubling,[16] and most eschew the language of balkanization, most communitarians nevertheless propose essentially the same alternative in their extensive reliance on the institutional recommendations of the neighborhood movement literature. To communitarians, the empowered neighborhood—of five to twenty-five thousand citizens[17]—is the ideal vehicle for developing citizenship. What makes these proposals similar in effect is the communitarians' insistence that neighborhood assemblies must be more than debating societies: they must be given genuine authority and responsibility.[18] Such empowerment is expected to engender the strong democracy of amateur government and direct communal self-help,[19] the very preferences of public choice liberals.[20] *Such empowerment, at least implicitly, would have the same fragmenting effect as in the public choice alternative in that the metropolitan area would now consist of many separate units of governance, each with considerable independence.* Indeed, one neighborhood movement analyst has gone so far as to suggest that their goal is "the shifting of the suburban model of community resources to the inner city."[21] In short, despite profound differences in their underlying interpretations of citizenship, neighborhood movement communitarians and public choice liberals share at least an implicit preference for the highly fragmented metropolis made up of largely independent empowered localities.

We believe, however, that both the public choice liberal and neighborhood movement communitarian perspectives on the relationship between urban institutions and citizenship may be wrong, that the rejected alternative of the reformed city promotes both conceptions of citizenship far better than the empowered locality. In the next section of this chapter, we develop this argument by specifying the behavioral implications of the two views of citizenship and linking those behaviors to urban institutions. In the following section, we outline a metropolitanist critique of citizenship in empowered localities. Finally, we test several of the propositions.

Citizenship and Institutions in the Metropolis

Before we can consider the metropolitanist case for citizenship in the reformed city, we need to specify better the arguments of those advocating the empowerment of localities. We do so in two steps, using the Exit, Voice, Loyalty, Neglect model (EVLN) outlined in chapter 3.

Modes of Problem Solving and Citizenship

Given that we cannot directly observe the affective content of behavior, how can we determine if institutions influence the exercise of citizenship? To communitarians, the answer lies in examining patterns of reliance on different "modes of social problem solving."[22] This focus should be equally appropriate from a public choice perspective, for how interdependent individuals resolve competing needs is what distinguishes liberal government from anarchy and the leviathan. The EVLN model provides such a typology. Recall that the model consists of four types of responses, arrayed on both active-passive and constructive-destructive dimensions, that individuals can invoke when facing a problem. Thus, *exit* is an active-destructive approach to problems in that it involves an explicit severing of the relationship between city and citizen; the most characteristic expression of exit is, of course, the Tiebout response of voting with one's feet. *Voice*, including most of the behaviors usually studied under the rubric of participation, is active and constructive effort to improve conditions that give rise to dissatisfaction. *Loyalty* involves passively, but constructively, responding to problems by optimistically waiting for conditions to improve, and includes many of the less active regime-supportive attitudes and behaviors studied in the standard participation literature. Or, as we have seen in our reinterpretation of the EVLN in chapter 4, *loyalty* can be the response of the satisfied citizen in the form of ritual support for the regime. Finally, *neglect* is a passive–destructive response to problems by withdrawal into disaffection, alienation, cynicism, and distrust.

How would liberals and communitarians interpret effective citizenship in terms of these four modes of problem solving? Our answers to this question are less clear than they might be because neither view is articulated in a single voice. Indeed, the extensive literatures on liberalism and communitarianism offer any number of fine distinctions between their respective sects, subschools, and factions. More to the point, although our interest is in the public choice institutional recommendations as one example of the promotion of a liberal conception of citizenship, the public choice reforms certainly do not exhaust the structural implications of liberal political thought. And although there is a somewhat greater correspondence between the institutional recommendations of the neighborhood movement literature and the communitarian understanding of citizenship, that correspondence is not complete. Therefore, we need to consider at least two interpretations of each view of citizenship.

The first, as seen in the second section of Table 8.1, which we denote as *Watchdog Liberalism*, is based on the most extreme public choice interpretation of citizenship, and one that has been most vigorously pilloried by communitarians. In this view, citizenship is defined by a contractual arrangement to establish a government and/or to provide a particular collective good or service.[23] When contract problems arise, as seen in the third section of Table 8.1, two modes of problem-solving response would be appropriate. Initially, *voice* behaviors might be used to call the parties to the requirements or terms of the contract. But if the problem is not resolved, the appropriate mode of response for the effective citizen is to sever the contract or *exit* the relationship. Indeed, voice behaviors are considered effective only if enforced by the threat of exit. In the urban political behavior literature, this is best represented by the Tiebout exiting hypothesis, which posits a quasi-market of jurisdictions from among which the citizen votes with his or her feet to select the preferred package of taxes and expenditures, and stands ready to move again.[24]

What of the other modes of problems solving? *Neglect* has two distinct meanings to Watchdog Liberalism. In the Whig tradition of Buchanan's liberalism,[25] neglect as distrust and alienation is an admirable orientation toward government, even when it is adhering to its contractual obligations, if only because the state is ever poised to trample individual rights. But our concern is with neglect as a passive-destructive problem-solving behavior. As a response to dissatisfaction, neglect clearly represents a failure of citizenship; it would mean that leviathan government had redefined the terms of the contract while leaving the citizen with no recourse but disaffection and alienation. More interestingly, under this strict interpretation of liberal citizenship there is little room for the problem-solving activity of *loyalty*—passively, but optimistically, waiting for conditions to improve. Political loyalty would be analogous to brand loyalty in private consumption in that it disrupts efficient operation of the market.

In this view, then, effective problem solving for the citizen is limited to contract management through exit or the threat of exit; nothing more is required of citizenship than eternal vigilance to ensure that all parties adhere to the contract. To communitarians, this is dreadful. As Barber notes, "When the citizenry is a watchdog that waits with millennial patience for its government to make a false move but that submits passively to all other legitimate governmental activity, citizenship [as communitarians interpret it] very quickly deteriorates into a latent function."[26] To Watchdog Liberals, however, this is the only meaningful form of citizenship behavior open, given the leviathan's omnipresent threat to individual rights.

While communitarians have (with some justification) explored the limits of this conception of citizenship,[27] Watchdog Liberalism is really something of a strawman. Recognizing the large transaction and information costs of exiting,[28] public choice proponents have slowly stepped back from exclusive reliance on the Tiebout model. And they have relied more heavily on a rich, older understanding of the public virtues of a liberal regime that allows for a broader range of appropriate problem-solving behaviors.[29]

Liberal theorist William Galston argues that under *Virtuous Liberalism*, as we call our second type of citizenship, the citizen must do more than simply respect others' rights and obey the law as required in Buchanan's contractual view.[30] To Galston,[31] he or she must be truly tolerant of fellow citizens, and, in regard to society, the virtuous citizen must exhibit loyalty—"The developed capacity to understand, to accept, and to act on the core principals of one's society." In relation to one's government, the virtuous liberal citizen is "moderate in demands and self-disciplined enough to accept painful measures." Just as importantly, citizens cannot be detached from public life, even if they have no duty to participate actively in governmental affairs. "Because liberalism incorporates representative government, the liberal citizen must have the capacity to discern the talent and character of candidates vying for office, and to evaluate the performance of individuals who have attained office." Liberal leaders must possess certain virtues as well, including "the capacity to forge a sense of common purposes against the centrifugal tendencies of an individualistic and fragmented society." Thus, while still adhering to the dichotomy of public and private life, advocates of virtuous liberalism argue that the liberal tradition embodies civic virtues that go far beyond Buchanan's watchdog citizenship.

As seen in the third section of Table 8.1, this view of liberalism legitimates a broader behavioral definition of citizenship. Assuming that leaders are virtuous and merit popular trust, *loyalty*—passively, but optimistically, waiting for citizens and their government to solve problems or ritually supporting the regime when satisfied—becomes a valid and valued response to problems by virtue of its resonance with the liberal virtues of temperance, tolerance, and patience. Indeed, if exit is a costly, if still ultimate sanction, loyalty becomes the most highly prized form of problem-solving behavior. *Voice* also becomes more important. It is no longer simply a preliminary to exit, as seen in the increased intrinsic importance assigned to participation in the recent public choice literature.[32] Still, there is no special emphasis on the exercise of voice as the defining behavior of citizens. As Galston notes, "In a liberal polity there is no duty to participate actively in politics, no requirement to place the public above the private."[33] Virtuous Liberalism, then, would downplay, though not dismiss, exit, and it would recognize voice as a legitimate form of citizenship behavior. But it is loyalty that is given a special place among the characteristic behaviors of effective citizens.

What of the communitarian interpretation? The position of Barber and Elkin, which we will denote as *Strong Democracy Communitarianism*, is very clear: only broad and deep political participation—*voice* behaviors—constitute effective democratic citizenship. For Barber, "the strong democratic solution to the political condition issues out of a self-sustaining dialectic of participatory civic activity and continuous community-building in which freedom and equality are nourished and given political being. Community grows out of participation and at the same time makes participation possible."[34] And for Elkin, democratic citizenship can only develop when citizens engage in active struggle and debate.[35] In the absence of such constructive problem solving, Strong Democracy Communitarians argue, citizens can neither constitute a true community nor integrate their social, economic, and personal lives into an encompassing political existence.

To Strong Democracy Communitarians, as seen in the third section of Table 8.1, neither of the passive forms of problem solving constitutes effective citizenship. Indeed, they would draw little distinction between *loyalty* and *neglect*. Both are evidence of an atrophying of citizenship. Even more ineffective is *exit*. If one is embedded in a social community and the civil and social communities are mutually defined through active participation in problem solving, then exit from the civil community is tantamount to abandoning one's social community. Exit would not be severing a limited contractual relationship, but destruction of the social fabric.

While the "strong democracy" understanding of communitarianism dominates the communitarian literature to the exclusion of almost all else, we think it reasonable to recognize another form of communitarianism, one that moderates Strong Democracy's exclusive emphasis on participation as evidence of meaningful citizenship. The starting point for this account of citizenship is the realization that there are very real practical limitations on participation in even the most democratic of settings.[36] Under the institutional reforms of Elkin and Barber, it would simply be impossible for all citizens to participate actively on all issues at all times, and they admit that some elements of representative democracy, however undesirable, will of necessity survive in the communitarian polity.

Until recently, however, communitarians have not given much attention to the democratic foundations of representation. But in *The Blue Guitar: Political Representation and the Community*, Nancy Schwartz has developed a controversial communitarian justification for representation.[37] She starts by arguing that realistic communitarianism must accommodate larger-sized communities given the need for sufficient social diversity in establishing meaningful frames of citizenship, a point that will become important later. This fourth view, then, can be identified as *Representative Communitarianism*.

What are the implications of at least some compromises in strong democracy communitarianism's commitment to complete and constant participation? Most importantly, and as seen in the third section of Table 8.1, *loyalty* must play at least a small, supplemental role in the Representative Communitarian's approach to problem solving. An individual must participate actively on some, and hopefully many, issues to be a fully engaged citizen. But on those issues where direct participation is not possible or is mediated through the selection of representatives, loyalty will be a valid indicator of citizenship. But while passive in comparison to voice, the loyalty of Representative Communitarians still has stringent requirements. Citizens must conscientiously deliberate over issues and candidates and monitor representative deliberations; simply voting and turning inward toward one's private life, as a liberal might, is not sufficient. And, in any case, loyalty is only supplemental; voice in other arenas and on other issues is still required.

Without knowing the affective content of any given behavior or the linkages an individual makes between his or her public and private lives, it may initially appear difficult to distinguish empirically between Virtuous Liberalism and Representative Communitarianism. Both value voice and loyalty. But there are differences. To the Virtuous Liberal, voice is a supplement to the more characteristic response of loyalty. To the Representative Communitarian, the reverse is true; loyalty as a problem-solving mode is valued only when voice— direct and active participation—is not possible. Moreover, exit would be an appropriate mode of problem solving to only the Virtuous Liberal, if in a considerably diluted form in comparison to Watchdog Liberalism.

Institutions and Modes of Problem Solving

Having specified how the four models of citizenship view the elements of the EVLN model, we next need to consider the way in which institutions influence reliance on the modes of behavior. In chapter 3, we hypothesized that three variables govern how citizens select among the four responses to dissatisfaction. First, *prior satisfaction*, having been satisfied in the past, is expected to encourage use of the constructive responses of voice and loyalty and discourage reliance on neglect and exit. Second, social, psychological, and tangible (e.g., homeownership) *investments* in the community are hypothesized to enhance the use of constructive responses: loyalty and voice. In the absence of investments there is little cost to invoking exit or neglect, the destructive modes of problem solving. And third, the availability of *alternatives*, having a Tiebout-type of local institutional environment, is expected to enhance the use of the active responses of exit and voice. Simply put, one cannot "vote with one's feet" if there is nowhere else to go. And based on the work of Hirschman,[38] they suggest that alternatives are necessary to make voice credible. In the absence of alternatives, then, citizens must rely on more passive responses. Given these considerations, both the neighborhood movement and public choice models must recognize that institutions can have direct as well as indirect influence on the play of citizenship.

The direct effect of institutions inheres in how they generate *alternatives:* institutionally fragmented metropolitan areas offer a large number of alternative civic communities to the dissatisfied citizen. Thus, given the EVLN specification of how alternatives influence reliance on the four modes of problem solving, fragmenting the metropolis into empowered localities can be expected to increase the use of the active responses of exit and voice and to diminish use of the passive responses of loyalty and neglect.

How does this outcome meet the expectations of our four models of citizenship? For Watchdog Liberals, the increased possibility of exit associated with fragmentation would be indicative of enhanced citizen control of popular government. And the same would be true for communitarians and Virtuous Liberals in regard to the increased use of voice behaviors expected to result from fragmentation. Beyond this, the direct effects are rather grim for several of our schools of citizenship. For communitarians, increased exit would be indicative of the demise of organic social communities. And for Representative Communitarians and Virtuous Liberals, the diminishment of loyalty associated with fragmentation must be troubling. In short, at least three of our four citizenship models, all but Watchdog Liberalism, would be less than satisfied with the probable direct effects of their preferred institutional arrangement. Moreover, even if they were satisfied, we saw in chapter 4 that the impact of ALTERNATIVES was the weakest of the EVLN predictor variables.

Clearly, Virtuous Liberals and communitarians must base their preference for fragmentation on more than their direct impact in generating exit alternatives. The indirect role of institutions, they might suggest, is found in one part of the *investment* component of the EVLN Model, for which strong support was found in the tests presented in chapter 4. More specifically, each of these three models implies that citizens are very attached to their localities, and that this deep psychological attachment is an important resource their empowered localities can call upon to encourage use of the constructive problem-solving modes of loyalty and voice. This hypothesized attachment has two sources.

First, citizens are assumed to be very attached to their local communities because it is there that they most immediately struggle with important issues affecting their lives. Virtuous Liberals and communitarians might then argue that empowered localities, therefore, will be better able to activate constructive problem solving than more remote governments addressing less vital issues. Thus, Elkin argues that "struggle and debate over the public interest must be connected to the day-to-day vital interests of citizens."[39] Ostrom, Bish, and Ostrom similarly attribute the "energy and enthusiasm," "robust power," and "animation and effort" of local government to its posing of issues directly important to the daily lives of citizens.[40]

Second, citizens are assumed to be more attached to their localities because they provide networks of personal relationships that are missing when the locus of involvement moves outside of the neighborhood. This form of investment provides an important resource that empowered localities can rely upon to encourage constructive problem-solving behaviors. As Elkin notes: "The second motive to be harnessed is the deep interest that each of us has in enjoying the esteem of others."[41] To communitarians, although probably not to even Virtuous Liberals, the importance of this motive implies that civil society must be firmly rooted in the face-to-face relations of private society. And as government becomes more remote from the day-to-day life of the citizen, those roots become more tenuous. Thus, larger jurisdictions cannot rely on the esteem rising from personal affect to encourage greater reliance on loyalty and voice.

In sum, the case for an indirect effect of institutions on the use of modes of political problem solving rests on the relationship between localized institutions and attachment to the community. Thus, Virtuous Liberalism and Representative Communitarianism implicitly assume that citizens residing in empowered localities will exhibit higher levels of loyalty and voice and diminished reliance on exit and neglect than their neighbors in the professionalized, centralized, and consolidated cities of progressives. And this indirect link provides the basis for the Strong Democracy Communitarians' hope that empowered neighborhoods will lead to exclusive use of voice.

The Metropolitanist Critique

The metropolitanist critique of these hypotheses is not new. Indeed, it was fully articulated by H. G. Wells for the Fabian Society as early as 1904.[42] In general, metropolitanism can be characterized as a set of institutional recommendations—those supporting the elimination of institutional fragmentation through creation of metropolitanwide governments—and the arguments supporting them. But does metropolitanism subscribe to a particular view of citizenship? Generally, metropolitanists, like public choice liberals, rarely say anything explicit about citizenship, focusing instead on the efficiency of goods and services delivery. They reach, however, remarkably different conclusions about which institutions are most likely to generate efficient delivery of services. But this concern for efficiency as part of the contractual relationship between governors and the governed implies something of a liberal understanding of citizenship. And, in the main, metropolitanists posit a "good government" version of Virtuous Liberalism, rather than the Watchdog Liberalism of Buchanan and other public choice proponents. Within the Virtuous Liberal understanding of citizenship, then, and as seen at the bottom of Table 8.21, the choice between fragmented governmental institutions and metropolitanwide government hinges on their relative efficiency advantages.

There is, however, another strain of metropolitanism, best represented by Norton Long in *The Polity*,[43] that places an almost communitarian view of citizenship at the heart of its support of metropolitanwide government. As Long has written:

> The apostles of metropolitanism are coming to realize that the vision they are seeking is something more than a better means of moving traffic, an improvement in the plumbing, or even an increase in the competitive position of the local economy. It is the possibility of attaining a shared common goal of a better life. The recreated city of the metropolitan area offers the hope of a significant manageable field of civic action in which a warmer sense of fraternity can be realized.[44]

This interpretation of the goals of metropolitanism is at best, however, a weak version of communitarianism. The very structure of metropolitanwide government necessarily precludes the immediate, close, and continued contact among citizens required of strong democracy proponents. Instead, Long's understanding of citizenship most closely resembles that of representative communitarianism, although probably even weaker in its adherence to core communitarian norms.

This "communitarian" strain of metropolitanism prescribes a strikingly different set of institutions than those discussed earlier, as seen in the last row of Table 8.1. Rather than metropolitan federation with a strong emphasis on neighborhood empowerment as a compromise between the ideals of the classic neighborhood government model and the practicalities of participation in the modern city, the "communitarian" metropolitanists offer full-scale metropolitan government as the most likely vehicle to achieve communitarian goals. In developing their understanding of the relationship between governmental structure and citizenship, metropolitanists do not question the importance of the indirect relationship between institutions, psychological attachment to the community, and varying patterns of reliance on the modes of problem solving posited by at least three of our models of citizenship. Instead, they question the locus of community attachment arising from (i) social embeddedness, and (ii) citizens' concern for vital issues. We consider each issue in turn.

First, metropolitanists dismiss as hopeless nostalgia the notion that social identity can be embedded in localized settings. In the modern metropolis, the social lives of citizens become fragmented. As Robert Wood notes, "As the metropolis extends . . . [d]iscrete local communities disappear; friendships become scattered randomly throughout the area; associations made in the course of work are different from those developed in residential neighborhoods."[45] The older boundaries do not disappear, but they no longer encompass an integrated social community. As Wells noted, "it is no longer the case that all who dwell in these old limits are essentially local inhabitants and mutually interdependent as once they would have been. A large proportion of our population, a large and increasing proportion, has no localized interests at all as an eighteenth century person would have understood locality."[46] Due to mobility within and among metropolitan communities, citizens are unlikely to give their neighborhood or suburb their primary political or social allegiance. Nor are temporary residents likely to have sufficient information to understand the services and policies of a small governmental unit. Even if one rejects Dahl's comment that "the village probably never was all that it is cracked up to be,"[47] its tattered remnants in suburbia and urban neighborhoods hardly constitute communities like those of times past.

To metropolitanists, social fragmentation is dangerous.[48] Thus, Wood writes, "as men wander in the lonely crowd, the capacity of existing units of government to function vigorously and effectively is impaired for they no longer engender civic consciousness and a sense of belonging."[49] But rather than recreate the village, they propose new institutions that will encompass our expanded social lives and our expanded community. As Wells noted, "It is not that all of these people do not belong to a community, but that they belong to a larger community of a new type which your administrators have failed to discover and which your working theory of local government ignores."[50] Indeed, they suggest that existing boundaries preserve social fragmentation, for "without regional institutions, no loyalty to a higher order is possible . . . .So regional problems find no vehicle for their solution and the capacity . . . to awake a regional consciousness is lost."[51]

This spatially expanded attachment is clearly something other than the older social attachments to small, organic communities. Yet, at the same time, they are not totally dissimilar in origin and makeup. Thus, "Chicagolanders," whether from Chicago, Skokie, or even Chesterton, in nearby northwest Indiana, share the tragedy of the Cubs and such cultural icons as Ernie Banks and George Hallas. And while their "strong talk" is less personal than communitarians would desire, it is no less real when broadcast over Wally Phillip's morning program on WGN radio or late-night talk shows on WBBM. Similarly, being an "Angelino" has little to do with living in Los Angeles, Anaheim, or North Hollywood, but with identifying with a social community, albeit a large one. A few analysts believe that this new locus of attachment has become more important than the older ties central to the hypotheses of public choice liberals and neighborhood movement communitarians.[52]

For metropolitanists, the best way to link citizens' social and civic lives so as to promote use of the constructive problem-solving modes of loyalty and voice is to create an encompassing urban government "great enough and fine enough to revive the dying sentiment of local patriotism."[53] Thus, instead of responding to the "lonely crowd" of the modern metropolis by recreating the mythic past, as they would say both public choice liberals and neighborhood movement communitarians have done, metropolitanists seek to establish a new type of community that they consider appropriate for a modern era.

The *second element of the communitarian and public choice attachment hypotheses is their assumption that the most vital interests are those that are local in the sense of the independent town or city or empowered neighborhood.* Again, the metropolitanists do not question the importance of considering, discussing, and debating important issues to stimulate attachment to the political and/or social community. Instead, they question whether the locus of such issues is still the small, independent town or neighborhood. Rather than encouraging debate over vital issues, they suggest that for several reasons such communities more often than not stifle openness and "democratic talk."

While metropolitan areas as a whole evidence substantial diversity, the homogeneous character of specific empowered localities reduces the diversity of perspectives needed for rational resolution of conflict over vital issues. The most characteristic trait of metropolitan demographic patterns is the segregation of citizens into what Robert N. Bellah and his colleagues identified in *Habits of the Heart* as "life-style enclaves."[54] Wood has argued that such communities evolved to avoid meaningful consideration of many important issues, that the suburbanite can "abjure political discussion and debate by joining a constituency which shares his values, and his tensions, anxieties, and uncertainties are relieved."[55] Thus, the same homogeneity that makes such communities so "neighborly" deprives them of the diversity needed to generate the meaningful discussion of vital public issues so important to communitarians like Barber and Elkin.[56]

It is not as if such people do not have the same vital concerns as those in Elkin's imagined empowered neighborhood. But many of the concerns of this type listed by Elkin as potential topics to be addressed in the empowered locality arise *outside* the locality of residence.[57] For example, the empowered locality of residence will offer an inadequate venue for discussing work life issues if they arise in the altogether different locality of employment.[58] The scale of many issues of personal vital concern to residents of empowered localities is inappropriate for that venue because social existence is now scattered across localities.

Also, a vital issue may be transformed by the parochial nature of enclave communities into forms hardly anticipated by the two schools of citizenship. The key examples are race and land use, where the questions are often redefined from asking how authority might be used to promote equality in the provision of services or promote equitable land use to how to keep certain groups—especially minorities and those with lower incomes—from entering the neighborhood/town. Moreover, the civil independence of the empowered locality will provide the necessary tools of zoning restrictions and land use controls to enforce de facto segregation.[59] Thus, many observers have concluded that the empowered localities exhibit a "politics of exclusion."[60] Discussion of these redefined issues may be as energetic and enthusiastic as communitarians could want, but their substance will often entail an exclusionary logic, substituting the language of NIMBYism for the languages of community or social contract.[61]

If empowered localities are demographically organized in such a way that they are able to avoid some issues, are able to redefine others narrowly, and are incapable of addressing still others because of social fragmentation, what can provide the basis for the "strong talk" of communitarians or even the local civic involvement of hypothetical Tieboutites? The answer is that their preferred jurisdictions are "empowered" only for the mundane tasks of service delivery. While important, these are not the sort of issues considered to be of vital personal concern to citizens on a day-to-day basis. For this reason, Long concluded that the principal limit to meaningful local citizenship is the "sheer lack of significance at the local level."[62] Organization of the political community around lifestyle enclaves precludes the kind of constructive conflict, debate, and discussion of vital issues (e.g., strong talk) that neighborhood movement communitarians and public choice liberals themselves take to be important. Indeed, as Wood argues, "It is at least an open question whether this creation of political boundaries around disparate groups and classes is an appropriate development in a democracy, or whether it truly frees the individual in the manner its advocates intend."[63] A more appropriate way to engender such debate is to develop institutions that encompass sufficient scale and scope to bring these vital issues to the fore.[64] If addressing vital issues is important to developing the community attachment needed to activate recourse to the constructive problem-solving modes of loyalty and voice, consolidation—not fragmentation—is required.

We have, then, two competing views of the relationships between institutions, community attachment, and modes of citizen problem solving. To liberal public choice proponents and communitarian neighborhood movement advocates, citizens residing in empowered localities should exhibit higher psychological attachment to their community, which should facilitate use of their respective preferred patterns of problem solving. To metropolitanists, the consolidated city–county government is more likely to foster the community attachment needed to encourage voice and loyalty. We now turn to testing these hypotheses.

Testing the Hypotheses

Variables and Their Measurement

We have three sets of variables to measure: government structure, citizen problem solving, and psychological attachment to the community. The first includes the structural factors that define the governmental institutions of fragmented and consolidated city government systems. Given our selection of research sites, these are summarized in the simple distinction between the Louisville–Jefferson County and Lexington–Fayette County respondents, with the latter residing in a consolidated city with a strong mayor, centralized bureaucratic provision of services, and partial at-large representation.

Our modes of problem solving—EXIT-MOVE, VOICE, LOYALTY, and NEGLECT—are measured in the same manner as outlined in chapter 4. Of these measures, the most problematic to communitarians will be the VOICE measure, made up of six standard indicators of political participation. Of course, we do not mean to imply that participating in just these ways is sufficient to satisfy the communitarian's requirement for effective voice. Participation for communitarians includes many more forms and deeper levels of participation. At the same time, though, if citizens engage in "full communitarian" participation, they will certainly be involved in the kinds of activities included in our VOICE index. Our measure, therefore, should enable us broadly to assess differences in the overall levels of participation associated with different institutional structures and levels of attachment.

In the models presented in chapter 3 and tested in chapter 4, we did not employ a separate measure of PSYCHOLOGICAL ATTACHMENT, our variable of central interest in assessing the liberal and communitarian citizenship hypotheses. Instead, several indicators of psychological attachment were included in the more general INVESTMENT index. To tap fully the hypotheses underlying the liberal and communitarian understandings of citizenship behaviors, two of the five items of the INVESTMENT index were used to construct our measure of PSYCHOLOGICAL ATTACHMENT. These two items focused on degree of attachment to the community and how sorry the respondent would be to leave the city. The remaining items of the more general INVESTMENT index address social ties to the community (i.e., number of friends in the community) that have little directly to do with the affective relationship between the citizen and his or her community, and were combined to create a separate indicator of SOCIAL INVESTMENT.

Findings

We suggested above that institutions can directly influence problem solving by opening or foreclosing alternatives, thereby shifting problem solving on the active–passive dimension. This relationship was examined in chapter 3 and need not be considered in more detail here. We found that the ALTERNATIVES variable, indicating high and low levels of Tiebout-like alternatives, generated weak and inconsistent coefficients. Thus, the direct impact of institutions as hypothesized by the EVLN model is not very strong, providing little support for this part of the analysis of both public choice liberals and neighborhood movement communitarians.

As noted above, we did not, however, examine the indirect impact of institutional fragmentation/consolidation as exercised through psychological attachment. Therefore, we reestimated the complete EVLN models using separate indicators of SOCIAL INVESTMENT and PSYCHOLOGICAL ATTACHMENT, our variable of central concern. In general, this minor respecification changed very little else in the full results reported earlier. The coefficients of determination change slightly. And the coefficients and standard errors of the remaining EVLN (ALTERNATIVES, CURRENT DISSATISFACTION, and HOMEOWNERSHIP) and control variables (GENERAL EFFICACY, RACE, INCOME, EDUCATION, AGE, and GENDER) were generally similar. We discuss here, therefore, only the results specific to the PSYCHOLOGICAL ATTACHMENT variable, as seen in Table 8.2. When that variable was regressed on the remaining independent variables in the EVLN model, the resulting R^2 value was only 0.24, suggesting that collinearity will not inhibit interpretation of these coefficients. As in the earlier tests, largely consistent results were found across all five matched sets of communities when they were estimated separately; therefore, we present the EVLN results for the full sample including all ten of the surveys.

The ATTACHMENT coefficient from a Probit estimate of the EXIT-MOVE model was strongly negative ($b = -0.352$; s.e. $= 0.078$; $t = -4.517$; $p < 0.01$, one-tailed test; $x^2 = 972.57$; $n = 1497$) indicating that those who are weakly attached are more likely to consider invoking the active–destructive response of leaving the jurisdiction. However, the response is not neatly linear, as evidenced

Table 8.2

PROBIT and OLS Estimates of Extended EVLN Models

Response to Dissatisfaction

Variable	EXIT-MOVE[a]	VOICE[b]	LOYALTY[b]	NEGLECT[b]
EVLN variables:				
RELDIS	0.012	0.364***	−0.979***	0.281***
	(0.071)[c]	(0.045)	(0.057)	(0.041)
PSYCHOLOGICAL ATTACHMENT	−0.352‡	0.070†	0.622‡	0.316‡
	(0.078)	(0.043)	(0.054)	(0.039)
INVEST-SOCIAL	0.021	0.219***	0.054	0.056
	(0.073)	(0.039)	(0.048)	(0.035)
HOMEOWNERSHIP	−0.091	0.664***	0.146	−0.098
	(0.272)	(0.159)	(0.199)	(0.145)
ALTERNATIVES	0.167	−0.011	0.522***	−0.208**
	(0.193)	(0.098)	(0.123)	(0.089)
CONTROL Variables:				
EDUCATION	−0.112*	0.210***	−0.147***	−0.047
	(0.062)	(0.033)	(0.041)	(0.030)
INCOME	−0.005	0.121***	−0.037	−0.017
	(0.054)	(0.027)	(0.033)	(0.024)
AGE	0.001	0.006*	0.013***	−0.001
	(0.006)	(0.003)	(0.004)	(0.003)
GENDER	−0.059	0.006	0.241**	0.141
	(0.084)	(0.094)	(0.118)	(0.086)
RACE	0.197	−0.011	0.287*	−0.275**
	(0.245)	(0.139)	(0.174)	(0.127)
GENERAL EFFICACY	0.076	−0.084*	0.001	0.356***
	(0.082)	(0.043)	(0.054)	(0.039)
Constant	3.679	−1.162	7.645	4.196
R^2	—	0.18	0.36	0.24
x^2	972.6	—	—	—
N	1497	1233	1233	1233

* = $p < 0.10$; ** = $p < 0.05$; *** = $p < 0.01$; † = $p < 0.10$; ‡ = $p < 0.01$, one-tailed tests.
[a]Estimated with Probit.
[b]Estimated with OLS regression; coefficients are unstandardized.
[c]Figures in parentheses are standard errors.

Figure 8.1. **Mean Levels of EXIT by levels of PSYCHOLOGICAL ATTACHMENT**

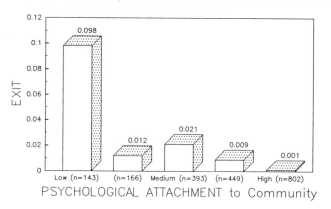

PSYCHOLOGICAL ATTACHMENT to Community

by the simple relationship between the two variables. The mean levels of EXIT for each of the five levels of PSYCHOLOGICAL ATTACHMENT are reported in Figure 8.1. The high mean level of EXIT found for the lowest level of AT-TACHMENT (0.098) drops off very sharply when we move up the scale of ATTACHMENT. Thus, EXIT is the response of the very unattached. The model was reestimated using the squared value of PSYCHOLOGICAL ATTACH-MENT. The reestimated coefficient ($b = -0.085$; s.e. $= 0.022$; $t = -3.867$; $p < 0.01$, one-tailed test; $x^2 = 1015.31$; $n = 1497$) generated no stronger results, however.

Our expectations were also met in regard to the NEGLECT model. The ATTACHMENT coefficient in the NEGLECT model was also negative and significant ($b = -0.316$; s.e. $= 0.039$; $t = -8.105$; $p < 0.01$, one-tailed test; $R^2 = 0.235$; $n = 1,233$), indicating that those who are weakly attached are more likely to use the passive–destructive response to problems of withdrawal and alienation. This is also illustrated by looking at the simple relationship between the variables, as seen in Figure 8.2. The mean levels of NEGLECT reported for each of the five levels of ATTACHMENT decline consistently from 5.226 to 3.546 as we move up the scale of ATTACHMENT. Thus, high attachment inhibits NEGLECT.

As expected, the ATTACHMENT coefficient in the EVLN VOICE model was positive and significant ($b = 0.070$; s.e. $= 0.043$; $t = 1.637$; $p < 0.10$, one-tailed test; $R^2 = 0.180$; $n = 1,233$), but only at the 0.10 level, indicating that those who are strongly attached are more likely to invoke the active–constructive response of VOICE to problems. But the weakness of these results is evident in the simple relationship between the variables, as seen in Figure 8.3. The mean levels of VOICE reported for each of the five levels of ATTACHMENT increase only slightly as we move up the scale of ATTACHMENT, and even decline slightly for the highest attachment level (2.809). So, while attachment does pro-mote VOICE, its impact is neither very strong nor entirely consistent.

Figure 8.2. **Mean Levels of NEGLECT by levels of PSYCHOLOGICAL ATTACHMENT**

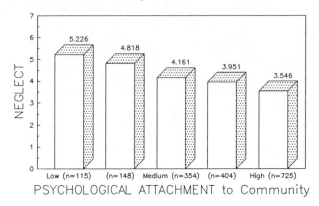

LOYALTY was found to be strongly associated with attachment. The AT-TACHMENT coefficient was positive and significant ($b = 0.622$; s.e. $= 0.054$; $t = 11.585$; $p < 0.01$, one-tailed test; $R^2 = 0.363$; $n = 1,233$), indicating that the weakly attached are far less likely to use this passive–constructive response. This is evident in the simple relationship between the variables, as seen in Figure 8.4. The mean levels of LOYALTY reported for each of the five ATTACHMENT levels increase sharply and consistently from 5.584 to 9.461 as we move up the ATTACHMENT scale. Thus, high attachment strongly promotes the positive and constructive LOYALTY response.

Our first set of hypotheses is therefore supported. That is, we fully expected that PSYCHOLOGICAL ATTACHMENT would be positively related to the constructive responses of VOICE and LOYALTY and negatively related to the destructive problem-solving modes of NEGLECT and EXIT. But the real contro-versy between metropolitanists and proponents of empowered localities lies not

Figure 8.3. **Mean Levels of VOICE by PSYCHOLOGICAL ATTACHMENT**

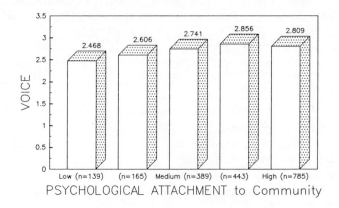

Figure 8.4. **Mean Levels of LOYALTY by Levels of PSYCHOLOGICAL ATTACHMENT**

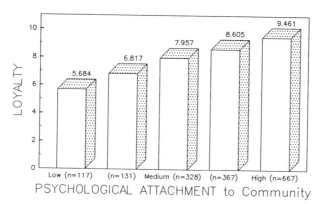

in these hypotheses; the key differences lie in their respective hypotheses about the relationship between local institutional structure and levels of psychological attachment.

To test these different expectations, difference-of-means tests were conducted on PSYCHOLOGICAL ATTACHMENT for the five matched pairs of communities. As seen in Table 8.3, the empowered locality expectations of public choice liberals and neighborhood movement communitarians were *not* supported. Mean attachment is considerably higher in each of the Lexington–Fayette neighborhoods than in their corresponding Louisville–Jefferson independent cities. Moreover, four of those differences are significant at the 0.01 level. The respondents living in the small, suburban governments in greater Louisville are considerably *less* psychologically attached to their cities than are their counterparts in the consolidated jurisdiction. Because of these differences in psychological attachment, and given the earlier findings on the relationships between psychological attachment and the four modes of problem solving, we expect that use of the constructive responses to problems of VOICE and, especially, LOYALTY is greater among consolidated government respondents, while use of the destructive responses of EXIT and NEGLECT should be more pronounced in the fragmented system.

Discussion

Our findings clearly provide little support for the citizenship hypotheses of neighborhood communitarians and public choice liberals. Given the observed differences in attachment, the institutions of the metropolitan reformers appear to promote use of the constructive problem-solving behaviors better than empowered localities. But what of citizenship more generally?

The greater attachment-induced reliance on destructive modes of problem

Table 8.3

PSYCHOLOGICAL ATTACHMENT Difference-of-Means Tests for Alternative Institutional Arrangements—Matched Lexington and Louisville Sites

Consolidated/fragmented government matched sets		Mean attach- ment	Standard deviation	n	Difference of means	t-value
LEX:	Blueberry	2.64	(1.09)	215		
LOU:	Minor Lane Heights	1.86	(1.49)	152	−0.78**	−5.56
LEX:	Chinoe	3.32	(1.05)	218		
LOU:	Beechwood Village	3.21	(1.14)	181	−0.11	−0.96
LEX:	Stonewall	3.08	(1.11)	249		
LOU:	Barbourmeade	2.49	(1.22)	170	−0.59**	−5.01
LEX:	Crestwood/Shadeland	3.35	(1.00)	242		
LOU:	Windy Hills	2.88	(1.14)	163	−0.47**	−4.31
LEX:	Green Acres	2.74	(1.20)	200		
LOU:	Newburg	2.03	(1.36)	157	−0.71**	−5.18

$* = p < 0.05; ** = p < 0.01.$

solving (EXIT and NEGLECT) found for the empowered localities is compatible with only the most extreme form of the Watchdog Liberalism understanding of citizenship. Heavy reliance on exit is a form of citizenship that can be pleasing to only the most extreme public choice liberals: those opting for the Tiebout model as the ideal form of institutional structure. But given our findings in chapter 5 about the infrequency of intentions to exit in fragmented communities, it is difficult to say that the results presented here actually provide much support for this extreme view of citizenship, even if one were willing to buy into its underlying premises about the appropriate relationship between citizens and their governments.

Supporters of the other three interpretations of citizenship also must find the patterns of problem solving in the fragmented communities disconcerting; empowered localities do not seem to provide much of a home for their preferred citizenship behaviors of voice and/or loyalty. Nor would communitarians of either stripe find much solace in our results for the consolidated government of Lexington–Fayette County; only a marginal increase in the use of voice was found for its citizens despite higher levels of attachment to it.

Only Virtuous Liberals would find the attachment-induced enhancement of loyalty in the consolidated government setting to be entirely satisfying (if perhaps surprising given its institutional locus) because of their preference for this mode of citizen response to dissatisfaction. If, as Elkin suggests, city institutions play a formative role in citizenship, then the empowered locality tends to create Watchdog Liberals, and the consolidated government of the metropolitanists is the school of Virtuous Liberals.

These conclusions, of course, are subject to several caveats. First, we should not attempt to generalize too broadly from these results. Such reticence is not characteristic of either the public choice or neighborhood communitarian literatures. For example, despite Elkin's stated intention to examine institutions,[65] they are at best stereotypes in his analysis; he characterizes all city governments as large, reformed, and centralized. Similarly, when public choice proponents discuss "gargantua," their examples are inevitably New York and Chicago,[66] neither of which is especially typical, or even consolidated. And beyond caricature, there may still exist many small, independent towns and urban neighborhoods like those that appeal to some feeling of nostalgia. Our conclusions do not apply to such localities, but are applicable to the mid-sized metropolitan areas in which most Americans now reside.[67]

Second, public choice proponents might object that all of this is irrelevant to assessing the merits of consolidation and fragmentation since the proof lies in the efficiency of service delivery. And they assert that on this score, the evidence supports fragmentation.[68] The evidence is more ambiguous than they admit, however,[69] and to the extent that efficiency differences exist, their models imply that they result in part from variations in responses citizens invoke when dissatisfied under alternative institutional structures[70]—precisely the behaviors we have examined. Thus, the argument underlying this potential objection to our analysis attempts to salvage the purported efficiency advantages of the public choice institutional recommendations by abandoning at least some of the means alleged to produced them.

Third, communitarians might claim that we have failed to test the full complement of reforms needed to engender real participation. Barber, for example, suggests that communitarian reforms cannot be evaluated except as a complete package.[71] This argument, however, only serves to insulate the communitarian view from empirical assessment of even its most basic causal claims. But even granting the argument for the moment, our findings add a new burden of proof to the communitarian campaign for neighborhood government. We have found that for at least the beginning of the institutional continuum running from settings totally nonsupportive to completely supportive of communitarian aspirations, the relationships between institutions, attachment, and political behavior run exactly opposite of what Barber thinks they are. Thus, communitarians must now account for this obverse relationship: why do local government institutions produce one set of results at one level of institutional reform, and then reverse at some unobserved and hypothetical threshold level?

Finally, what is the role of nonlocalized attachment in enhancing citizenship? It is clearly a more shallow and diffuse attachment based on shared symbols of *metropolitan* pride and shared experiences of *metropolitan* life. As such, it cannot replace the attachments associated with rural villages and ethnic neighborhoods of years past. This poses problems for Strong Democracy Communitarianism, with its exclusive focus on empowered localities; the older attachments are gone and their newer analogs are too weak to bear the demands of communitarian citizenship. Barring some rather drastic remaking of the social community, such as Elkin's proposal to restrict mobility or Dagger's option of dispersing citizens from the cities into smaller, presumably heterogeneous sites, "Strong Democracy" cannot be built on metropolitan attachment of the type noted by metropolitanists.[72]

For Virtuous Liberals and, to a lesser extent, Representative Communitarians, however, such attachments, when coupled with appropriate institutions, offer the prospect for realizing their understandings of citizenship. Although they often focus on empowered localities as their preferred instruments, they, unlike the other two views of citizenship, are not conceptualized in a manner that *strictly requires* empowered localities. Virtuous Liberalism, in comparison to Watchdog Liberalism, is far less tied to the public choice literature on fragmented institutions. The prospects for Representative Communitarianism, however, are less clear; although Schwartz's controversial understanding of communitarianism is certainly compatible with nonlocal institutions, as indicated by Long's rationale for metropolitan government, it is also a view that many communitarians do not consider to be "communitarian enough." In any case, metropolitanists would be on solid ground if they were to say to supporters of both schools that, to the extent that their understandings of citizenship depend on attachment, they should look to the modern metropolis, and not to the past of parochial localism. As Robert Wood has written, "The plea for gargantua is not an attack against neighborhoods, against the importance of 'moral integration' or against the need for fellowship and companionship. It is simply a plea against confusing these socially desirable qualities with the prerequisites of good government, against equipping neighborhoods with political prerogatives."[73]

Notes

1. Dahl (1967, p. 959).
2. Dahl (1967, pp. 965–67).
3. Buchanan (1975, pp. 21–22); and Galston (1988).
4. Buchanan (1975, pp. 162–63).
5. Galston (1988).
6. Barber (1984).
7. Long (1962, p. 177).
8. Barber (1984, p. 219); Elkin (1987, pp. 109, 152).
9. Barber (1984, p. 155).
10. Tiebout (1956); Bish and Ostrom (1973); Bish (1971); and V. Ostrom, Bish, and Ostrom (1988).
11. Kotler (1969); Fredrickson (1973); and Zimmerman (1972).
12. Elkin (1987, pp. 30, 143); Schwartz (1988, pp. 123–24); V. Ostrom, Tiebout, and

Warren (1961, p. 837); V. Ostrom, Bish, and Ostrom (1988, pp. 63–71).

13. Curiously, "citizenship" is noted in the indexes of neither *Local Government in the United States* by V. Ostrom, Bish, and Ostrom (1988) nor Buchanan's *The Limits of Liberty* (1985).

14. Most citizens have little knowledge about and less control over special districts (see Bennett and DiLorenzo, 1982) and COGs because they represent cities rather than citizens, and are incapable of overcoming the veto power of constituent units (Harrigan, 1989, pp. 345–47).

15. Advisory Commission on Intergovernmental Relations (1987); and V. Ostrom, Bish, and Ostrom (1988).

16. Dagger (1981).

17. Barber (1984).

18. Barber (1984, p. 264).

19. Barber (1984, pp. 264, 269).

20. V. Ostrom (1977, pp. 35–36); and Whitaker (1980).

21. Perry (1973, p. 85).

22. Elkin (1987, pp. 5, 95).

23. Buchanan (1975, pp. 162–63); and Barber (1984, p. 220).

24. Tiebout (1956); V. Ostrom, Tiebout, and Warren (1961); and Lowery and Lyons (1989).

25. Bailyn (1967).

26. Barber (1984, p. 220).

27. Elkin (1987, pp. 196–99).

28. Oakerson, Parks, and Bell (1987).

29. V. Ostrom (1977).

30. Galston (1988); Galston (1982); Thigpen and Downing (1987).

31. Galston (1988, pp. 1282–84).

32. Oakerson, Parks, and Bell (1987).

33. Galston (1988, p. 1284).

34. Barber (1984, p. 152).

35. Elkin (1987, p. 169).

36. Schwartz (1988, p. 731); Dahl (1967).

37. Schwartz (1988).

38. Hirschman (1970).

39. Elkin (1987, p. 153).

40. V. Ostrom, Bish, and Ostrom (1988, p. 25).

41. Elkin (1987, p. 153).

42. Wells (1961).

43. Long (1962).

44. Long (1962).

45. Wood (1961b, pp. 179–80).

46. Wells (1961, p. 146).

47. Dahl (1967, p. 961).

48. Long (1962, pp. 184–85).

49. Wood (1961b, p. 180).

50. Wells (1961, p. 147).

51. Wood (1961b, pp. 179–80).

52. Long (1962, pp. 156–64).

53. Wells (1961, p. 154).

54. Bellah et al. (1985, p. 73); Harrigan (1989, p. 250).

55. Wood (1961b, p. 190).

56. Schneider and Logan (1982b).

57. Elkin (1987, p. 153).

58. Wood (1961b, p. 179).

59. Danielson (1976); Hamilton, Mills, and Puryear (1975); and Mills and Oates (1975a).

60. Harrigan (1989, pp. 284–302); Wood (1966, pp. 95–98); Fainstein and Fainstein (1980, p. 259).

61. Communitarians usually sidestep this issue via the sometimes unstated and usually weakly supported (e.g., Elkin, 1987, p. 183) inadequate reference to Crenson's (1983) assumption that enough diversity exists. Public choice proponents simply assert that segregation has nothing to do with fragmentation per se, and suggest that it be handled by a higher level of government, which fails to recognize that fragmentation provides the ability to segregate.

62. Long (1962, p. 179).

63. Wood (1961b, p. 191).

64. Wood (1961b, p. 191).

65. Elkin (1987, pp. 12–15).

66. E. Ostrom and Whitaker (1974); and V. Ostrom, Bish, and Ostrom (1988, p. 71).

67. More generally, both communitarians and public choice scholars seldom acknowledge the many Chinese boxes *within* even the most consolidated and professionalized metropolitan government. Gargantua is assumed to consist of only one box when nearly all consolidated governments are composed of many subboxes—district versus at-large representation, neighborhood organizations, little city halls, and such. Thus, the reality of reformed governmental institutions is far more complex than acknowledged.

68. V. Ostrom, Bish, and Ostrom (1988).

69. Harrigan (1969, pp. 321–23).

70. Oakerson, Parks, and Bell (1987).

71. Barber (1984, p. 263).

72. Elkin (1987, p. 193); Dagger (1981, p. 733).

73. Wood (1961b, pp. 191–192).

9

Designing Urban Institutions

Two sets of concerns have dominated the debate over the virtues of the traditional civic reform versus the public choice (or Tiebout) models for governing urban America. One focuses on the economic claims made by both sides regarding the impacts of their particular institutional design recommendations on the actual efficiency with which various local services can be produced and delivered.[1] Supporters from both camps have engaged in endless arguments over whether larger scale or consolidated local governments generate sufficient economies of scale to produce more cost-effective services, as the civic reformers claim, or whether the existence of numerous smaller units competing in a quasi-market model for highly mobile citizens will result in more efficient service delivery, as supporters of the public choice model assert.[2]

Clearly, none of the data obtained from the Lexington and Louisville surveys can be used to address these efficiency concerns, although we believe that the basic research design used in these studies would enable researchers interested in such questions to engage in a more sophisticated and theoretically relevant discussion of the actual costs and benefits of various service packages offered by consolidated versus more fragmented systems of local government serving similar types of spatially defined communities. At minimum, it would enable researchers to confront the economic assertions associated with these two models in a more tractable manner than by continuing the din of claims and counterclaims over such things as whether the per capita cost of running a small, suburban police department will be less than that incurred by a large, central city police department serving a quite different and more complex set of needs and circumstances.

The other set of concerns focuses on much less discussed, but equally important, political and administrative consequences that allegedly flow out of adopting the particular design recommendations of these two schools of thought. Here the often implicit questions are framed in terms of the effects of more integrated or consolidated versus more fragmented systems of local government on such things as power, access, influence, representation, responsiveness, participation, and the general nature of the civic bonds that define the relationship between citizens and their local governments. It is within this political and administrative framework that we are also obliged to consider the effects of consolidation versus fragmentation on how citizens evaluate local services and what they do in response to being dissatisfied with some or all of those services.

Summary of Results

This latter set of concerns provided the impetus for the research reported in this book—research that we believe makes two important contributions to the study of local government institutions and local political behavior. *First*, we developed and simultaneously tested comprehensive models of citizens' satisfaction with local government and their political responses to dissatisfaction. As noted in chapter 1, prior work on these topics is both too limited theoretically and relies all too heavily on research designs that are not sufficiently robust to provide for an integrated account of these fundamental relationships between citizens and their local governments. In contrast, we have established a better linkage between theory and data in several respects.

- Our simultaneous assessment of the three major accounts of the sources of citizen satisfaction with local government in chapter 2 led to a parsimonious model that highlights the citizen's investment in the community and local efficacy as well as the government's provision of a broad range of high-quality services.

- The EVLN model as respecified and tested in chapter 4 linked theoretically what had previously been a disparate set of literatures on local political behavior and provided a parsimonious explanation of how citizens select among these alternative responses to dissatisfaction.

- Both of these analyses were developed in the context of a unique research design that effectively allowed us to control for both individual- and jurisdiction-level variance in factors thought to be important in prior theoretical analyses. While not without problems of its own, this design, we hope, will set a standard for future comparative work on urban politics.

- We demonstrated in our analyses of citizen attribution errors and modes of urban citizenship how these general models can be usefully employed to address other, more specific questions about local political behavior and institutional design.

Our *second* contribution inheres in our findings on the comparative merits of the prescriptions of traditional civic reformers and public choice theorists on local government consolidation/fragmentation. The results were strong in two respects. We found, in chapter 5, little support for the underlying premises of the

Tiebout exiting hypothesis as elaborated upon by public choice theory. And just as important, we found substantial evidence that local government consolidation enhances the civility of political behavior in an urban setting.

- We found in the end of chapter 2 that consolidation has a strong, if indirect, and positive influence on citizens' satisfaction with local government. A greater number of local services is positively associated with satisfaction, and consolidated governments tend to provide more services. Therefore, citizens of consolidated systems will tend to be more satisfied with their local governments than will residents of cities in fragmented systems.

- The results in chapter 6 indicate that citizens in consolidated systems make far fewer errors in attributing responsibility for the provision of local services, and that such errors can bias mean community assessments of service quality. Therefore, citizens in consolidated systems will tend to evaluate their local governments more accurately.

- In chapter 7, we saw that minority citizens are provided more comprehensive services, are less dissatisfied and disaffected, and participate at least as much in consolidated systems as in fragmented systems featuring independent cities in which they are a majority.

- And in chapter 8, we found that residents of consolidated systems are more psychologically attached to their communities than are residents of fragmented systems. Because attachment was found to be positively associated with the constructive problem solving behaviors of voice and loyalty, their use will be enhanced under consolidated government.

The combination of negative evidence on the underlying premises of the public choice model and these four findings on the political benefits of consolidation provide new support for the traditional reform prescriptions that have long been dismissed as an intellectual guide to urban structure and organization.

Future Research Directions

We fully recognize that both of these contributions to the urban literature are strongly stated, and that no single analysis or even a set of analyses will end debates that have defined the local political behavior and local institutional design literatures for most of this century. Strong knowledge claims, like the communitarian's "strong talk," are often essential if one hopes to initiate and maintain a fruitful dialog. But the forcefulness of our claims is more than strategic rhetoric in the game of scientific discovery. For the reasons we have outlined, we believe that our tentative answers to these questions are superior on theoretical and empirical grounds to those upon which we admittedly build. There are, however, a number of limitations in the analysis, only some of which have been pointed out in previous chapters, that suggest several specific research efforts that need to be made to advance the quality of the debate over how best to analyze and organize local governments in urban America.

For one thing, the Lexington and Louisville surveys still need to be replicated in a variety of other urban settings as suggested in our original proposal to the National Science Foundation. We need to examine the attitudes and behaviors of individuals living in similar kinds of spatially defined areas or neighborhoods located in highly fragmented urban settings typical of many of our older, Rust Belt urban complexes, versus those living in larger, more integrated, but not formally consolidated, systems that are typical of many of the growing urban areas in the Sun Belt. After all, the kinds of massive annexation efforts carried out in many Sun Belt cities have produced situations not unlike the Lexington setting in terms of placing central city residents within the same local jurisdictional boundaries as those drawn from a wide variety of spatially defined suburban areas. And many comparable fragmented systems both within and outside the Sun Belt share a wide range of characteristics found in our Louisville setting that are important for making cross-sectional comparisons.

Just as important, these analyses need to be replicated using panel data to assess several important longitudinal relationships that we were able to address only indirectly. The central issue concerns the role of loyalty as a response to dissatisfaction in the EVLN model presented in chapter 3. Lacking the kind of data needed to separate prior satisfaction and current dissatisfaction effectively, we were not able to distinguish this response from the more general regime supportive attitudes and behaviors of those who are fully satisfied with their local government and the services it provides. It would also be useful to assess the temporal elements of the satisfaction and responses to dissatisfaction models in a full quasi-experimental setting, where one of the local research settings actually undergoes extensive consolidation during the course of the analysis. Given the infrequency of consolidation in recent years, such an analysis must wait for events beyond the control of researchers. But this kind of design would be far stronger in terms of internal validity than the analyses presented here, even though ours are superior to most of the designs found in the urban politics literature.

We also need to examine simultaneously in a single research design both the objective and subjective nature of local service delivery under alternative institutional arrangements. As noted in the introduction to this chapter, the extensive public choice literature on actual service delivery patterns suggests that fragmented systems are more efficient. As we have noted at several points, we believe the evidence is far more mixed than public choice proponents admit. But even if we accept their interpretation of these research findings, our results raise something of a paradox. That is, if fragmented systems provide more efficient services, then why do consolidated systems offer a more fertile ground for effective democratic control of local government? And if there is a disjunction between the economic and political advantages of consolidation or fragmentation, how are we to choose between these two forms of organizing local government? At this time, our results can provide no answers to these questions. Nor can the many public choice studies on objective service provision. By focusing respectively on political or economic consequences of organization, neither the Lexington and Louisville study nor the public choice analyses of St. Louis, for example, can speak to the overall impact of local government structure. Thus, a single analysis focusing on both implications of local institutions is required if we are comprehensively to evaluate the civic reform and public choice prescriptions for metropolitan governance.

The matched comparison research design may also prove to be useful in answering other types of research questions that were not addressed in the Lexington and Louisville study. First, the present study and the EVLN model have not looked at the responses of local public officials to the various problem-solving behaviors by citizens in the two metropolitan systems. To what extent, and under what conditions, will public officials attempt to respond to exit, voice, loyalty, and neglect? Do officials operating under the fragmented versus more integrated systems react to these behaviors in ways that are systematically different?

Second, this research design could be utilized to examine the kinds of questions raised in this study with respect to the actions and behaviors of other key actors in the metropolitan system, such as owners and managers of business organizations. Although the literature on business location suggests that businesses do not respond solely to local tax and service packages when making locational choices, there is sufficient evidence to suggest that economic leaders do engage in voice behaviors to influence local policies. This would also provide an opportunity to engage in a more meaningful discussion of the extent to which local political elites may respond differentially to the EVLN behaviors of ordinary citizens compared to business leaders. However, it should be clear that if evidence is uncovered suggesting that the mechanisms of the Tiebout model work more clearly and precisely with respect to economic leaders than found in this study concerning ordinary citizens, this would seriously undercut the model's assumption that consumer sovereignty or citizen choice is a dominant influence in the local political system. Shifting the focus to elites would represent a fundamental change in the model.

Third, the research strategy used in the Lexington and Louisville study can also be employed to investigate the political and administrative implications of the traditional civic reform and public choice models in other areas of public policy. Perhaps the most obvious application is to education. A very large body of literature has developed over the past several decades concerning the alleged impacts of cross-district busing, the consolidation of central city and suburban schools to achieve racial balance, and the use of such public choice approaches as vouchers and magnet schools that must compete for students. Yet, much of this literature remains poorly integrated in both theoretical and empirical terms despite its obvious connections to the same kinds of basic structural and institutional questions posed in the larger debate over the traditional civic reform versus the public choice or Tiebout models.

Another potential area that needs to be examined in this manner is environmental policy. While some of the major dimensions of this policy area have been coopted by state and/or federal agencies, major responsibilities for such things as zoning and controlling the nature and rate of economic and population growth still remain in the hands of local governments in most parts of the United States. When coupled with some of the more recent debates over who should control such things as the siting of landfills or toxic and biological waste incinerators that may be used to handle waste products from other communities and even other states, there is a rather wide-ranging set of issues that clearly involve claims and counterclaims regarding the political and administrative virtues of local control (fragmentation) versus more regional, statewide, or even federal control (consolidation). Regardless of the substantive parameters of such debates, they involve many of the same basic theoretical questions raised in the long-standing dispute between traditional reformers and public choice advocates.

Updating the Civic Reform Model

One very critical step, however, needs to be taken before anyone begins to tackle the important task of replicating this study in other urban areas, or applying its comparative research design to other policy areas. We need a more detailed and a more realistic version of the traditional civic reform model with which to make these important comparisons. Although the findings presented in this volume raise serious doubts about many of the assertions and assumptions regarding the political and administrative consequences of adopting the public choice model, it must be noted that supporters of this model have been much more willing to advance specific, testable propositions about these aspects of their model than their traditional civic reform counterparts. Aside from the general assertion that more integrated and preferably totally consolidated systems of local government in urban areas will lead to more focused responsibility, few specific guidelines are offered in the civic reform literature about the political consequences of their recommendations for organizing local governments within our urban areas.

It is true that many of the civic reformers who have been interested in reducing the levels of governmental fragmentation found in most of our urban areas over the years have also been involved in endorsing such structural and institutional arrangements as the city-manager system, nonpartisan elections, and at-large representation. Since many of these so-called "reformed" structures have been characterized in the empirical literature as being insensitive to the segmental needs of urban societies, it is not difficult to link these various recommendations to create a version of the civic reform model that assumes a single tax–service package offered by a single local government that is structured internally to be insensitive to anything other than the larger, areawide needs and concerns of its citizens. This, of course, is the view of the traditional reform theory that has been promulgated by public choice scholars. But this interpretation, we believe, constitutes an unfair caricature of the traditional reform model that is no longer consistent with the kinds of institutional design recommendations that contemporary civic reform efforts have actually embraced.

As suggested at several points in this volume, even the most extensive versions of the civic reform model combining the reorganization of internal structures with efforts to consolidate local governments that have actually been proposed or put into effect in the United States during the past fifty years or more have provided for at least two levels of services tied to differing tax levels. Most of them have also incorporated such structural features as district representation, mayor–council systems, formalized opportunities for citizen input into public policy discussions, and even such ideas as citizen complaint bureaus. Even when reorganizing solely the internal structures of local government, the "new" reform tradition has emphasized such things as district representation since at least the mid-1960s. Local reformers have been willing to recognize and respond to numerous contingencies in designing institutional solutions balancing segmental and areawide interests.

If we are to compare the civic reform and public choice models for local government organization meaningfully, then our comparisons should be founded on an accurate understanding of just what each entails, not caricatures that predetermine research conclusions. We have tried to accomplish this for the former by focusing on more than the Tiebout exiting hypothesis in our characterization of public choice theory, although Tiebout's ideas remain central to that school's analyses of local service delivery systems. But neither public choice scholars, nor, frankly, proponents of consolidation have done much in the way of accurately characterizing the core elements of the civic reform model *as it is actually applied in contemporary urban America*. We have suggested the outlines for a more accurate understanding of the reform model by focusing on the political consequences of consolidation and highlighting the many institutional complexities that have been appended to the reform prescriptions in order to introduce concerns for segmental interests in a community. We will have more meaningful scholarly debate about the consequences of local institutions if our attention is focused on these realities of two major competing designs for metropolitan government.

Such attention on the actual structures and consequences of local governmental organization will also, we suspect, lead to more meaningful public consideration of proposals for consolidation. As has often been noted,[3] public support for consolidation is tepid at best. Indeed, the voters of Louisville and Jefferson County have rejected two separate proposals for consolidation within recent years. In part, this lack of support represents a failure of the proponents of consolidation to articulate accurately just what consolidation can and cannot do.

Instead of highlighting the political advantages of metropolitan integration in terms of information, equity in service provision, and democratic control, supporters of consolidation all too often make insupportable claims about economies of scale that shift the terms of the debate to the wrong issues. Thus, it is not just public choice scholars who have caricatured the civic reform model; many proponents of consolidation are inadvertent co-conspirators. A more accurate representation of the real advantages of consolidation, we believe, would focus debates over proposals for structurally streamlining fragmented systems on issues that are more likely to win support among voters for metropolitan government.

Implications for the Literature on Reform

This disjunction between the academic and applied understandings of the traditional reform theory extends far beyond its application to metropolitan governance. The propositions of the traditional reform theory as developed by the progressives also speak to a wider variety of concerns, including administrative reform, centralization versus decentralization, intergovernmental relations, and neutral competence of public employees. While we have not addressed these broader concerns of the larger reform model, the conclusions we have offered may bear on their consideration.

Criticism of the more general reform model, if anything, has exceeded that addressed to the specific proposal on consolidating local governments. Indeed, scholarly accounts of the entire progressive approach to structural reform have been highly critical for many decades. From Herbert Simon's 1945 dethroning of the "principles of administration" in *Administrative Behavior*, we learned that the reform tradition of the first decades of this century was constructed on a foundation of sand; there were no "principles," only mutually contradictory "proverbs" with no criteria for selecting among them.[4] By the early 1970s, Vincent Ostrom not only echoed Simon on the vacuity of the principles of administration, but elevated public choice theory to paradigmatic status.[5] Similarly, Knott and Miller's recent text, *Reforming Bureaucracy: The Politics of Institutional Choice*,[6] severely critiques traditional reform theory and practice as a foil for their institutional prescriptions, which are, in part, informed by the public choice approach, as does Bendor in *Parallel Systems*.[7] In these and many other important scholarly works, spanning nearly forty-five years, the ideas of the civic reformers are belittled as atheoretical myths, dismissed as lacking empirical foundation, and, most damning of all, viewed as inconsistent with democratic control.

What is strange about all of this is that virtually no scholarly defense has been made of the classic interpretation of traditional reform theory. How are we to explain this imbalance? One simple explanation is that the intellectual status of any theory is enhanced by being viewed as successfully superseding a powerful challenger. As philosopher of science David Hull has observed, scientific progress requires ongoing competition among theories, not theoretical hegemony or even a succession of dominant theories.[8] From this perspective, Ostrom and the others would have had to create from scratch a reform tradition to oppose if they had failed to breathe just enough life into the ideas of the progressives to constitute a plausible devil. Indeed, public choice theory is largely defined by its opposition to the traditional reform theory.[9]

Yet, it must also be emphasized that the thoughts of the traditional reformers continue to persist in the real world of institutional design. For even though there has been no serious scholarly defense of the traditional reform model in its pure or original form in nearly fifty years, it survives and even prospers in informing the practice of government, if, as we have seen, in a very evolved form. From state administrative reforms through Reagan-era calls for a comprehensive response to illegal drugs to journalistic comparisons of Detroit's decay with Toronto's civility,[10] many elements of the traditional reform theory survive seemingly unaffected by decades of academic inattention and neglect.

So why does the traditional reform theory remain so attractive to practitioners of the art of government? We believe that our assessment of what has happened with respect to the application of this model to metropolitan governance may also apply to these broader dimensions of the classic reform theory. Practitioners have been prepared to modify the prescriptions of the reform theory to fit the varied circumstances of actual governance. So, the traditional theory in practice is often quite different and more complex than the classic model which has been the object of derision for four decades. Thus, notions like centralization and bureaucratic neutrality have been made more sensitive to the realities of policymaking in a diverse society and politically charged environment. Just as it is unfair to judge public choice theory without reference to the many concessions some of its advocates have made to practical constraints on implementation,[11] so both supporters and critics of the traditional reform theory need to address the many ways it has adapted and evolved in practice under varying circumstances.

We strongly suspect that it would be useful to reexamine many of the tenets of the larger reform theory as they have actually been implemented using the kinds of theoretical and research design tools employed here to assess the specific question of consolidation or fragmentation. And just what is the nature of those tools? It may come as something of a surprise for us to note that our approach is greatly informed by public choice theory, even though its empirical analyses generate results supportive of the hypotheses drawn from the reform tradition. The fundamental contribution of public choice theory lies not in its design prescriptions, but in its theoretical analyses linking individual incentives to real and complex institutions in order to generate hypotheses about the consequences of structural change. And, lacking such a foundation, the general traditional reform approach was justly criticized as a set of atheoretical prescriptions. In our study, though, the EVLN model in particular and our analyses of citizenship, attribution error, and the equity of service distribution are developed on an analytic foundation linking individual incentives to the opportunities and costs arising from alternative institutions as they are actually realized in urban settings. In a critical sense, then, our work constitutes a public choice analysis of metropolitan government, albeit one leading to recommendations more commonly housed with the civic reform tradition.[12]

We suspect that similar "public choice" analysis of the many other structural proposals that collectively constitute the general reform model will lead to results that are equally surprising. Public choice scholars will no doubt counter this expectation with a very different set of hypotheses. This does not trouble us, for it is central to the nature of scientific debate. Empirical analysis will help to resolve these issues. What is more troubling is that some public choice scholars may object to our claim of analytic kinship. And in doing so, they will mistake contingent prescription for essential method, thereby falling into the same error that led to the demise of the older reform tradition.

Notes

1. See Zimmerman (1970) and Freisema (1972) for insightful reviews of the classic civic reform tradition.
2. Harrigan (1989).
3. For example, see Baldassare (1989).
4. Simon (1945).
5. V. Ostrom (1973).
6. Knott and Miller (1987).
7. Bendor (1985).
8. Hull (1988).
9. V. Ostrom, Bish, and Ostrom (1988).
10. For example, see, in order, Michigan State (1976); General Accounting Office (1983); and The Economist (1990).
11. Zodrow (1983).
12. For another example of public choice methods and a traditional reform outcome, see Lowery (1982).

Appendix A: Glossary of Multi-item Variables

CURRENT DISSATISFACTION is an inverse scored variation of the SATIS-FACTION index.

GENERAL EFFICACY is a five point index ranging from zero to four combining responses to the following questions with the available responses including agree and disagree, and with the high efficacy responses coded one and the low efficacy responses coded zero:

> Voting is the only way that people like me can have any say about how the government runs. Agree / Disagree
>
> Sometimes politics and government seem so complicated that a person like me can't really know what's going on. Agree / Disagree
>
> I don't think that public officials in this country care very much about what people like me think. Agree / Disagree
>
> People like me don't have any say about what the government does. Agree / Disagree

INVESTMENT is a fourteen-point index generated from summing the SOCIAL INVESTMENT and PSYCHOLOGICAL ATTACHMENT indices.

LOCAL EFFICACY is an inversely scored variation of the NEGLECT index.

LOYALTY is sixteen point index ranging from zero to fifteen made up of responses to the following question where high loyalty responses were coded a value of three:

> Generally speaking, how much do you trust the officials of [name of local government] to do the "right thing" about problems that may arise in the community? Almost Always / Most of the Time / Only Sometimes / Almost Never
>
> If someone criticized the overall performance of the [Name of Local Government] during a conversation, how strongly would you defend the government? Very Strongly / Somewhat Strongly / Not Very Strongly / Not Defend At All
>
> Problems with public services in [name of local government] usually work themselves out. Strongly Agree / Agree / Disagree / Strongly Disagree
>
> People are too quick to blame local officials when things go wrong in [name of local government]. Strongly Agree / Agree / Disagree / Strongly Disagree
>
> As far as people like me are concerned, the best thing to do is to believe in the honesty and wisdom of those who run [name of local government]. Strongly Agree / Agree / Disagree / Strongly Disagree

NEGLECT is a thirteen-point index ranging from zero to twelve made up of responses to the following questions where high neglect responses were coded a value of three:

> When there are problems like garbage in the streets or potholes in the roads, it is useless to complain to officials of the [name of local government].
> Strongly Agree / Agree / Disagree / Strongly Disagree
>
> I don't care what happens in the [name of local government] as long as things are OK for me and my family. Strongly Agree / Agree / Disagree / Strongly Disagree
>
> The [name of local government] doesn't care about people like me.
> Strongly Agree / Agree / Disagree / Strongly Disagree
>
> It's not worth paying attention to issues facing the [name of local government] because all the local politicians care about is serving their own interests. Strongly Agree/ Agree / Disagree/ Strongly Disagree

PRIOR SATISFACTION is a seven-point index ranging from zero to six combining responses to the following two questions with the high satisfaction responses coded three:

> Would you say that in past years you were generally very satisfied, satisfied, dissatisfied, or very dissatisfied with the way the [name of local government] did its job?
>
> Regardless of how you may feel right now, how would you rate the overall performance of the [name of local government] in past years? Would you say that in past years its overall performance was excellent, good, fair, or poor?

PSYCHOLOGICAL ATTACHMENT is a five-point index ranging from zero to four made up of responses to the following questions where high investment responses were coded a value of two:

> Suppose that for some reason you had to move away from the area you now live in, how sorry or pleased would you be to leave?
> Very Sorry / Somewhat Sorry / Not Sorry At All
>
> Do you feel a Strong, Moderate, or Weak attachment to living in [name of local government]?

SATISFACTION is seven-point index ranging from zero to six combining responses to the following two questions with the high satisfaction responses coded three:

> Would you say that you are currently very satisfied, satisfied, dissatisfied, or very dissatisfied with the way the [name of local government] is doing its job?
>
> In general, how good a job do you feel [name of local government] is currently doing in providing services—would you say that it is doing excellent, good, fair, or a poor job?

SOCIAL INVESTMENT is a ten-point index ranging from zero to nine made up of responses to the following questions where high social investment responses were coded a value of three:

How many of your friends live in your most immediate neighborhood—none, a few, more than half, almost all?

How many of your relatives live in your most immediate neighborhood—none, a few, more than half, almost all?

How long have you lived in [name of local jurisdiction]? Has it been less than a year, one to five years, six to ten years, or more than ten years?

VOICE is a seven-point index ranging from zero to six made up of responses to the following questions, where Yes responses were coded one and No responses were coded zero:

Have you ever attended a meeting or meetings called to discuss problems in your neighborhood or local community? Yes / No

Have you ever belonged to any organization attempting to solve problems in your neighborhood or local community? Yes / No

Have you ever helped to organize a petition drive regarding problems in your neighborhood or local community? Yes / No

Have you ever telephoned or written to an elected official or agency of [name of local government] regarding problems in your neighborhood or local community? Yes / No

Have you ever signed a petition regarding any particular problem in your neighborhood of local community? Yes / No

Have you ever met informally with neighbors to work on solving problems concerning local government services in your neighborhood or local community? Yes / No

Appendix B: Citizen Response to Dissatisfaction Questionnaire

UK-SRC   OCTOBER/NOVEMBER 1986

/ 1 /   / __ / __ / __ / __ /   / __ / __ /
101   102 103 104 105   106 107
CARD   ID #   INTERVIEWER#

/ __ /
108
COUNTY CODE

                    1= LEXINGTON-FAYETTE COUNTY
                    2= JEFFERSON COUNTY
                       [obj. Alternative var.]

1. Record SEX of respondent.

    (109)
            1. MALE
            2. FEMALE

2. Skip this item for Lexington-Fayette respondents.

    (110)
            Code as a 9 in col. 8 -- Go to Q-4

3. Skip this item for Lexington-Fayette respondents.

    (111)
            Code as a 9 in col. 9 -- Go to Q-4

4. How would you describe the people who live, say, within a four or five
    block area of where you live? Would you say that they are basically **VERY
    MUCH LIKE YOU, SOMEWHAT LIKE YOU,** or **NOT AT ALL LIKE YOU** in terms of such
    things as income, education, and general life style?

    (112)
                    1. VERY MUCH LIKE ME
                    2. SOMEWHAT LIKE ME
                    3. NOT AT ALL LIKE ME
                    9. DK/NA

5. Overall, how would you rate (**Lexington-Fayette County**) area as a place
    to live? Would you say that it is an **EXCELLENT, GOOD, FAIR,** or **POOR** place
    to live?

    (113)
            1. EXCELLENT
            2. GOOD
            3. FAIR
            4. POOR
            9. DK/NA

198

6. How long have you lived in (**LEXINGTON-FAYETTE COUNTY**)? Has it been **LESS THAN A YEAR, ONE TO FIVE YEARS, SIX TO TEN YEARS,** or **MORE THAN TEN YEARS?**

    (114)
        1. LESS THAN ONE YEAR
        2. ONE TO FIVE YEARS
        3. SIX TO TEN YEARS
        4. MORE THAN TEN YEARS
        5. DK/NA

7. Do you **OWN** or **RENT** the residence you now live in? **YES or NO?**

    (115)
        1. OWN
        2. RENT
        3. DK/NA

8. How many of your <u>friends</u> live in your immediate neighborhood-- **NONE, A FEW, MORE THAN HALF, ALMOST ALL?**

    (116)
        1. NONE
        2. A FEW
        3. MORE THAN HALF
        4. ALMOST ALL
        5. DK/NA
                        [hint: within 5 or 6 blocks]

9. How many of your <u>relatives</u> live in your immediate neighborhood-- **NONE, A FEW, MORE THAN HALF, ALMOST ALL?**

    (117)
        1. NONE
        2. A FEW
        3. MORE THAN HALF
        4. ALMOST ALL
        5. DK/NA
                        [hint: within 5 or 6 blocks]

10. How many children <u>under 18</u> currently live at this address? [Do not count those away at school etc.]

    (118)
        1. NONE
        2. ONE
        3. TWO
        4. MORE THAN TWO
        5. DK/NA

                        IF NONE CODE 10a AND 10b AS 1
                        AND SKIP TO Q-11

10a. If any children under 18 living at home, ask: How many of these children
     attend school?

     (119)
          1. NONE
           2. ONE
               3. TWO
                   4. MORE THAN TWO
                       5. DK/NA

```
--------------------------------------
               IF NONE CODE 10b AS 1 AND
               SKIP TO Q-11
--------------------------------------
```

10b. If any children under 18 attending school, ask: How many of these
     children attend <u>public</u> school?

     (120)
          1. NONE
           2. ONE
               3. TWO
                   4. MORE THAN TWO
                       5. DK/NA

11. Looking to the future for a moment, how likely are you to move in the next
     two or three years? Will you **DEFINITELY MOVE, PROBABLY MOVE, PROBABLY NOT
     MOVE, or DEFINITELY WILL NOT MOVE?**

     (121)
          1. DEFINITELY WILL MOVE
           2. PROBABLY WILL MOVE
               3. PROBABLY NOT MOVE
                   4. DEFINITELY WILL NOT MOVE
                       5. DK/NA

```
--------------------------------------
               IF PROBABLY NOT MOVE OR DEFINITELY
               WILL NOT MOVE CODE 11a AND 11b
               AS 9 AND SKIP TO Q-12
--------------------------------------
```

11a. If DEFINITELY WILL MOVE or PROBABLY WILL MOVE, ask: Would such a
     move involve leaving (**LEXINGTON-FAYETTE COUNTY**)-- **YES or NO?**

     (122)
          1. YES
           2. NO
               9. DK/NA

11b. If DEFINITELY WILL MOVE or PROBABLY WILL MOVE to Q-11, ask: What are the
     two or three most important reasons you will move or might move out of
     (LEXINGTON-FAYETTE COUNTY)?

     _____

     _____

     _____

                        IF ANY MENTION OF TAXES, LOCAL
                        GOVERNMENT   SERVICES,   POLITICAL
                        CORRUPTION, OR ANYTHING PERTAINING TO
                        LOCAL GOVERNMENT PERFORMANCE code as
                        REGIME GOVERNMENT TYPE REASONS.

                        ALL OTHER TYPES OF RESPONSES--JOBS, JOB
                        TRANSFERS, GET CLOSER OR FURTHER AWAY
                        FROM RELATIVES, DIVORCE, RETIREMENT,
                        HEALTH, ETC.-- code as PERSONAL-ECONOMIC
                        TYPE RESPONSES

     (123)
            1. REGIME-GOVERNMENT TYPE REASONS
            2. PERSONAL-ECONOMIC TYPE REASONS
            9. DK/NA

12. OK, let's talk a bit about how you CURRENTLY feel about the overall
     performance of the (LEXINGTON-FAYETTE URBAN COUNTY GOVERNMENT). Would
     you say that you are currently VERY SATISFIED, SATISFIED, DISSATISFIED, or
     VERY DISSATISFIED with the way the (LEXINGTON-FAYETTE URBAN COUNTY
     GOVERNMENT) is doing its job?

     (124)
            1. VERY SATISFIED
            2. SATISFIED
            3. DISSATISFIED
            4. VERY DISSATISFIED
            9. DK/NA

13. In general, how good a job do you feel the (LEXINGTON-FAYETTE URBAN
     COUNTY GOVERNMENT) is currently doing in providing services -- Would you
     say that it is doing an EXCELLENT, GOOD, FAIR, or POOR job?

     (125)
            1. EXCELLENT
            2. GOOD
            3. FAIR
            4. POOR
            9. DK/NA

14. Let's get a bit more specific. I'm going to read you a short list of services that local governments often provide. Please tell me how you would rate the performance of the (**LEXINGTON-FAYETTE URBAN COUNTY GOVERNMENT**) when it comes to providing each of the following services. Would you say that the service provided is **EXCELLENT, GOOD, FAIR, POOR,** or **IS NOT PROVIDED** by the (**LEXINGTON-FAYETTE URBAN COUNTY GOVERNMENT**)?

EXCEL/ GOOD/ FAIR/ POOR/ NOT PROV/ DK/
1.   2.   3.   4.   5.   9.

(126) POLICE
       PROTECTION

(127) TRASH &
       GARBAGE
       COLLECTION

(128) STREET
       LIGHTING

(129) PARKS &
       RECREATION

(130) ROAD/STREET
       MAINTENANCE

(131) PUBLIC
       TRANSPORTATION

(132) PUBLIC HEALTH
       SERVICES

(133) SANITARY SEWERS

(134) PLANNING &
       ZONING

(135) STORM SEWERS

(136) SOCIAL SERVICES

----

15. Now I'd like you to try and recall how you felt about the services provided by the (**LEXINGTON-FAYETTE URBAN COUNTY GOVERNMENT**) in past years. Would you say that in past years you were generally **VERY SATISFIED, SATISFIED, DISSATISFIED,** or **VERY DISSATISFIED** with the way the (**LEXINGTON-FAYETTE URBAN COUNTY GOVERNMENT**) did its job?

(137)
       1. VERY SATISFIED
         2. SATISFIED
           3. DISSATISFIED
             4. VERY DISSATISFIED
               5. DK/NA

16. Regardless of how you may feel right now, how would you rate the overall performance of the (**LEXINGTON-FAYETTE URBAN COUNTRY GOVERNMENT**) in past years?   Would you say that in <u>past</u> <u>years</u> its overall performance was **EXCELLENT, GOOD, FAIR, or POOR?**

(138)
  1. EXCELLENT
  2. GOOD
    3. FAIR
      4. POOR
        9. DK/NA

17. OK. Let's get back to talking about <u>today</u>!   How would you rate the chances of someone like yourself finding another neighborhood in the (**LEXINGTON-FAYETTE COUNTY**) area that is similar to the one you now live in?   Would you say that the chances are **VERY GOOD, ONLY FAIR, or RATHER POOR?**

(139)
  1. VERY GOOD
  2. ONLY FAIR
    3. RATHER POOR
      4. DK/NA

18. How would you rate your chances of finding another place to live within the (**LEXINGTON-FAYETTE COUNTY**) area that has the kind of local tax and service package that you prefer?   Would you say that the chances of finding such an arrangement are **VERY GOOD, ONLY FAIR, or RATHER POOR?**

(140)
  1. VERY GOOD
  2. ONLY FAIR
    3. RATHER POOR
      4. DK/NA

19. The next several items concern things that some people say they do when problems arise in their local community or neighborhood. You can give a **YES** or **NO** answer as I read each item.

	YES/	NO /	DK/
	1.	2.	9.

(141) Have you ever attended a meeting or meetings called to discuss problems in your neighborhood or local community?   ___/ ___/ ___/

(142) Have you ever belonged to any organization attempting to solve problems in your neighborhood or local community?   ___/ ___/ ___/

(143) Have you ever helped to organize a petition drive regarding problems in your neighborhood or local community?   ___/ ___/ ___/

(144)   Have you ever telephoned or written to
an elected official or agency of the
(**LEXINGTON-FAYETTE URBAN COUNTY
GOVERNMENT**) regarding problems in
your neighborhood or local community?   ___/ ___/ ___/

(145)   Have you ever signed a petition
regarding any particular problem in
your neighborhood or local
community?   ___/ ___/ ___/

(146)   Have you ever met informally with
neighbors to work on solving
problems concerning local government
services in your neighborhood or
local community?   ___/ ___/ ___/

While we are asking for YES-NO kinds of answers, let me ask for your thoughts
concerning another subject.

20. In recent years private companies have started to offer a number of
services that were traditionally provided by local governments like the
(**LEXINGTON-FAYETTE URBAN COUNTY GOVERNMENT**).

How about you? Have you or members of your household ever considered
looking for some way to have a private company provide a service that is
<u>currently</u> offered by the (**LEXINGTON-FAYETTE URBAN COUNTY GOVERNMENT**)--
YES or NO?

(147)
        1. YES
          2. NO
            3. DK/NA

                              **IF "NO" CODE Q-20a AS 9 AND SKIP
                              TO Q-21.**

20a. If "YES" to Q-20 above, ask: What kinds of service or services that are
currently being provided by the (**LEXINGTON-FAYETTE URBAN COUNTY
GOVERNMENT**) have you purchased or thought about purchasing from a private
company?

        _____
        _____

                              **CODE AS 1 IF MENTION ANY OF THE
                              FOLLOWING; CODE 0 IF NOT MENTIONED.**
                              ----

(148)   PRIVATE SECURITY CO., POLICE, ETC.

(149)   TRASH/GARBAGE COLLECTION

(150)   OTHER

21. Supposing that for some reason you had to move away from the area you now live in, how sorry or pleased would you be to leave-- **VERY SORRY, SOMEWHAT SORRY, or NOT SORRY AT ALL?**

(151)
    1. VERY SORRY
     2. SOMEWHAT SORRY
      3. NOT SORRY AT ALL
       4. DK/NA

22. Generally speaking, how much do you trust the officials of the (**LEXINGTON-FAYETTE URBAN COUNTY GOVERNMENT**) to do the "right thing" about problems that may arise in the community-- **ALMOST ALWAYS, MOST OF THE TIME, ONLY SOMETIMES, ALMOST NEVER?**

(152)
    1. ALMOST ALWAYS
     2. MOST OF THE TIME
      3. ONLY SOMETIMES
       4. ALMOST NEVER
        5. DK/NA

23. If someone criticized the overall performance of the (**LEXINGTON-FAYETTE URBAN COUNTY GOVERNMENT**) during a conversation, how strongly would you defend the government-- **VERY STRONGLY, SOMEWHAT STRONGLY, NOT VERY STRONGLY, NOT AT ALL?**

(153)
    1. VERY STRONGLY
     2. SOMEWHAT STRONGLY
      3. NOT VERY STRONGLY
       4. NOT DEFEND AT ALL
        5. DK/NA

24. Do you feel a **STRONG, MODERATE,** or **WEAK** attachment to living in (**LEXINGTON-FAYETTE COUNTY**)?

(154)
    1. STRONG
     2. MODERATE
      3. WEAK
       9. DK/NA

25. When it comes to elections for Mayor or Council members in the (**LEXINGTON-FAYETTE URBAN COUNTY GOVERNMENT**), how often would you say that you vote-- **REGULARLY, ONLY OCCASIONALLY, or ALMOST NEVER?**

(155)
    1. REGULARLY
     2. ONLY OCCASIONALLY
      3. ALMOST NEVER
       4. DK/NA

26. We understand that one of the reasons some people buy houses these days is so they can sell them later at a profit. Would you say that, in your particular case, this consideration was **VERY IMPORTANT, IMPORTANT, UNIMPORTANT, VERY UNIMPORTANT, or NOT RELEVANT SINCE YOU ARE RENTING?**

   (156)
   >   1.   VERY IMPORTANT
   >   2.   IMPORTANT
   >   3.   UNIMPORTANT
   >   4.   VERY UNIMPORTANT
   >   5.   NOT RELEVANT SINCE AM RENTING
   >   9.   DK/NA

27. Some people say that "You can't fight city hall." How true is that statement for you-- **VERY TRUE, SOMEWHAT TRUE, or NOT TRUE AT ALL?**

   > [Prompt for response-you can't change things, etc.]

   (157)
   >   1.   VERY TRUE
   >   2.   SOMEWHAT TRUE
   >   3.   NOT TRUE AT ALL
   >   4.   DK/NA

28. OK. I'm now going to read you several statements. In each case I'd like to know whether you **STRONGLY AGREE, AGREE, DISAGREE, or STRONGLY DISAGREE** with the statement that I read.

	/ SA/	A /	D /	SD/	DK/

(158) Problems with public services in (**LEXINGTON-FAYETTE URBAN COUNTY GOVERNMENT**) usually work themselves out.

/ 1./	2./	3./	4./	9./

(159) People are too quick to blame local officials when things go wrong in (**LEXINGTON-FAYETTE COUNTY**).

/ 1./	2./	3./	4./	9./

(160) When there are problems like garbage in the streets or potholes in the roads, it is useless to complain to officials of the (**LEXINGTON-FAYETTE URBAN COUNTY GOVERNMENT**).

/ 1./	2./	3./	4./	9./

(161) I don't care what happens in (**LEXINGTON-FAYETTE URBAN COUNTY**) government or politics as long as things are OK for me and my family.

/ 1./	2./	3./	4./	9./

/ SA/ A / D / SD/ DK/

(162)   The thing to do when the
        (**LEXINGTON-FAYETTE URBAN**
        COUNTY GOVERNMENT) fails to
        respond to problems is for
        people like me to move to
        another local governmental
        jurisdiction that can better
        serve their needs.   / 1./ 2./ 3./ 4./ 9./

(163)   The best kind of citizen is
        one who goes about his or her
        own business and doesn't cause
        trouble.   / 1./ 2./ 3./ 4./ 9./

(164)   The (**LEXINGTON-FAYETTE URBAN**
        COUNTY GOVERNMENT) doesn't
        care about people like me.   / 1./ 2./ 3./ 4./ 9./

(165)   It's not worth paying attention
        to issues facing the (**LEXINGTON-**
        FAYETTE URBAN COUNTY GOVERNMENT)
        because all the local politicians
        care about is serving their own
        interests.   / 1./ 2./ 3./ 4./ 9./

(166)   As far as people like me are
        concerned, the best thing to do
        is to believe in the honesty and
        wisdom of those who run the
        (**LEXINGTON-FAYETTE URBAN COUNTY**
        GOVERNMENT).   / 1./ 2./ 3./ 4./ 9./

----

29.   OK. We've been talking a lot about your feelings about your neighborhood
      and the (**LEXINGTON-FAYETTE URBAN COUNTY GOVERNMENT**). Now I'd like to
      ask you to shift gears a bit and think about your feelings about
      government in general in this country.

      I'm going to read you just a few statements that people have made about
      government and politics in the UNITED STATES. Would you tell me if you
      AGREE OR DISAGREE with these statements?

	AGREE	DISAGREE	DK/NA
	1.	2.	9.

(167)   Voting is the only way that
        people like me can have any say
        about how the government runs
        things.   / 1. / 2. / 9. /

		AGREE	DISAGREE	DK/NA
		1.	2.	9.

(168) Sometimes politics and
government seem so complicated
that a person like me can't
really know what's going on.   / 1. /   2.   /   9. /

(169) I don't think that public
officials in this country
care very much about what
people like me think.   / 1. /   2.   /   9. /

(170) People like me don't have
any say about what the
government does.   / 1. /   2.   /   9. /

We have just a few more items and then we're done.

---

30. In what year were you born?

(171-172)   [Code last two digits]

          19 __ __

31. What is the highest grade or year of school you have completed?   (Read
responses)

     (173)
          1. 8 YEARS OR LESS
             2. 9-11 YEARS
                3. COMPLETED HIGH SCHOOL
                   4. HIGH SCHOOL PLUS BUSINESS OR TECHNICAL TRAINING
                      5. SOME COLLEGE
                         6. COMPLETED COLLEGE
                            7. GRADUATE OR PROFESSIONAL SCHOOL BEYOND
                               COLLEGE
                            8. DK/NA

32. What is your race?   (Read Responses If Necessary)

     (174)
          1. WHITE
             2. BLACK
                3. OTHER
                   9. DK/NA

33. Considering ALL sources of income before taxes for everyone living in your
    household, what was the total household income for 1985?   I'll read a
    series of income categories.   Please stop me when I get to your household
    income level.

    (175)
            0. UNDER $10,000
            1. $10,000 to $20,000
              2. $20,000 to $30,000
                3. $30,000 to $40,000
                  4. $40,000 to $50,000
                    5. $50,000 to $60,000
                      6. $60,000 to $70,000
                        7. $70,000 to $80,000
                          8. OVER $80,000
                            9. DK/NA

34. Does anyone living in your home currently work for or serve as an elected
    official in the (**LEXINGTON-FAYETTE URBAN COUNTY GOVERNMENT**)?

    (176)
            1. YES
            2. NO
              3. DK/NA

OK. HERE IS OUR VERY LAST ITEM

35. Are you currently **EMPLOYED OUTSIDE THE HOME, TEMPORARILY LAID OFF,
    UNEMPLOYED, RETIRED, A STUDENT, A HOUSEWIFE, or WHAT?**

    (177)
            1. YES, EMPLOYED OUTSIDE THE HOME
            2. TEMPORARILY LAID OFF
              3. RETIRED
                4. STUDENT
                  5. HOUSEWIFE
                    6. OTHER   -------------------------------------
                      9. DK/NA   **IF "EMPLOYED OUTSIDE THE HOME," GO
                                     TO Q-36. IF "NOT"--CODE Q-36 AS 9.**
                                     ----

36. Which of the following categories best describes the kind of work that you
    do? (Read category items.)

    (178)
            1. LABORER, MACHINE OPERATOR
            2. CLERICAL OR RETAIL SALES
              3. SKILLED TECHNICIAN
                4. MANAGER OR SUPERVISOR
                  5. OWNER OR CHIEF EXECUTIVE OFFICER
                    6. PROFESSIONAL (i.e. Medical doctor, Dentist,
                        Engineer, Professor, etc.)
                      7. OTHER
                        9. DK/NA

**THANK YOU VERY MUCH FOR YOUR COOPERATION. YOUR WILLINGNESS TO HELP US COMPLETE
THIS SURVEY IS MOST APPRECIATED. LET ME AGAIN ASSURE YOU THAT YOUR ANSWERS
WILL REMAIN COMPLETELY CONFIDENTIAL.**

References

Aberbach, Joel D. and Jack L. Walker. (!970). "The Attitudes of Blacks and Whites toward City Services: Implications for Public Policy." In *Financing the Metropolis*, ed. John P. Crecine. Beverly Hills, CA: Sage Publications.

Abramson, Paul R. (1983). *Political Attitudes in America: Formation and Change*. San Francisco: W. H. Freeman.

Advisory Commission on Intergovernmental Relations. (1987). *The Organization of Local Public Economies*. Washington, DC: Advisory Commission on Intergovernmental Relations.

Agger, Robert E., Daniel Goldrich, and Bert E. Swanson. (1964). *The Rulers and the Ruled: Political Power and Impotence in American Communities*. New York: John Wiley.

Almond, Gabriel A., and Sidney Verba. (1963). *The Civic Culture: Political Attitudes and Democracy in Five Nations*. Princeton, NJ: Princeton University Press.

Bachrach, Peter, and Morton S. Baratz. (1970). *Power and Poverty: Theory and Practice*. New York: Oxford University Press.

Bailyn, Bernard. (1967). *The Ideological Origins of the American Revolution*. Cambridge, MA: Harvard University Press.

Balch, George I. (1974). "Multiple Indicators in Survey Research: The Concept Sense of Political Efficacy." *Political Methodology 1:* 1–43.

Baldassare, Mark (1989). "Citizen Support for Regional Government in the New Suburbia." *Urban Affairs Quarterly 24:* 460–69.

Barber, Benjamin. (1984). *Strong Democracy*. Berkeley: University of California Press.

Beck, Paul Allen, Hal G. Rainey, and Carol Traut. (1986). "Public Views of Local Services and Taxes: Divergent Sources of Fiscal Policy Thinking." Paper Presented at the Annual Meeting of the Midwest Political Science Association, Chicago, Illinois, April.

Beck, Paul Allen, Hal G. Rainey, Keith Nicholls, and Carol Traut. (1986). "Citizen Views of Taxes and Services: A Tale of Three Cities." *Social Science Quarterly 68:* 223–43.

Bellah, Robert N., Richard Madsen, William M. Sullivan, Ann Swindler, and Steven M. Tipton. (1985). *Habits of the Heart*. New York: Harper and Row.

Bendor, Jonathan B. (1985). *Parallel Systems: Redundancy in Government*. Berkeley: University of California Press.

Bennett, James T., and Thomas J. DiLorenzo. (1982). "Off-Budget Activities of Local Government: The Bane of the Tax Revolt." *Public Choice 39:* 333–42.

Berelson, Bernard R., Paul F. Lazersfeld, and William N. McPhee. (1954). *Voting*. Chicago: University of Chicago Press.

Bish, Robert L. (1971). *The Public Economy of Metropolitan Areas*. Chicago: Markham.

Bish, Robert L., and Vincent Ostrom. (1973). *Understanding Urban Government.* Washington, DC: American Enterprise Institute.

Boyle, John, and David Jacobs. (1982). "The Intracity Distribution of Services: A Multivariate Analysis." *American Political Science Review 76:* 371–79.

Broder, J. M., and A. Allan Schmid. (1983). "Public Choice in Local Judicial Systems." *Public Choice 40:* 7–20.

Brown, Karin, and Philip B. Coulter. (1983). "Subjective and Objective Measures of Police Service Delivery." *Public Administration Review 43:* 50–58.

Brudney, Jeffrey L., and Robert E. England. (1982a). "Analyzing Citizen Evaluations of Municipal Services: A Dimensional Approach." *Urban Affairs Quarterly 17:* 359–69.

———. (1982b). "Urban Policy Making and Subjective Service Evaluations: Are They Compatible?" *Public Administration Review 42:* 127–35.

Buchanan, James M. (1975). *The Limits of Liberty.* Chicago: University of Chicago Press.

Campbell, Angus, Gerald Gurin, and Warren E. Miller. (1954). *The Voter Decides.* Evanston, IL: Row, Peterson.

Campbell, Angus, Philip E. Converse, Warren E. Miller, and Donald E. Stokes. (1960). *The American Voter.* Chicago: University of Chicago Press.

Cebula, R. J. (1974). "Interstate Migration and the Tiebout Hypothesis: An Analysis According to Race, Sex, and Age." *Journal of the American Statistical Association 69:* 876–79.

———. (1976). "A Note on Non-White Migration, Welfare Levels, and the Political Process." *Public Choice 28:* 117–19.

———. (1977). "An Analysis of Migration Patterns and Local Government Policy toward Public Education." *Public Choice 33:* 113–21.

———. (1978). "An Empirical Note on the Tiebout-Tullock Hypothesis." *Quarterly Journal of Economics 92:* 705–11.

Cebula, R. J., and K. L. Avery. (1983). "The Tiebout Hypothesis in the United States: An Analysis of Black Consumer-Voters, 1970–75." *Public Choice 41:* 307–10.

Cingranelli, David L. (1981). "Race, Politics, and Elites: Testing Alternative Models of Municipal Service Distribution." *American Journal of Political Science 25:* 664–92.

Clark, T. A. (1979). *Blacks in Suburbs: A National Perspective.* New Brunswick, NJ: Center for Urban Policy Research.

Cole, Richard. (1975). "Citizen Participation in Municipal Politics." *American Journal of Political Science 19:* 761–81.

Conlan, Timothy J., and David B. Walker. (1986). "Reagan's New Federalism." In *American Intergovernmental Relations Today,* ed. Robert Jay Dilger. Englewood Cliffs, NJ: Prentice-Hall.

Connolly, H. X. (1970). "Black Movement into the Suburbs." *Urban Affairs Quarterly 8:* 91–111.

Coulter, Philip. (1988). *Political Voice.* Tuscaloosa: University of Alabama Press.

Cox, Kevin. (1973). "Alienation and Political Apathy." *Social Forces 38:* 185–89.

Crenson, Matthew A. (1983). *Neighborhood Politics.* Cambridge, MA: Harvard University Press.

Dagger, Richard. (1981). "Metropolis, Memory, and Citizenship." *American Journal of Political Science 24:* 715–37.

Dahl, Robert. (1967). "The City in the Future of Democracy," *American Political Science Review 61:* 953–70.

Danielson, Michael N. (1976). *The Politics of Exclusion.* New York: Columbia University Press.

DeHoog, Ruth Hoogland, David Lowery, and W. E. Lyons. (1990). "Citizen Satisfaction with Local Governance: A Test of Individual, Jurisdictional, and City Specific Explanations." *Journal of Politics 52:* 807–37.

DiLorenzo, Thomas J. (1983). "Economic Competition and Political Competition: An Empirical Note." *Public Choice 40:* 203–209.

Durand, Roger. (1976). "Some Dynamics of Urban Service Evaluations among Blacks and Whites." *Social Science Quarterly 56:* 698–706.

Economist, The. (1990). "Toronto and Detroit: Canadians Do It Better." May 19, p. 17–20.

Elazar, Daniel. (1970). *Cities on the Prairie.* New York: Basic Books.

———. (1972). *American Federalism: A View from the States.* New York: Crowell.

Elkin, Stephen L. (1987). *City and Regime in the American Republic.* Chicago: University of Chicago Press.

Engstrom, Richard, and Michael McDonald. (1981). "The Election of Blacks to City Councils: Classifying the Impact of Electoral Arrangements on the Seats/Population Relationship." *American Political Science Review 75:* 344–54.

Fainstein, Norman I., and Susan S. Fainstein. (1980). "Mobility, Community, and Participation: The American Way Out." In *Residential Mobility and Public Policy,* ed. W. A. V. Clark and Eric G. Moore. Beverly Hills, CA: Sage Publications.

Fantini, Mario, and Marilyn Gittell. (1982). *Decentralization: Achieving Reform.* New York: Praeger.

Farley, R. (1970). "The Changing Distribution of Negroes with Metropolitan Areas: The Emergence of Black Suburbs." *American Journal of Sociology 75:* 512–29.

Farrell, Daniel. (1982). "Exit, Voice, Loyalty, and Neglect as Responses to Job Dissatisfaction: A Multidimensional Scaling Approach." Paper presented at the Annual Meeting of the American Academy of Management.

Farrell, Daniel, and Caryl E. Rusbult. (1981). "Exchange Variables as Predictors of Job Satisfaction, Job Commitment, and Turnover: The Impact of Rewards, Costs, Alternatives, and Investments." *Organizational Behavior and Human Performance 27:* 78–95.

———. (1985). "Understanding the Retention Function: A Model of the Causes of Exit, Voice, Loyalty, and Neglect." *Personnel Administrator 30:* 129–40.

Farrell, Daniel, Caryl E. Rusbult, Glenn Rogers, and A. G. Mainous III. (1985). "An Integrative Approach to the Study of Responses to Job Dissatisfaction: The Impact of Investment Model Variables on Exit, Voice, Loyalty, and Neglect." Department of Psychology, University of Kentucky, mimeo.

Ferman, Barbara. (1985). *Governing the Ungovernable City: Political Skills, Leadership and the Modern Mayor.* Philadelphia: Temple University Press.

Finifter, Ada W. (1972). *Alienation and the Social System.* New York: John Wiley.

Fitzgerald, Michael R., and Robert F. Durand. (1980). "Citizen Evaluations and Urban Management: Service Delivery in an Era of Protest." *Public Administration Review 40:* 585–94.

Fowler, Floyd J., Jr. (1974). *Citizen Attitudes toward Local Government, Services, and Taxes.* Cambridge, MA: Ballinger.

Fredrickson, George, ed. (1973). *Neighborhood Control in the 1970s.* New York: Chandler Publishing.

Freisema, H. Paul. (1972). "The Metropolis and the Maze of Local Governments." *Urban Affairs Quarterly 2:* 68–90.

Galston, William A. (1982). "Defending Liberalism." *American Political Science Review 76:* 621–29.

———. (1988). "Liberal Virtues." *American Political Science Review 82:* 1277–92.

Gans, Herbert. (1962). *The Urban Villagers.* New York: Free Press.

General Accounting Office. (1983). *Federal Drug Interdiction Efforts Need Strong Central Oversight.* Washington, DC: General Accounting Office.

Goel, A. J., W. J. Lovett, R. Patten, and R. L. Wilkins. (1988). "Black Neighborhoods Becoming Black Cities: Local Control and the Implications of Being Darker than Brown." *Harvard Civil Rights–Civil Liberties Law Review 23:* 415–81.

Goodman, Jay S. (1977). "Trends in Urban Theory: The Search for Rational Strategies." *Urban Affairs Quarterly 13:* 243–53.

Greer, Scott. (1962). *The Emerging City: Myth and Reality.* New York: Free Press.

Guest, Avery M. (1978). "The Changing Racial Composition of Suburbs, 1950–1970." *Urban Affairs Quarterly 14:* 195–206.

Guest, Avery M., and Barrett Lee. (1983). "The Social Organization of Local Areas." *Urban Affairs Quarterly 19:* 217–40.

Hallman, Howard. (1974). *Neighborhood Government in a Metropolitan Setting.* Beverly Hills, CA: Sage Publications.

Hamilton, Bruce W., Edwin S. Mills, and David Puryear. (1975). "The Tiebout Hypothesis and Residential Income Segregation." In *Fiscal Zoning and Land Use Controls,* ed. Edwin S. Mills and Wallace E. Oates. Lexington, MA: D. C. Heath.

Harrigan, John J. (1989). *Political Change in the Metropolis.* Glenview, IL: Scott, Foresman/Little Brown.

Hero, Rodney E. (1986). "Explaining Citizen-Initiated Contacting of Government Officials: Socioeconomic Status, Perceived Need or Something Else?" *Social Science Quarterly 67:* 626–35.

Hero, Rodney E., and Roger Durand. (1980). "Explaining Citizen Evaluations of Urban Services: A Comparison of Some Alternative Models." *Urban Affairs Quarterly 20:* 344–54.

Hill, Richard Child. (1974). "Separate and Unequal: Governmental Inequality in the Metropolis." *American Political Science Review 68:* 1557–68.

Hirschman, Albert O. (1970). *Exit, Voice and Loyalty.* Cambridge: Harvard University Press.

Hull, David. (1988). *Science as a Process.* Chicago: University of Chicago Press.

Janowitz, M. (1967). *The Community Press in an Urban Setting.* Chicago: University of Chicago Press.

Jones, Bryan D. (1980). *Service Delivery in the City: Citizen Demand and Bureaucratic Rules.* New York: Longman.

———. (1989). "Why Weakness Is a Strength." *Urban Affairs Quarterly 25:* 30–40.

Jones, Bryan D., Saadia Greenberg, Clifford Kaufman, and Joseph Drew. (1978). "Service Delivery Rules and the Distribution of Local Government Services: Three Detroit Bureaucracies." *Journal of Politics 40:* 332–68.

Kantor, Paul. (1983). *The Dependent City: The Changing Political Economy of Urban America.* Glenview, IL: Scott, Foresman and Company.

Karnig, Albert. (1975). "Private-Regarding Policy, Civil Rights Groups, and Mediating Impact of Municipal Reforms." *American Journal of Political Science 19:* 91–106.

Kenyon, D. A. (1984). "Preference Revelation and Supply Response in the Arena of Local Government." *Public Choice 42:* 147–60.

Knott, Jack H., and Gary J. Miller. (1987). *Reforming Bureaucracy: The Politics of Institutional Choice.* Englewood Cliffs, NJ: Prentice-Hall.

Kotler, Milton. (1969). *Neighborhood Government.* Indianapolis, IN: Bobbs-Merrill.

Kotter, John, and Paul Lawrence. (1974). *Mayors in Action: Five Approaches to Urban Governance.* New York: John Wiley.

Lake, R. W. (1981). *The New Suburbanites: Race and Housing in the Suburbs.* New Brunswick, N.J.: Center for Urban Policy Research.

Lineberry, Robert L. (1977). *Equality and Urban Policy: The Distribution of Municipal Services.* Beverly Hills, CA: Sage Publications.

Lineberry, Robert L., and Louis H. Masotti, eds. (1976). *The New Urban Politics.* Cambridge, MA: Ballinger.

Logan, John R., and Mark Schneider. (1982). "Governmental Organization and City/Suburb Income Inequality, 1960–1970." *Urban Affairs Quarterly 17:* 303–18.

Long, Norton E. (1962). *The Polity.* Chicago: Rand McNally.

————. (1967). "Political Science and the City." In *Urban Research and Policy Planning,* ed. L. F. Schnore and H. Fagin. Beverly Hills, CA: Sage Publications.

Lowery, David. (1982). "Public Choice When Services Are Costs: The Divergent Case of Assessment Administration." *American Journal of Political Science 26:* 57–76.

————. (1985). "Public Opinion, Fiscal Illusion, and Tax Revolution: The Political Demise of the Property Tax." *Public Budgeting and Finance 5:* 76–88.

Lowery, David, and William E. Lyons. (1989). "The Impact of Jurisdictional Boundaries: An Individual-Level Test of the Tiebout Model." *Journal of Politics 51:* 73–97.

Lowery, David, W. E. Lyons, and Ruth Hoogland DeHoog. (1990). "The Composition and Impact of Institutionally Induced Attribution Errors on Citizen Satisfaction with Local Governmental Services." *American Politics Quarterly 18:* 169–96.

Lyons, William E. (1971). "Measuring Life-style: Some Findings Concerning the Empirical Basis for Aggregate Measures of Familism and Non-Familism." *Social Science Quarterly 52:* 398–408.

————. (1977). *The Politics of City-County Merger.* Lexington: University of Kentucky Press.

Lyons, William E., and Richard Engstrom. (1971). "Life-style and Fringe Attitudes toward the Political Integration of Urban Governments." *Midwest Journal of Political Science 15:* 475–94.

Lyons, William E., and David Lowery. (1986). "The Organization of Political Space and Citizen Responses to Dissatisfaction in Urban Communities: An Integrative Model." *Journal of Politics 48:* 321–46.

————. (1989a). "Citizen Responses to Dissatisfaction in Urban Communities: A Partial Test of a General Model." *Journal of Politics 51:* 841–68.

————. (1989b). "Governmental Fragmentation and Consolidation: Five Public Choice Myths About Creating Informed, Involved, and Happy Citizens." *Public Administration Review 49:* 533–43.

McDougall, G. S., and H. Bunce. "Urban Services and the Suburbanization of Blacks." *Social Science Quarterly 67:* 596–603.

Michigan, State of. (1976). *Final Report of the Governor's Advisory Task Force on Property Tax Revision.* Lansing, MI: Department of Management and Budget.

Milbrath, Lester W. (1968). "The Nature of Political Beliefs and the Relationship of the Individual to Government." *American Behavioral Scientist 12:* 28–36.

————. (1971a). "Individuals and the Government." In *Politics in the American States,* ed. Herbert Jacob and Kenneth N. Vines. Boston, MA: Little Brown.

————. (1971b). "A Paradigm for the Comparative Study of Local Politics." *Politico 36:* 5–35.

————. (1971c). *People and Government.* Buffalo: State University of New York.

Milbrath, Lester, and M. L. Goel. (1977). *Political Participation.* Chicago: Rand McNally.

Miller, Gary J. (1981). *Cities by Contract: The Politics of Municipal Incorporation.* Cambridge, MA: MIT Press.

Mills, Edwin S. and Wallace E. Oates, eds. (1975). *Fiscal Zoning and Land Use Controls.* Lexington, MA: D. C. Heath.

Mladenka, Kenneth. (1981). "Citizen Demands and Urban Services: The Distribution of Bureaucratic Response in Chicago and Houston." *American Journal of Political Science 25:* 693–714.

Mladenka, Kenneth, and Kim Hill. "The Distribution of Benefits in an Urban Environment: Parks and Libraries in Houston." *Urban Affairs Quarterly 13:* 73–94.

Neiman, M. (1976). "Communication: Social Stratification and Governmental Inequality." *American Political Science Review 70:* 1557–68.

Oakerson, Ronald J., Roger B. Parks, and H. A. Bell. (1987). "How Fragmentation Works—St. Louis Style." Paper presented at the Meeting of the Midwest Political Science Association, Chicago, April.

Orbell, John, and Toru Uno. (1972). "The Theory of Neighborhood Problem Solving: Political Action vs. Residential Mobility." *American Political Science Review 66:* 471–89.

Ostrom, Elinor. (1972). "Metropolitan Reform: Propositions Derived from Two Traditions." *Social Science Quarterly 53:* 474–93.

———., ed. (1976). *The Delivery of Urban Services.* Beverly Hills, CA: Sage Publications.

———. (1985). "The Social Stratification–Government Inequality Thesis Explored." *Urban Affairs Quarterly 19:* 91–112.

Ostrom, Elinor, and Dennis C. Smith. (1976). "On the Fate of Lilliputs in Metropolitan Policing." *Public Administration Review 36:* 192–99.

Ostrom, Elinor, and Gordon P. Whitaker. (1974). "Community Control and Governmental Responsiveness: The Case of Police in Black Communities." In *Improving the Quality of Urban Management,* ed. David Rogers and Willis D. Hawley. Beverly Hills, CA: Sage Publications.

Ostrom, Vincent. (1973). *The Intellectual Crisis in American Public Administration.* University: University of Alabama Press.

———. (1977). "Structure and Performance." In *Comparing Urban Service Delivery Systems,* ed. Vincent Ostrom and Francis Pennel Bish. Beverly Hills, CA: Sage Publications.

Ostrom, Vincent, Robert L. Bish, and Elinor Ostrom. (1988). *Local Government in the United States,* San Francisco: Institute for Contemporary Studies.

Ostrom, Vincent, Charles M. Tiebout, and Robert Warren. (1961). "The Organization of Government in Metropolitan Areas: A Theoretical Inquiry." *American Political Science Review 55:* 831–42.

Pachon, Harry P., and Nicholas P. Lovrich. (1977). "The Consolidation of Urban Services: A Focus On Police." *Public Administration Review 37:* 38–49.

Pack, Howard, and Janet Pack. (1978). "Metropolitan Fragmentation and Local Public Expenditures." *National Tax Journal 31:* 349–62.

Parks, Roger B. (1984). "Linking Objective and Subjective Measures of Performance." *Public Administration Review 44:* 118–27.

———. (1985). "Metropolitan Structure and Systematic Performance: The Case of Police Service Delivery." In *Policy Implementation in Federal and Unitary States,* ed. K. Hanf and T. A. J. Toonen. Dordrecht, The Netherlands: Martinus Nijhoff.

Parks, Roger B., and Ronald J. Oakerson. (1989). "Metropolitan Organization and Governance: A Local Public Economy Approach." *Urban Affairs Quarterly 25:* 18–29.

Parks, Roger B., and Elinor Ostrom. (1981). "Complex Models of Urban Service Systems." *Urban Policy Analysis: Directions for Future Research,* Urban Affairs Annual Reviews, no. 7, ed. Terry N. Clark. Beverly Hills, CA: Sage Publications.

Percy, Stephen L. (1986). "In Defense of Citizen Evaluations as Performance Measures." *Urban Affairs Quarterly 22:* 66–83.

Perry, David C. (1973). "The Suburb as a Model for Neighborhood Control." In *Neighborhood Control in the 1970s,* ed. George Fredrickson. New York: Chandler Publishing.

Peterson, Paul E. (1981). *City Limits*. Chicago: University of Chicago Press.

Phares, Donald. (1989). "Bigger Is Better, or Is It Smaller? Restructuring Local Government in the St. Louis Area." *Urban Affairs Quarterly 25:* 5–17.

Quigley, John. (1980). "Local Residential Mobility and Local Government Policy." In *Residential Mobility and Public Policy,*. ed. W. A. V. Clark and Eric Moore. Beverly Hills, CA: Sage Publications.

Rakove, Milton. (1975). *Don't Make No Waves—Don't Back No Losers*. Bloomington: Indiana University Press.

Rogers, Bruce D., and C. McMurdy Lipsey. (1974). "Metropolitan Reform: Community Size and the Perception of Public Services," Paper Presented at the Annual meeting of the Southern Sociological Association, Atlanta, Georgia, April.

Rose, Harold. (1976). *Black Suburbanization: Access to Improved Quality of Life or Maintenance of the Status Quo?* Cambridge, MA: Ballinger.

Rusbult, Caryl E. (1980). "Commitment and Satisfaction in Romantic Associations: A Test of the Investment Model." *Journal of Experimental Social Psychology 16:* 172–86.

Rusbult, Caryl E., and Daniel Farrell. (1985). "A Longitudinal Test of the Investment Model: The Impact on Job Satisfaction, Job Commitment, and Turnover of Variations in Rewards, Costs, Alternatives, and Investments." *Journal of Applied Psychology 15:* 80–103.

Rusbult, Caryl E., and David Lowery. (1985). "When Bureaucrats Get the Blues: Responses to Dissatisfaction among Federal Public Employees." *Journal of Applied Social Psychology 15:* 80–103.

Rusbult, Caryl E., and I. M. Zembrodt. (1983). "Responses to Dissatisfaction in Romantic Involvements: A Multidimensional Scaling Analysis." *Journal of Experimental Psychology 19:* 274–93.

Rusbult, Caryl E., I. M. Zembrodt, and L. K. Gunn. (1982). "Exit, Voice, Loyalty, and Neglect: Responses to Dissatisfaction in Romantic Involvements." *Journal of Personality and Social Psychology 43:* 1230–42.

Savas, E. S. (1983). *Privatizing the Public Sector: How to Shrink Government*. Chatham, NJ: Chatham House Publishers.

Schneider, Mark. (1989). "Intermunicipal Competition, Budget-Maximizing Bureaucrats, and the Level of Suburban Competition." *American Journal of Political Science 33:* 612–28.

Schneider, Mark, and John R. Logan. (1982a). "The Effects of Local Government Finances on Community Growth Rates." *Urban Affairs Quarterly 18:* 91–105.

———. (1982b). "Suburban Racial Segregation and Black Access to Local Public Resources." *Social Science Quarterly 63:* 762–70.

Schuman, Howard, and Barry Gruenberg. (1972). "Dissatisfaction With City Services: Is Race an Important Factor?" In *People and Politics in Urban Society,* ed. Harlan Hahn. Beverly Hills, CA: Sage Publications.

Schwartz, Nancy L. (1988). *The Blue Guitar*. Chicago: University of Chicago Press.

Sears, David O., and John B. McConahay. (1973). *The Politics of Violence*. Boston: Houghton Mifflin.

Seligson, Mitchell. (1980). "A Problem-Solving Approach to Measuring Political Efficacy." *Social Science Quarterly 60:* 630–42.

Sharp, Elaine B. (1980). "Citizen Perceptions of Channels for Urban Service Advocacy: The Role of Citizen Organizations." *Public Opinion Quarterly 33:* 362–76.

———. (1982). "Citizen-Initiated Contacting and Socioeconomic Status: Determining the Relationship and Accounting for It." *American Political Science Review 76:* 109–15.

———. (1984a). "Citizen Demand-Making in the Urban Context." *American Journal of Political Science 28:* 654–70.

———. (1984b). "Exit, Voice, and Loyalty in the Context of Local Government Problems." *Western Political Quarterly 37:* 67–83.

———. (1984c). "Need, Awareness, and Contacting Propensity Study of a City with a Central Complaints Unit." *Urban Affairs Quarterly 20:* 22–30.

———. (1986). *Citizen Demand-Making in the Urban Context.* University: University of Alabama Press.

Shevsky, Eshref, and Wendell Bell. (1955). *Social Area Analysis.* Stanford, CA: Stanford University Press.

Simon, Herbert A. (1945). *Administrative Behavior.* New York: Free Press.

Stein, Robert M. (1987). "Tiebout's Sorting Hypothesis." *Urban Affairs Quarterly 23:* 140–60.

Stipak, Brian. (1977). "Attitudes and Belief Systems Concerning Urban Services." *Public Opinion Quarterly 41:* 41–55.

———. "Citizen Satisfaction with Urban Services: Potential Misuse as a Performance Indicator." *Public Administration Review 39:* 46–52.

Svara, James. (1977). "Unwrapping Institutional Packages in Urban Government." *Journal of Politics 39:* 166–75.

Swanstrom, Todd. (1985). *The Crisis of Growth Politics: Cleveland, Kucinich, and the Challenge of Urban Populism.* Philadelphia: Temple University Press.

Talbot, Allan R. (1969). *The Mayor's Game: Richard Lee of New Haven and the Politics of Change.* New York: Praeger.

Thibaut, John W., and H. H. Kelly. (1959). *The Social Psychology of Groups.* New York: John Wiley.

Thigpen, Robert B., and Lyle A. Downing. (1987). "Liberalism and the Communitarian Critique." *American Journal of Political Science 31:* 637–55.

Thomas, John Clayton. (1982). "Citizen-Initiated Contacts with Government Agencies: A Test of Three Theories." *American Journal of Political Science 26:*504–22.

Tiebout, Charles M. (1956). "A Pure Theory of Local Expenditures." *Journal of Political Economy 64:* 416–24.

Vedlitz, Arnold, and Eric P. Veblen. (1980). "Voting and Contacting: Two Forms of Political Participation in a Suburban Community." *Urban Affairs Quarterly 16:* 31–48.

Verba, Sidney, and Norman H. Nie. (1972). *Participation in America: Political Democracy and Social Equality.* Chicago: University of Chicago Press.

Wagner, Richard E., and Warren E. Weber. (1975). "Competition, Monopoly, and the Organization of Government in Metropolitan Areas." *Journal of Law and Economics 18:* 661–84.

Wells, H. G. (1961). "Administrative Areas." In *Democracy in Urban America,* ed. Oliver P. Williams and Charles Press. Chicago: Rand McNally.

Whitaker, Gordon P. (1980). "Coproduction: Citizen Participation in Service Delivery." *Public Administration Review 40:* 240–46.

Willbern, York. (1960). *The Withering Away of the City.* Bloomington, IN: Indiana University Press.

Williams, Oliver P. (1981). *Metropolitan Political Analysis: A Social Access Approach.* New York: Free Press.

———. (1975). "Urban Politics as Political Ecology." In *Essays on the Study of Urban Politics,* ed. Ken Young. London: Macmillan.

Williams, Oliver P., Harold Herman, Charles S. Liebman, and Thomas Dye. (1965). *Suburban Differences and Metropolitan Policies.* Philadelphia: University of Pennsylvania.

Wong, Kenneth K. (1988). "Economic Constraint and Political Choice in Urban Policymaking." *American Journal of Political Science 32:* 1–18.

Wood, Robert C. (1961). *1400 Governments*. Cambridge, MA: Harvard University Press.
———. (1961b). "The New Metropolis." In *Democracy in Urban America*, ed. Oliver P. Williams and Charles Press. Chicago: Rand McNally.
———. (1966). "Suburbia: The Fiscal Roots of Political Fragmentation and Differentiation." In *Metropolitan Politics,* ed. Michael N. Danielson. Boston: Little Brown.
Yates, Douglas. (1977). *The Ungovernable City: The Politics of Urban Policy Making.* Cambridge, MA: MIT Press.
Zemans, F. Z. (1973)."Legal Mobilization: The Neglected Role of Law in the Political System." *American Political Science Review 77:* 690–703.
Zimmerman, Joseph F. (1970). "Metropolitan Reform in the U.S.: An Overview." *Public Administration Review 30:* 531–43.
———. (1972). *The Federated City.* New York: St. Martin's Press.
Zodrow, George R., ed. (1983). *Local Provision of Public Services: The Tiebout Model After Twenty-Five Years.* New York: Academic Press.

Index

Accountability, 117–18
Administrative Behavior (Simon), 192
Age, 26, 34, 72
Aggregate-level errors, 120–21
Alternatives, 27, 43, 51–52, 56, 59,
    67*n.43*, 168
  citizen awareness of, 91–92, 98–99
  and correspondence, 62
  and loyalty, 75
  variable, 71
Apathy, 117
Assessment error, 30, 118
Attachment, 75–76. *See also* Investment;
    Psychological attachment
Attribution error, 30, 100, 187
  average bias in satisfaction by average
    number of, 141
  bias, 140–41
  decomposition of, 123
  institutions and, 115–43

Bachrach, Peter, 52, 59
Balch, George I., 19, 26
Baratz, Morton S., 52, 59
Barber, Benjamin, 161, 165, 166,
    181
Beechwood Village, predicted satisfaction
    scores, 139
Bell, Wendell, 46
Bellah, Robert N., 172
Bias, 120–21, 131–43
  and general satisfaction, 134–36
  predicted satisfaction with, 139
Bish, Robert L., 46, 90, 93, 117, 169
Blacks, 146–59
Blueberry (Fayette County), 134

*Blue Guitar: Political Representation and
    the Community, The* (Schwartz), 167
Buchanan, James M., 165
Bunce, H., 147

Campbell, Angus, 71
Children, 87*n.5*
Chinoe (Fayette County), 126, 133
Citizen satisfaction
  city and neighborhood-specific
    explanations of, 23–24
  individual-level explanations of, 19–20
  jurisdiction-level explanations of, 20–23,
    34, 36
  OLS regression results of five models of,
    35–37
  research on, 4–7
  sources of, 18–45
  survey findings, 33–42
  testing and estimation procedures, 33
  testing the explanations, 25
  variables and measurement, 25–33
Citizenship, urban, 160–84
  findings, 175–79
  and institutions, 163–70
  metropolitanist critique, 170–74
  and nonlocal attachment, 181–82
  and problem solving, 164–68
  testing the hypotheses, 174–79
  two interpretations of, 160–63
  variables and measurement, 174–75
"City and the Future of Democracy, The"
    (Dahl), 160
COGs. *See* Councils of Governments
Collinearity, 33, 72, 78
Columbus (Ohio), 49

Communitarianism, 160–63, 168–69, 174, 180, 181
Community, 161
Community dissaffection, 19
Competition, 94
Consolidated government, 93, 96, 104–05, 181, 187, 188–89
  and citizen awareness, 97, 99–100
  and minority communities, 151
  OLS regression of satisfaction with, 137
  public support for, 191–92
Correspondence, 49, 59–65
Councils of Governments (COGs), 157, 163
Cox, Kevin, 46
Current dissatisfaction, 57–59, 71, 72, 76
  and correspondence, 62–63
  EVLN model excluding, 74–75, 78
  and jurisdiction structure, 100–101
  in minority communities, 151–52
  in minority versus white communities, 152–54

Dagger, Richard, 117
Dahl, Robert, 160, 171
Democratic control, 120, 141
Demographic variables, 19
Discrimination, 145–46
Dissatisfaction, research on, 4–7
Dissatisfaction, responses to, 5–7, 46–47
  determinants of, 56–59
  four models of, 53–55, 86
  political participation as, 52–53
  sequential choice model of, 85, 86

Education, 26, 72, 87n.4, 139–40, 189–90
Effective citizenship, 120, 141
Efficacy. See General efficacy; Local efficacy
Elkin, Stephen L., 166, 169, 181
Environmental policy, 190
Evaluation errors
  difference of means on biases in, 132
  difference of means on numbers of, 130
  frequency distribution of numbers of, 128
  impact of, 129–40
  and institutional structures, 115–18
  testing institutionally induced, 125–40
  types and decomposition of, 188–25

EVLN model, 8, 46–67, 164
  applying in urban settings, 52–59
  estimates for original, 73, 74
  existing models and limitations, 47–50
  PROBIT and OLS estimates of extended, 176
  respecifying, 78–84
  results for respecified, 80–84
  testing, 68–88
  variables and measures, 69–72
Exclusion, politics of, 173
Exit, 6, 48, 51, 54, 55, 58, 69–70, 77, 86, 164
  and correspondence, 63–64
  and psychological attachment, 177
  and relative dissatisfation, 79–80
  Tiebout model of, 90, 94–95, 97, 104
  and Virtuous Liberalism, 166
  and Watchdog Liberalism, 165, 180
EXIT-PRIV. See Privatization
Exit, Voice, Loyalty, Neglect model. See EVLN model

Fabian Society, 170
Familism, 11
Farrell, Daniel, 51
Fayette County (Kentucky). See Lexington-Fayette County
Fragmented government, 5, 92–93, 118, 181, 188–89
  and bias, 142
  and citizen awareness, 97, 98, 99–100, 107
  and exit response, 95–96
  loyalty and neglect in, 96
  OLS regression of satisfaction with, 138
  and racial inequality, 157
  and relative differences between whites and blacks, 154–55
  and suburban ghettos, 144–59

Galston, William, 165–66
Gender, 26, 34 72, 139–40
General efficacy, 26, 34, 72
Green Acres (Fayette County), 38–39, 126, 133, 149–56
Greer, Scott, 49
Guest, Avery M., 49
Gurin, Gerald, 71

Habits of the Heart (Bellah), 172
Hero, Rodney E., 26
Hill, Richard Child, 145
Hirschman, Albert O., 7, 51, 168
Homeownership, 26, 34, 70–71, 72, 78
Household clustering. *See* Spatial
        clustering
Housing discrimination, 157
Hull, David, 193

Income, 21, 26, 28, 33–34, 39–40, 72
Individual-level errors, 120–21
Institutional arrangements, 21–23
    designing, 185–94
    and evaluation errors, 115–18
    likelihood of exit response, 101–02,
        111–12
    perceptions of alternatives by, 98–99,
        107–08
    and problem solving, 168–70
    and racial inequality, 144–59
    service level perception difference of
        means tests, 99–100, 108
    and urban citizenship, 163–70
Investment, 20, 27, 42, 43, 51, 56, 58, 59,
        70–71, 72, 174
    and citizen satisfaction, 33–34
    and citizenship, 168, 169
    and correspondence, 62
    difference of means tests, 101, 111
    and fragmented government, 92–93

Janowitz, M., 49
Jefferson County (Kentucky), 9–14, 131
Jones, Brian, 6
Jones, James, 148

Kansas City, 97
Kelly, H.H., 51

Land-use controls, 157
Lee, Barrett, 49
Lexington and Louisville study, 3–17
    characteristics of matched
        cities/neighborhoods, 12
    difference in means/proportions, 14
    households and response rates, 12–13
    purpose, data, and methods, 7–9
    summary of results, 186–87
    surveys, 9–14

Lexington-Fayette County (Kentucky),
        9–14
Liberalism, 160–63
Life-style-maintaining conditions, 47–48,
        53
Lineberry, Robert, 3
Lipsey, C. McMurdy, 38
Local efficacy, 19–20, 26–27, 33–34, 42,
        43
Local efficacy indicator, 69
Local political jurisdictions, 50
Locational choice, 47–48, 50, 90, 91
Logan, John R., 145, 147
Long, Norton, 145, 170, 173
Louisville-Jefferson County (Kentucky),
        9–14
Loyalty, 48, 51, 54, 55, 59, 76–77, 85–86,
        88*n.17*, 164, 167
    and alternatives, 75
    and correspondence, 64
    difference of means test, 103, 114
    estimates for respecified model, 83
    and psychological attachment, 178, 179
    and relative dissatisfaction, 79
    and Virtuous Liberalism, 166
    and Watchdog Liberalism, 165

McDougall, G.S., 147
Metropoltanism, 170–74
Miller, Gary J., 106*n.19*
Miller, Warren E., 71
Minorities. *See* Race
Minor Lane Heights (Jefferson County),
        134
MISSET errors, 45*n.31*, 119–23, 125–26,
        131, 133, 142

National Science Foundation, 8
Neglect, 51, 54, 55, 59, 86, 164
    and correspondence, 64
    difference of means test, 103, 114
    estimates for respecified model, 84
    index, 69
    in minority communities, 151–52
    in minority versus white communities,
        152–54
    and psychological attachment, 178
    and relative dissatisfaction, 79–80
    and Watchdog Liberalism, 165
Neighborhood movement literature, 161
Neighborhoods, 50

Newburg (Kentucky), 30, 38–39, 139, 148–56, 159*n.29*
Nonfamilism, 11
NONSET errors, 45*n.31*, 119, 122, 126, 128, 133

Observed evaluation, 121–22
  bias in mean, 135
OLS regression, 33
  for black and white research sites, 40
  for consolidated/ nonconsolidated research sites, 39
  of jurisdiction level determinants, 41
Orbell, John, 49, 85–86
"Organization of Government in Metropolitan Areas: A Theoretical Inquiry, The" (Ostrom, Tiebout, and Warren), 90
Ostrom, Elinor, 46, 117, 146, 147, 157, 169
Ostrom, Vincent, 90, 93, 96, 117, 169, 192

Parallel Systems (Bendor), 192
Partial Service Districts, 105
Participation, 161
  local, 52–53
  see also Voice
Police services, 147
Political boundaries, 49, 59–65
Political efficacy, 19–20
Polity, The (Long), 170
Prior satisfaction, 51, 56, 58, 59, 168
  and correspondence, 61–62
  impact on voice, 74–75
  variable, 70
Privatization, 106*n.19*
  considered by institutional arrangement, 102–03, 113
  and consolidated government, 96
  and ELVN model, 55, 67*n.42*, 69, 70, 72, 74, 77–78, 86, 88*n.17*
Problem solving, 164–70
Psychological attachment, 174–80, 187
  difference-of-means tests, 180
  exit by levels of, 177
  loyalty by levels of, 178, 179
  neglect by levels of, 177, 178
  voice by levels of, 177, 178
Public choice theory, 5–6, 117–18, 141, 161, 187, 191, 193–94
"Pure Theory of Local Expenditures, A" (Tiebout), 90

Race, 21, 26, 72
  and citizen satisfaction, 33–34, 187
  and government structure, 145–48
Racial composition, 27–28, 38–39
Reagan, Ronald, 3
Reforming Bureaucracy: The Politics of Institutional Choice (Knott and Miller), 192
Relative dissatisfaction, 78–80
Representational Communitarianism, 167–68, 182
Research design
  future directions in, 187–90
  limits of, 24–25
Rogers, Bruce D., 38
Rusbult, Caryl E., 51

SAS LOGIST, 26, 33
Satisfaction. *See* Citizen satisfaction
Schneider, Mark, 145, 147
Schwartz, Nancy, 167
Segregation, 145, 156–57
Seligson-Sharp indicator, 26
Service evaluation, 124–25
Service quality, 28–30
  bias in, 30–32
  and satisfaction, 32
Services, 28
  in black communities, 150–51
  citizen evaluation of, 22, 30
  defining universe of, 125–29
  discrimination in, 146
  efficiency of delivery, 181
  expectations of, 21
  in Lexington/Fayette and Jefferson County sites, 29
  perceived versus actual, 109
Sharp, Elaine B., 48, 49, 91, 97
Shevsky, Eshref, 46
Simon, Herbert, 192
Social identity, 171
Social investment. *See* Investment
Socioeconomic boundaries, 49, 59–65
Socioeconomic status, 11
Sorting hypothesis, 94
Spatial clustering, 21, 50
Spillover communities, 145, 149
Stakeholding. *See* Investment
Standard error, 72
Stein, Robert M., 94
Stonewall (Fayette County), 126

Strong Democracy Communitarianism, 166–67, 170, 182
SUBSET errors, 45*n.31*, 118–23, 126–27, 131, 142
Suburban ghettos, 144–59
Survey Research Center (SRC) index, 19
Systemic error, 120

Thibaut, John W., 51
Tiebout, Charles M., 46, 94, 96
Tiebout model, 5, 21, 53, 61, 89–114, 187, 191
  limits of, 47–49
  operation of, 94–96
  testing, 97–103
  underlying assumptions of, 91–94
Traditional reform theory, 4–7, 116–17, 141, 191, 193–94
  updating, 190–92
True evaluation, 121–22
  bias in mean, 135

University of Kentucky Research Center (UKSRC), 12
Uno, Toru, 49, 85–86
Urbanism, spatial dimensions of, 46–47, 49

Virtuous Liberalism, 165–66, 168–69, 180–81, 182

Voice response, 6, 51, 54, 55, 58–59, 86, 164
  and availability of exit, 95
  and consolidated government, 96
  and correspondence, 63
  difference-of-means tests, 102, 112
  estimates for respecified, 82
  in minority communities, 151–52
  in minority versus white communities, 152–54
  and psychological attachment, 177, 178
  and relative dissatisfaction, 79–80
  variable, 69
  and Virtuous Liberalism, 166
  and Watchdog Liberalism, 164–65

Warren, Robert, 96
Watchdog Liberalism, 164–65, 168, 180
Wells, H.G., 170, 171–72
Whitaker, Gordon R., 147
Willbern, York, 50
Williams model, 47–48, 49, 53
Williams, Oliver P., 21, 46
Windy Hill, 139
Wood, Robert, 171, 172, 173, 182

Zoning restrictions, 157

About the Authors

W. E. Lyons is Professor of Political Science and Public Administration at the University of Kentucky. He is a specialist in urban government and politics, bureaucratic politics, intergovernmental relations, and land use regulation and growth management. In addition to having published numerous articles in a variety of leading social science journals, Dr. Lyons is author of two other books: *One Man One Vote in Canada* (McGraw Hill–Ryerson Press), and *The Politics of City-County Merger: The Lexington Experience* (University Press of Kentucky).

David Lowery is Professor and Chair of the Department of Political Science of the University of North Carolina at Chapel Hill where he teaches public budgeting, bureaucratic politics, and research methods. He has published extensively on these topics in the *American Political Science Review*, the *American Journal of Political Science*, and the *Journal of Politics*. He is the coauthor (with William D. Berry) of *Understanding U.S. Government Growth: An Empirical Analysis of the Post-War Era*.

Ruth Hoogland DeHoog is Associate Professor of Political Science and Director of the Master of Public Affairs Program at the University of North Carolina at Greensboro. She is author of *Contracting Out for Human Services* (SUNY Press), and of articles in several leading political science and public administration journals. Her research interests include privatization, urban administration, and bureaucratic politics.